THE ULTIMATE ENCYCLOPEDIA OF
PICKUPS

THE ULTIMATE ENCYCLOPEDIA OF
PICKUPS

PETER HENSHAW

CHARTWELL
BOOKS

This edition published in 2010 by
CHARTWELL BOOKS
an imprint of Book Sales
a division of Quarto Publishing Group USA Inc.
142 West 36th Street, 4th Floor
New York, NY 10018
USA

Copyright © 2016 Regency House Publishing Limited
The Manor House
High Street
Buntingford
Hertfordshire
SG9 9AB
United Kingdom

For all editorial enquiries, please contact:
www.regencyhousepublishing.com

ISBN-13: 978-0-7858-2252-3

10 9 8 7 6 5 4

Printed in China

The Publisher wishes to thank Garry Stuart, who took
most of the photographs in this book and also the
following:-

Page 105: © General Motors
Page 174: Flickr/Roger Blake
Page 175: Flickr/Ricardo Pérez
Page 254: Flickr/Kecko
Page 255: Wikimedia Commons/Michael Gil
Page 261: Flickr/Nick Ares
Page 300: Flickr/Brain Cantoni
Page 301: Flickr/Steve Cornelius
Page 361: © General Motors
Page 365: Wikimedia Commons/Mj-Bird
Page 376: Flickr/Peter PZ
Page 385: Courtsey of Mazda
Page 395: Courtesy of Mitsubishi Motors
Page 441-442: Courtesy of Toyota

CONTENTS

INTRODUCTION

Even pickups get the hot-rod treatment, as on this 1929 Model A Ford.

'I was a lonely teenage broncoing buck,' sings Don McLean, 'with a pink carnation and a pickup truck.' Few things are so closely associated with American culture as the pickup. If the modern automotive myth is true, then America was built on the backs of a heavy-duty Mack, an International tractor, a Harley-Davidson motorcycle and a Ford F-series pickup, probably from 1952.

There's no denying that pickup trucks were the workhorses of an entire nation for the best part of a century – a constant presence throughout American history. In the 1920s, hard-working Midwestern farmers relied on their Model Ts and Chevys to coax a living from the land before loading up and fleeing to California as fields turned to dust in the 1930s. Militarized pickups helped to chase Hitler into his bunker, though by the 1950s and '60s pickups were back on the farm, on the building site, or acting as carry-alls for rapidly-expanding businesses.

Other countries of the world didn't take to the pickup in quite the same way. The Europeans favoured small panel vans, while

in Africa bigger trucks were the norm and India had depended on the scooter-based tuk-tuk for decades. Only Australia with its 'utes' (utilities) has a similar feeling for the pickup, sharing a strong sense of the outdoor with America as well as the 'can-do' attitude that fits the image of the pickup like a glove. We are therefore concentrating on the American story, for even Japanese pickups from Toyota, Nissan and the rest would not have developed in quite the same way without a huge American market at their disposal.

The reason for the bond between Americans and their pickups isn't hard to find. After half a century of hard work, these little trucks have become firmly linked with the nation's great outdoors and the call of the wild to which many urbanites aspire, dreaming of the days when the American nation was in its infancy. The next best thing is to load one's truck with a camper unit or a trailer, and head off for the woods, mountains and prairies. Which is why, when *Car Life* magazine road-tested an International Scout in 1961, it described its appeal thus: 'You, feeling every inch the

Rust in peace: the final resting place for a 1930s Chevy.

man in the Marlboro ad, wend your way to work in your rugged, he-man Scout.' Or why Jeep offered a trim package on its 1975 pickups called 'the Pioneer'.

Until the early 1960s, pickups were working vehicles, but sales rocketed through the decade as they were used to haul boats and camping trailers or transport hunters shooting duck. It began to dawn, as two-car families became increasingly common, that two-seater pickups weren't quite as impractical as they seemed, and it was not unusual for the owner of a sedan or station wagon to buy a pickup as well. But weekend campers were still buying pickups to help them do a job of work, much as they liked the rugged image they conveyed.

All that changed in the 1970s when the

RIGHT
2001 Ford F-150. Ford's F-series was the most successful pickup of all time.

OPPOSITE
The Ram brought Dodge pickups to the forefront in the 1990s.

craze for customizing began and it was realized that pickup trucks could be private transport too. This accounts for the huge growth in pickup sales over the last three decades. Back in 1947, sales of all trucks, including the heavies, accounted for 21.7 per cent of the entire American market. By 1998, pickups alone constituted more than one in three sales, but the figure becomes almost half the entire market when SUVs are added to the equation, with sales of full-sized pickups nearly doubling by the early 1990s.

If more proof be needed, the Ford F-series was not only the best-selling pickup truck for 25 years, it was also the most successful vehicle of any type for a decade. Some say the growth of the SUV is a threat to the pickup's role as America's favourite transport, but there is little sign of that so far. In 2004, Ford sold over 900,000 F-series – up 11 per cent on the previous year – while Chevrolet shifted 700,000 Silverados and over 400,000 Dodge Rams found new homes. There is little doubt that pickups are one of the success stories of the American motor industry.

Of course there is a downside. Along with SUVs, pickups are the gas-guzzlers of the 21st century, pumping out more pollution than the equivalent sedan. They cause more damage in collisions, both to vehicles and people, and need bigger roads, garages and parking spaces. With the best will in the world they cannot be regarded as sustainable transport. So will they survive in the same recognizable form? As the Chinese say, the next 20 years should be interesting times.

CHAPTER ONE
CHEVROLET

OPPOSITE
1934 Chevrolet Model DB.

BELOW
A customized Model DB.

The name William C. Durant may not be as well known as that of Henry Ford, yet the companies he created, not only Chevrolet but also the entire General Motors empire, managed to outsell and outwit Ford for much of the 20th century. It is also worth remembering that while Chevrolet has always been regarded as Ford's arch-rival, it is only one division within General Motors.

Durant was a salesman/entrepreneur with a hand in the early fortunes of Buick, Cadillac, Oldsmobile and many other companies. He called this first grouping the General Motors Company, but soon ran out of money and was forced to resign. But it would take more than a mere business failure to discourage Durant: he decided to build a small car, for which he set up the Little Motor Car Co., and Chevrolet to make a large one. The name Chevrolet came from the Swiss-born racing driver, Louis Chevrolet, who designed an upmarket six-cylinder car for Durant bearing his name. This car, the Classic Six, was reasonably successful, but Durant's real intention had been to offer a cheap car as a way of undercutting Henry Ford. Louis Chevrolet washed his hands of it in disgust, but his name lived on: the low-priced Chevrolet 490 sold so well that Durant was able to use the profits to quietly buy up shares in his old General Motors company. By 1916, he owned 54 per cent, enabling him to pronounce himself the new president. Chevrolet was swiftly incorporated into General Motors and would remain the corporation's entry-level division for the

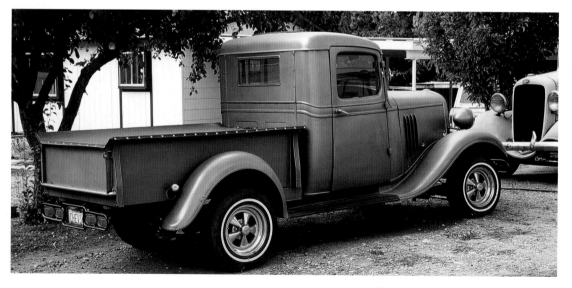

rest of the century. As for Durant, within five years he again ran out of cash, forcing him to leave the company he had started, this time with no prospect of return.

But Chevrolet prospered, and although it didn't produce what would now be recognized as a modern closed-cab pickup until the 1920s, it was offering light trucks rather earlier. The first were announced in 1918, the $^1\!/_2$-ton Light Delivery being a beefed up version of the 490 passenger car but with stronger springs. It was slightly more powerful than a Model T, giving 26bhp from its 170-ci (2786-cc) four-cylinder engine, driving through a conventional three-speed transmission. Like the T, it was sold as a bare chassis, in this case with only a cowl and windshield, to which customers fitted their own bodywork.

Alongside the Light Delivery was the heavier-duty 1-ton Series T, 'Sanely

OPPOSITE
A pickup like this is probably the best place from which to advertise a Harley or Corvette.

designed, properly constructed and built of known material', according to the *Chevrolet Review*, which went on to say: 'We have subjected these trucks to the most grueling tests! They have been driven the distance across the continent and back again. They have been put to the road tests and load tests. And from these we know just what these trucks will do under the most trying conditions.'

Like the 490, the one-ton Chevy was powered by a four-cylinder overhead-valved engine of 223ci (3654cc) and 37bhp. At $1,325, it was considerably more expensive than the ¹/₂-ton, reflecting its greater power, heavy-duty specification and longer 125-in (3.2-m) wheelbase. This was the price for the bare chassis, though Chevrolet's biggest truck also came from the factory as a Curtain Top Express or Flare Board Express, the latter a type of primitive pickup with short wooden sides to its load bed, flared to accommodate bulky loads and with no cab. Whatever its format, however, the Series T proved to be reliable and hard-working, and remained part of the Chevrolet line-up for five years.

Both the 490 and the T remained virtually unchanged during their lifetimes, though it didn't prevent Chevrolet from going to town with the publicity. Take this quote from the 'Commercial Cars' catalogue of 1920. 'The Chevrolet Light Delivery Wagon is designed to meet the requirements of those who have need of a commercial car with slightly less capacity and a considerably lighter weight than is afforded by a 1-ton truck. It is sturdily constructed and amply

powered for all transportation needs. It is light enough to be speedy, easy-riding and economical with fuel and tires.' The 490 now included electric lights, starter and horn, adjustable windshield, spare-wheel rim and a complete tool kit. As for the 1-ton, its Flare Board option measured 114.5in long and 44in wide (2.9 x 1.1m), so it was usefully large. However, there was still no cab and the driver had to wear oilskins to protect himself from the rain.

Although Chevrolet was by now firmly established in the truck business, it is necessary to see this in perspective. In 1920, it built 5,288 1-ton Series Ts, the product of four factories, compared with over 135,000 Model TT 1-tonners that Ford produced the same year. So while Chevrolet was slowly gaining on Ford as far as car production was concerned, it had a long way to go in terms of its trucks. It was also the year when Billy Durant was forced out due to financial problems within the company.

The company was undeterred, however, and launched a new truck for 1921, the ³/₄-ton Model G. Essentially it was a mix of existing components, the front half of the 490 married with the heavier-duty rear end, plus the Series T's 37-bhp four-cylinder engine. The 'product of years of experience', according to Chevrolet, it also came in Flare Board Express form, with a bed 2in (5cm) wider than that of the T but over 12in (30cm) shorter, due partly to the 120-in (3-m) wheelbase. Sales that year were lower than ever and only 855 Model Gs and less than 500 Ts were built.

Chevrolet decided that a little Ford-style

pricing was in order, so the ¹/₂-ton New Superior, available as the Series A and B for 1923, began at $325 for the bare chassis against $625 for that of the 1921 490. It was decided that a cut-price specification was no longer in order and it was given a similar 102-in (2.6-m) wheelbase to the 490, sharing the 171-ci (2802-cc) 37-bhp four-cylinder engine with the bigger trucks. These were now named the Series D Utility Express, all rated at one ton and with a choice of 120- or 125-in wheelbases.

Both ¹/₂- and 1-ton models were mildy updated for 1924, the lighter truck gaining a straight front axle and rod- rather than cable-operated brakes. The four-cylinder engine was redesigned the following year with a water pump and fan cooling, though quoted power was actually slightly down at 35bhp. The ¹/₂-ton became the Superior Series K, with an angled windshield, while the 1-ton became the Series H. All were sold as chassis only, but could later have a vestibule added, which was simply a closed cab. There were more minor engine changes for 1926, together with bigger brakes, while Chevrolet announced a roadster pickup – a passenger car with a load bed in place of the rumble seat. Meanwhile, the 1-ton gained 4in (10cm) in the wheelbase and became the Series R.

In 1927 the Superior series was supplemented by the Capitol AA, in both ¹/₂- and 1-ton forms with 103- and 124-in (2.6- and 3.1-m) wheelbases respectively. The bigger truck was offered for the first time with a factory-built stakesided load bed at $680, while the ¹/₂-ton AA bare chassis cost

just $395, slightly cheaper than the equivalent Superior. It was only offered in that form, publicized as a commercial chassis to which aftermarket bodywork could be fitted.

Nineteen-twenty-eight was the final year for this first generation of four-cylinder Chevrolet trucks. More power was offered from the faithful 171-ci overhead-valve four, due to a higher 4.5:1 compression ratio, bigger valves with higher lift, and a two-piece exhaust manifold. Oddly, it was still quoted at the same 45bhp as before, but now peaked at 2,200rpm. This was fitted to a longer 107-in (2.7-m) wheelbase chassis for the updated National AB Series, while the 1-ton became the LO, then LP series, with a 124-in wheelbase and standard four-speed transmission. Chevrolet listed the AB in ten different styles, for the first time including a pickup. Remember how Chevrolet trucks had been selling at only a tiny fraction of Ford's back in 1920? In 1928, this increased to 133,682; Ford was still in the throes of switching over to Model A production, so Chevrolet trucks were outselling those of its arch-rival for the first time.

Second-Generation Six-Cylinders
The year 1929 was highly significant for Chevrolet. Not only did it maintain market leadership over Ford, even though Ford's production lines were up to full speed with the new Model A, but it announced a six-cylinder engine. At the time, sixes were the preserve of more expensive middle-class cars, rather than trucks, but Chevrolet chose to use its new power unit across the range.

The engine in question was what would later be known as the 'Stovebolt six', due to the appearance of its cylinder-head bolts, and in a long career would power countless Chevrolet sedans, trucks and even the first Corvette. It was a conventional overhead-valve unit of 194ci (3179cc), with cast-iron block and a compression ratio of 5.02:1. Nicknamed the 'Cast-Iron Wonder', Stovebolt coming later, it produced 46bhp at 2,600rpm, which gave it a considerable advantage over the four-cylinder 40-bhp Ford, allowing Chevrolet to upgrade its 1-ton truck to 1½ tons. Of course, Dodge

OPPOSITE and LEFT
A 1946 pickup. Early post-war Chevrolet pickups were almost identical to the pre-war models.

would respond with its own six and Ford with the famous flathead V8 within a few years, but that was still in the future.

For the time being, Chevrolet was offering a truck that was smoother and faster than any of the opposition, and which enabled more deliveries to be made in a day. The advantages were especially marked in the short-wheelbased ¹/2-ton: as in previous years, Chevrolet had fitted the same engine to its light-duty trucks as to the big ones, so the renamed ¹/2-ton International AC gave sparkling performance. At $400 for the bare chassis, it was slightly more expensive than a Ford Model A chassis ($350), so it wasn't quite the 'six at the price of a four' that Chevrolet advertisements promised, but it was close enough to make the $50 worthwhile.

If 1929 had been a landmark in the history of Chevrolet trucks, then 1931 was almost as significant. The company bought up the Martin-Parry Co. of Indianapolis, a major supplier of aftermarket bodies. At long last the company could offer a full range of truck bodies, and these included pickups. The Open Cab Pickup offered a load bed 66in long, 45in wide and 13in deep (168 x 114 x 33cm), based on the same Independence AE 1/2-ton chassis that every other Chevrolet truck had that year. Listed at $440 (the bare chassis was still offered at $355) it was also referred to as a Roadster Pickup or Roadster Delivery, but one fact was clear – Chevrolet was now in the business of producing factory-built pickups.

It was joined by a closed-cab variant the following year when all the 1/2-tonners were renamed the Confederate Series BB. All had extra power as the Cast-Iron Wonder was coaxed up to 53bhp at 2,800rpm and 131lb ft, due in part to a slightly higher compression ratio of 5.2:1. This engine was produced to a truck specification distinct from the standard sedan motor. A silent synchromesh three-speed transmission was standard across the range, making the trucks easier to drive, while a new option was the Deluxe trim, which used the 1931 car fenders, running boards and other features, plus chrome headlights and horn. There were more improvements for 1933, with 56bhp from the Stovebolt and the option of a four-speed transmission on the 1/2-ton trucks for the first time, plus a windshield fitted with safety glass. As for the pickup, this now had an all-steel cargo box, with double security

chins and a left-hand mounted spare tyre. The price was down to $440, due to the Depression, not that Chevrolet was suffering too much. It produced almost 100,000 trucks that year, enough to take a 50 per cent share of the entire U.S. market.

There was smoother, car-like front-end styling the following year, with fully-crowned fenders, while the wheelbase was up to 112in (2.8m) and the Stovebolt was enlarged to 207ci (3392cc), though Chevrolet claimed the same 56bhp as before, albeit peaking at a slightly lower speed. Prices were also beginning to creep back up, indicating that the worst of the Depression was over, confirmed the following year when production leaped to over 167,000. There were few changes in 1935, though the ever-adaptable Stovebolt received another power boost to 79bhp at 3,200rpm in 1936 – not quite as strong as Ford's 85-bhp V8, but not far off it either. There were hydraulic brakes as well – another plus point over Ford – and an all-steel cab.

Heavier-duty trucks returned to the line-up in 1937 as the 3/4-ton GD and 1-ton GE joined the new 1 1/2-ton GC. The first two shared a 122.25in (3.1-m) wheelbase, while all three offered a pickup box, which measured 77 by 45in on the GC and was 16in deep (196 x 114 x 41cm). The GE had bigger brakes and 17-in tyres, but was otherwise very similar to the GD. The bigger trucks also had stakeside variants, which the 1/2-ton didn't, and these were slightly more expensive than the pickups by virtue of their larger capacity. To prove the mechanical reliability of the basic unit and show off its

new 'Diamond Crown' styling, racing driver Harry Hartz drove a 1/2-ton pickup off the production line in Flint, Michigan, and on to a 10,000-mile (1610-km) journey around the U.S.A. He achieved this in 72 days without a single breakdown.

Chevrolet sedans now had the same power as Ford's flathead, the latest 217-ci (3556-cc) version of the Stovebolt now delivering 85bhp. It had been slightly derated to 78bhp in the trucks, though was listed at the same 170lb ft, while internal changes were aimed at longer life rather than higher power. Added in 1938 was a larger water pump with ball-bearings and heavier valve springs, not to mention a diaphragm clutch, uprated electrics and a new starter motor. There was a styling update the following year, including fuller fenders and a two-piece V-shaped windshield, features shared by both 1/2-ton JC, 3/4-ton JD and 3/4-ton JE. Chevrolet trucks were increasingly coming to share the styling features of equivalent sedans, and were looking most stylish as a result. The new styling also brought a roomier cab with extra headroom and more comfortable seat, and the instruments were grouped together to make them easier to read.

The 3/4-ton JE was a heavy-duty version of the standard 3/4-ton, with 14-in diameter brakes and 17-in tyres. It effectively replaced the old 1-tonner, uprated as the 1 1/2-ton. Reflecting the increasing popularity of pickups, the new 3/4-ton had a pickup variant in both JD and heavy-duty JE forms. Due to an extra 10in (25cm) of wheelbase, it was notably bigger than the JC pickup, with a

ABOVE and OPPOSITE
New rear three-quarter windows are shown
to good effect on these 1950 Chevys.

length of 78in, width of just under 46in and depth of 14in (198 x 117 x 36cm), which added up to 13 per cent more capacity.

Motoring historian John Gunnell refers to them as 'Wurlitzers', and there could be no better description for Chevrolet's chrome-encrusted trucks of 1941. Fairing the headlight pods into the front fenders was regarded as 'modern' at the time, but the massive chrome grille, which dominated the entire front end, made even some 1950s sedans seem restrained by comparison. Still, it was distinctive, and the 1941 trucks did incorporate several worthwhile improvements. A longer 115-in (2.9-m) wheelbase on the 1/2-ton provided the driver with more legroom and the seat was placed at a more comfortable angle with improved padding. The Stovebolt six now produced 90bhp at 3,300rpm and 174lb ft at 1,200. By

now, the 3/4–ton truck had a longer wheelbase, up to 125.25in, and also boasted the Wurlitzer front end.

Chevrolet set a new record, with over 212,000 trucks sold that year. This high production rate carried over to the 1942 model year, when over 119,000 trucks were registered before production was halted in March 1942 to concentrate on the war effort. Until July 1945, the Government allowed Chevrolet to build only 56,128 light trucks for essential civilian use. All of these, as well as the 1942 trucks, were very little changed from their 1941 specification, Wurlitzer and all.

Production, when it resumed in August 1945, was composed of 1941–42 models, the pickup at the much increased price of $757. The factory made it clear that these were no more than stopgaps or 'interim' models 'not to be considered post-war models'. Moreover, because of the austerity of the times, trim was painted rather than chromed.

Chrome returned in May 1946, when the first official post-war trucks were launched, though a glance at the specifications revealed the same old 1941–42 trucks with a few refinements. The 1/2-ton was renamed 3100 and the 3/4-ton 3600, but the Stovebolt still came in 1941 90-bhp form. There were no other significant changes. However, in addition to the chrome detailing, the first post-war Chevrolet trucks now came in a range of colours. Most common in the 1945–46 interim trucks had been Turret Gray, but the choice was now altogether more cheerful. It included Omaha Orange, Apple Green and Swift's Red and two-tone

shades were offered as well – not a bad note on which to end this long line of Chevrolet pickups.

Advance, Advance!

Chevrolet's all-new 'Advance Design' light trucks went on sale on Saturday, 28 June 1947. It was a significant day not only for Chevrolet but also for the entire industry, these being the first genuinely new post-war trucks to hit the market. The most obvious piece of advanced design was the new cab, with its full-width styling, horizontal grille and integral headlights.

It was far bigger than before – 8in (20cm) wider and 7in longer – allowing Chevrolet to fit a three-passenger bench seat. Not only that but the seat was also adjustable to allow optimum vision, helped by the larger windshield, still V-shaped and in two pieces, and rear window. Truck owners, in an early example of market research, had let it be known that a roomier cab with better vision and more comfortable seating was what they wanted most and that is what they got. Larger, wider doors complemented the bigger cab, which sat on a three-point suspension system designed to give a softer ride, and was completely welded where previous cabs had been partly bolted together. There was also a new optional heater/defroster, with vents at the rear of the cab to expel used air.

Buyers of pickups had a choice of three models as the 1-ton returned this year, being the $^{1}/_{2}$-ton 3104, $^{3}/_{4}$-ton 3604 and 1-ton 3804. All three load beds were 50in wide and 16.2in deep (127 and 41cm), but lengths

RIGHT and OPPOSITE
At the other end of the scale, some owners
were spending long hours and many dollars
making their pickups better than new.

were 78, 87 and 108in (198, 221 and 274cm) respectively, reflecting wheelbases of 116, 125.25 and 137in (2.9, 3.2 and 3.5m). These were steel-sided cargo boxes with wooden floors and steel skid strips. There was a new cab and a new load bed, but what hadn't changed was the 90-bhp 217-ci (3556-cc)

overhead-valve six, apart from its new name – Thriftmaster. Something else had changed as well. Chevrolet produced over 335,000 trucks in the 1947 calendar year, as eager buyers clamoured for the only true post-war pickups available. It was little wonder that the division had to open three new factories

and double the capacity of its body plant.

Given this sort of demand, it's hardly surprising that major changes were not on Chevrolet's list of priorities for the next few years. Some controls were shifted to allow for a flat, unobstructed floor space and make more room for a third passenger, while the

OPPOSITE
A neat and clean custom job has been made of this 1950 model, which extends to the load bed.

gear change moved to the steering column and the parking brake became a foot-actuated pedal. The optional four-speed transmission fitted to the 1-ton 3800 now had synchromesh, while for 1949 the gas tank was moved inside the cab behind the back of the seat. That year, the pickup range began at $1,263 for the ½-ton 3104, increasing to $1,471 for the 1-ton 3804. Forest Green was the standard colour, but there were others available, with contrasting pinstriping, such as Sun Beige with Totem Scarlet, to set them off. Attractive colours and an up-to-date design were all that was neccessary to keep production humming in 1949, when over 383,000 trucks were built, enough for a 33.8 per cent share of the market. Ford had only 21.6 per cent that year, so life was sweet as far as Chevrolet was concerned.

But it couldn't afford to be complacent, and 1950 saw several improvements, such as double-acting, all-round shock absorbers and a circuit-breaker lighting system. By now, the Thriftmaster six offered slightly more power, due to a Rochester Power Jet down-draft carburettor, larger valves and a straight-through muffler, with 92bhp at 3,400rpm and 176lb ft at 1,000. An existing feature was Deluxe cab equipment, which included 'Nu Vue' rear quarter windows for improved visibility. Yet another production record was broken, with 494,573 trucks built in the calendar year – nearly 150,000 more than Ford and 368,000 ahead of Dodge. In other words, that year, one in three new trucks was a Chevrolet. Nineteen-fifty-one was less eventful, though ventipanes (opening quarter

windows) improved ventilation. But the shortage of materials, as a result of the Korean War, meant that once again Chevrolet trucks had to bid farewell to chrome, if only temporarily. Production fell that year, though it was still enough to maintain its market leadership with a 30 per cent share. It says a lot for the appeal of Chevrolet trucks that they kept their dominant position into the early 1950s, well after major rivals had launched their own new post-war trucks.

There were no major changes in either 1952 or '53, unless one counts push-button door handles in the first year and a left-handed mounting of the spare wheel in the second. There were new colours in 1953, Transport Blue, Burgundy Maroon and Coppertone, among others. But there were some genuine changes for 1954, chiefly because the 1947 Advance Design was now in its eighth year and Chevrolet needed to sustain interest before its all-new 1955 model was ready to launch. First and foremost there was more power, as the Thriftmaster was increased to 235ci (3851cc), with an increase in both bore and stroke. The extra cubic inches, plus a higher compression ratio of 7.5:1, resulted in 112bhp at 3,700rpm and 200lb ft at 2,000rpm. It still drove through a three-speed manual gearbox, with heavy-duty or four-speed floor-shift options, though the option of General Motors' Hydra-Matic automatic transmission on all trucks up to one ton was the most exciting change.

Customers would also have appreciated the reduced amount of kick-up on the rear of

the chassis, which reduced the load height and allowed the cargo box to have deeper sides, giving 28cu ft of space. This meant many parts had to be redesigned, but was worth it for its increased usability. All the trucks had a more substantial engine cross member and better cab mounting, and there were improvements to details such as the wiper system and an illuminated glove box. Most obvious of all, however, was the new one-piece windshield, available either clear or tinted, the new grille and square parking lights. Chevrolet truck production dropped by 10 per cent that year, reflecting a generally depressed market, but the company managed to keep its 30 per cent overall share. So the Advance Design had done a great job. As the first new post-war pickup, it had stolen a march on the opposition, consolidating its best-selling position, which it had held for eight years. Could the new generation for 1955 hope to do as well?

V8s & Sweep-Sights

The 'Task Force', Chevrolet's new pickups for 1955, had more of everything: more power than the trucks they replaced; more space, comfort, options and presence. Chevrolet had taken a huge step forward by replacing the entire range of light-, medium- and heavy-duty trucks in one fell swoop, maintaining its leadership of the light truck market as it had with the Advance Design.

The all-new styling was modern and forward-looking, with running boards hidden behind the doors and fashionable frenched visors on the headlights. The massive wraparound 'Sweep-Sight Windshield' was

derived from that of the Buick Le Sabre, and could be echoed in an optional wraparound rear window, while the familiar 235-ci Thriftmaster six was still the base engine, though now producing 123bhp at 3,800rpm.

But Chevrolet had to offer a V8 engine if it wished to keep ahead of the pack. A kind of mania was sweeping Detroit in the mid 1950s, as every manufacturer proceeded to drop their side-valve motors in favour of the hot new overhead-valve V8s, so it was odd that Chevrolet was one of the last to

RIGHT and OPPOSITE
This 1951 Chevrolet Series 3100 has been
nicely restored.

follow suit. When it did, however, Ford having followed this route the previous year, the small-block 265-ci (4343-cc) V8 made such an impact that it transformed Chevrolet's stolid image overnight. Even in its mildest form, the short-stroked, easy-breathing small-block was able to produce 154bhp at 4,000rpm.

Better still, Chevrolet had the sense to make the new wonder engine available right across the range for 1955, and that included the pickups. These were only offered in the lowest state of tune (154bhp, 7.5:1 compression, two-barrel carb) but the Sedan Delivery, basically the pickup with a panel-van rear end, could also be had with 162bhp or 180bhp 'Power Pack' V8s. They all bore the 'Trademaster' name, under the pickup hood, but nobody was fooled, the only justification for this sort of power being sheer driving enjoyment. Even the mildest V8 made the Chevrolet pickup one of the fastest trucks on the road. All came with a wide choice of transmissions: three-speed with or without overdrive, heavy-duty three-speed, four-speed or Hydra-Matic.

The range was expanded with a long-wheelbased ½-tonner alongside the standard models, its 123.5 inches (3.1m) allowing a load bed of 8ft (2.4m), compared with 6.5ft for the other ½-ton models. The ¾-tonners shared the 123.5-in wheelbase, with heftier springs, axles, shocks and tyres to cope with a GVW (gross vehicle weight) of 6,900lb (3130kg). The 1-ton wheelbase measured 135in (3.4m), and a four-speed transmission was part of the package. There was a host of other new standard features on all the

OPPOSITE and LEFT
By 1951, the marque dominated the U.S. pickup market, with nearly one in three new pickups now a Chevrolet.

pickups, such as tubeless tyres and 12-volt electrics, plus options that included power steering and power brakes, but the ultimate Chevrolet pickup was the Cameo.

This was something of a milestone in the history of pickups, where style was concerned, in that it was the first American pickup to come with flush sides. It looked far smoother than the traditional stepside, having a wider load bed, though in the Cameo's case it had been faked: fibreglass panels covered the stepsides, while another

OPPOSITE
Concealed running boards, panoramic
windshield and hooded headlights gave this
Chevy a modern appearance.

LEFT
The 1955 3200 Hydra-Matic, one of the
new generation of 'Task Force' Chevrolets.

smoothed the rear tailgate over. So although it looked wider, the cargo box was actually 2in (5cm) narrower than the standard stepside. Fake it may have been, but the Cameo was a pioneer, for one day most

pickups would be built with flush sides. Chevrolet marketed the Cameo as a stylish sort of car/truck, referring to it as the 'suburbanite pickup'. It was produced in limited numbers and with plenty of exclusive

touches such as a Bombay Ivory/Commercial Red paint job and red/white interior to match.

Because the new-generation Task Force had been so impressive, and the fact that

OPPOSITE
A Series 5100 from the mid 1950s.

BELOW
1954 saw the last of the old-look pickups.

OPPOSITE

There has been no loving restoration or elaborate customization, apart from non-standard wheels, for this pickup from 1955.

Chevrolet sold not far short of 400,000 trucks in its first year, one would have expected no changes to the range for 1956. But the power race was now in full swing so the pickups were given extra horses that year. Even the Thriftmaster got the treatment, with a higher 8.0:1 compression boosting power to 140bhp and torque to 210lb ft, the base 265 V8 now up to 155bhp.

Meanwhile, all the major manufacturers were beginning to offer factory-fitted four-wheel-drive on their light trucks and Chevrolet was no exception. For 1957, a selectable system, with a two-range, eight-speed transmission, was offered right across the pickup range as well as in most other Chevrolet light trucks. A rubber-mounted divider split the power 50/50 front/rear, and could be shifted between two- and four-wheel-drive while on the move. Another part of the package consisted of four power take-off points for driving machinery. Once again, Chevrolet captured over 32 per cent of the truck market, though sales were down to a little over 350,000. It couldn't have failed to notice, however, that Ford was narrowing the gap at almost 31 per cent.

There was much to do, therefore, in the Task Force's third year, and a spate of updates included new front-end styling with twin headlights and a new name – Apache. There was more power to go with the bolder front end: the Trademaster V8 had been upsized to 283ci (4637cc) the previous year, and now came with yet more power, the base 283, with an 8.5:1 compression ratio and single two-barrelled carburettor producing 160bhp and 270lb ft. Once again, if one was

able to dispense with the pickup bed and order the Sedan Delivery, there were 185-bhp two-barrel and 230-bhp four-barrel options as well. Still not enough? In theory, the Delivery could also be ordered with the Corvette's Rochester fuel injection, which promised 250bhp at 5,200rpm, plus exciting handling from the live-axled, leaf-sprung chassis. This would have been unlikely, however, as the Rochester set-up was an exotic and expensive piece of kit; even among Corvette buyers, only a handful were willing to pay extra for the privilege. More relevant to most Apache customers was the fact that the Thriftmaster six was boosted to 145bhp that year.

Probably of more significance to the history of Chevrolet pickups was the mid-year arrival of the Fleetside. This took over from the Cameo, sales of which had dwindled to only 1,405 by this time. Stylish though it was, the Cameo cost $500 more than the standard Apache. Ford had introduced its own Styleside equivalent the previous year, at the same price as the standard Flareside, which was a roaring success, leaving Chevrolet no choice but to drop the Cameo and replace it with an all-steel double-walled box, with the same stylish flush sides but more useful space. Offered on both 1/2- and 3/4-ton pickups, the Fleetside measured 75in (191cm) wide, a full 25in (63cm) more than the Stepside, which in short-box form made it nearly as wide as it was long. As a long box on the 123.25-in wheelbase, it offered an impressive 75.6cu ft. Unlike Ford, Chevrolet charged extra for that space, but as it was a

scant $6 it is unlikely that many buyers were in fact deterred.

There was a change of tack for 1959 as a recession caused American car buyers to look at fuel economy afresh. Sales of imported cars and trucks, such as VW's Transporter pickup, were increasing month on month, and traditional trucks like the Apache were beginning to seem thirsty and inefficient. Detroit was in the process of launching its own compact sedans though there was no sign of a compact pickup.

So Chevrolet tweaked the Thriftmaster six to improve economy, describing the V8 as 'efficient' instead of emphasizing its power. An Economy Contoured Camshaft, with lower valve lift in the six, cut power to 135bhp, though torque actually increased to 217lb ft. Chevrolet claimed a 10 per cent gas saving while driving and 25 per cent at idle. If that wasn't enough, a Maximum Economy Option added a smaller carburettor and taller 3.38:1 rear axle, for which the company claimed a further 10 per cent saving. However, this didn't prevent Ford truck production from overtaking Chevrolet for the first time in decades, while Chevrolet just managed to hang on to its sales lead but couldn't rely on it any more.

The Gold Rush

The early 1960s was a time of boom for Chevrolet pickups. The company built its ten-millionth truck during 1966, and it's a sobering thought that one-third of the entire output since 1918 had left the factories since 1960. At least part of the boom was down to the increasing recreational market. Sales of

travel trailers, truck campers and camping trailers tripled between 1961 and '66, and all of them needed a beefy pickup to haul them, preferably with a V8 beneath the hood. In spite of the hype given to the small-block V8, only a minority of Apache pickup buyers had actually ordered one, the Thriftmaster six outselling the V8 by six to one in 1960. But that had shifted to three to one by the middle of the decade, as private customers began to buy Chevrolet pickups; moreover, they were willing to buy the power to haul their camping trailers up to the mountains at weekends.

The new decade was greeted by all-new styling, the latest Chevrolet trucks having squared-off, more functional lines, combined with a roomier cab and stronger front end,

OPPOSITE and BELOW
A 1955 3100 with stylish additions such as whitewall tyres, chrome hubcaps, overriders and colour-matched sun visors. The cab is roomy, light and airy.

OPPOSITE and LEFT
A V8 option for the 1955 pickup allowed
Chevy to catch up with the competition on
the road.

OPPOSITE and LEFT
Every inch the good ole boy: Doug Brown
and his lived-in 1955 Chevy.

OPPOSITE
A fully customized 1955 Stepside.

the whole truck being up to 7in (18cm) lower. The three basic models were renamed C10 (1/2-ton), C15 (3/4-ton) and C20 (1-ton), while trucks with four-wheel-drive acquired a 'K' suffix. As before, there were Fleetside and Stepside cargo boxes, the bigger wraparound windshield emphasizing the wider cab. A significant change lurking underneath was independent front suspension for the two-wheel-drive 1/2- and 3/4-tonners. Using ball joints and torsion bars, this was thought to be the first independent front end on a U.S.-built pickup, and was complemented by rear coil springs. The 1-ton continued with variable-rate leaf springs and a solid front axle, while other changes were hardly world-shaking: the three-speed overdrive transmission was dropped, as was the Hydra-Matic automatic, replaced by General Motors' Powerglide: a Spicer front axle was fitted to the 4x4s.

There was a new four-wheel-drive pickup for 1961, the 4x4 driveline now being available on the long-box 1/2-ton C10, which had not been the case previously. But Chevrolet's thoughts were not with the traditional trucks that year, as it was launching a new range based on the Corvair. The pickup version of this was aimed fair and square at the VW Transporter, but offered rather more power from the Corvair's air-cooled flat-six mounted in the tail; at first, this had 80bhp/128lb ft, later 95bhp with a 110-bhp option. It also had a usefully long 105-in (2.7-m) load bed, offered as the Loadside with fixed double-walled steel sides or the Rampside with a side-loading tailgate that touched the ground, acting as a loading ramp. It was later supplemented by the Chevy

II-based 1/2-ton van, dropped in 1965.

Meanwhile, the names of the conventional pickups were changed for 1962, the Thriftmaster six becoming the 'High-Torque' while the trucks themselves became 'Jobmasters'. Single headlights made a comeback, though the only substantive change was a new engine option, the High-Torque 261, which was really the old 235-ci unit with a 3-in (76-mm) stroke. As the name suggests, it measured 261ci (4277cc) and produced 150bhp and 235lb ft at 2,000rpm. But the 261 was no more than a stopgap: for 1963 Chevrolet launched a new pair of overhead-valve sixes to replace the originals, which could trace their roots back to the first Stovebolt engine of 1929. These new sixes were lighter, due to their thin-walled construction, the smaller short-stroke version of the 230-ci (3769-cc) producing 140bhp at 4,400rpm and 220lb ft at 1,600rpm, while its 292-ci (4785-cc) brother, standard on the four-wheel-drive K-series, made 165bhp and 280lb ft. Both engines wore the same High-Torque label as their predecessors, also applied to the latest 283-ci (4637-cc) V8, now with 9.0:1 compression and 175bhp/275lb ft. Chevrolet was now selling more V8 trucks than ever before, achieving its 100,000th for the first time that year, though this was dwarfed by the 378,000 sixes sold.

There were no major changes during the pickup's final three years on the market. The torsion bar front suspension had been converted to coil springs for 1963, but attention was focused on the cab the following year; the windshield was conventional rather than wraparound and

allowed the A-pillars to slope backwards rather than forwards. Inside, there was a new dashboard and the Custom Comfort Option consisted of red or beige trim, an armrest, cigarette lighter and other minor touches. Air conditioning became a factory option the following year, and with sales of camper units still booming, Chevrolet now offered a Camper Special pickup, with beefed-up undercarriage and a standard V8.

The truck's final year was a happy one for Chevrolet, which posted its best 12 months yet, with 621,354 trucks sold. By far the biggest sellers (over 470,000) were the C- and K-series trucks, with the long-wheelbased 1/2-ton C1500 far and away the favourite. Chevrolet built over 200,000 of these in 1966, plus another 140,000 of the short-wheelbased C1400. The C2500 was next, at a little over 73,000, with four-wheel-drive pickups produced in tiny numbers – less than 8,500 in all.

Engine options were also interesting, by far the most popular that year being the 283-ci V8. Almost as popular were the High-Torque 292-ci (4785-cc) six and Chevrolet's small-block 327-ci (5359-cc) V8, which was a 220-bhp option in that final year, very few buyers staying with the base 230-ci (3769-cc) six. These early 1960s pickups did more to expand Chevrolet's sales of light trucks than any other.

Customs & Campers
Chevrolet's Custom Sport Truck option was fitted to only 3 per cent of its light trucks in 1967, which made it seem like a flop. But it was not: it was indicative of the way the

pickup market was changing, despite its carpet, cigarette lighter, sound insulation and extra brightwork. Under the snappier title, 'CST', it was aimed at younger buyers looking for fun with a truck at weekends rather than using it for work. There were Custom Appearance and Comfort & Convenience packages, too, reflecting the growing numbers of pickups now used to haul campers, surfboards and trail bikes into the great outdoors.

Sales of trucks increased by 40 per cent

OPPOSITE
Pickups and country music seem to go together, which is why this 1955 model found its way onto an album cover.

LEFT
High-riding and chrome-beamed, the ready-for-action 'Ole Yeller', a 1956 pickup.

PAGES 58 and 59
A 1957 3100s with all the trimmings. This was the final year for the single-headlight front end.

between 1967 and '72, and Chevrolet had a share in this growth, producing nearly three-quarters of a million trucks in the final year. So when it launched the latest pickup in 1967, it was in a rapidly changing market.

The styling was all-new, squared-off, chunky and modern, with more glass, plus a lower stance for easier access and better handling. The trucks may have been marketed as 'Job Tamers' but much of their convenience

engineering had been done with private buyers in mind.

The base power unit was now a 250-ci (4097-cc) six of 140bhp, but the 292-ci (4785-cc) six and 283-ci (4637-cc) V8 were

arried over unchanged, plus the newly-popular 220-bhp 327. These were given even more cubic inches in 1968, when Chevrolet's big-block 396-ci (6489-cc) V8 became available. With 310bhp and 400lb ft, it raised pickup power yet another notch, proving that muscle trucks weren't only an invention of the 1990s. There was a still more powerful

325-bhp high-compression version, but this was only for the El Camino. At the same time, the 283 V8 was replaced by the division's newer 307-ci (5031-cc), which itself offered 200bhp. In its turn the 327 was replaced for 1969 by Chevy's ubiquitous 350-ci (5735-cc) V8, really a 327 with a longer stroke, which came in three states of

tune: 215bhp (8.0:1 compression, two-barrel carb); 250bhp (9.0:1, two-barrel); and 255bhp (9.0:1, four-barrel). The mildest 350 was by far the most popular engine choice that year and over 120,000 were sold, while a mere 13,000-odd trucks were delivered with the ultimate 396. On the other hand, the CST option was gradually gaining

OPPOSITE
1959 Apache 32 Fleetside.

ABOVE
1959 Apache 32 Stakeside.

ABOVE and OPPOSITE
1959 El Camino, Chevrolet's attempt to
rival the Ford Ranchero.

popularity, having had just short of 30,000 buyers in 1969, while nearly 150,000 chose the Comfort & Convenience package instead. Chevrolet devoted a whole double-page advertisement to the virtues of the optional power steering, showing a camper-

equipped pickup wending its way through a forest, the driver not even breaking sweat: 'Just 2½ pounds of finger pressure moves that pickup around like a car,' went the blurb, making it plain that burly construction workers were no longer a target.

By 1970, the line-up would have been familiar to any buyer of Chevrolet pickups in the past ten years or more. As well as the ½-ton C10, ¾-ton C20 and 1-ton C30, there was a choice of Fleetside or Stepside cargo boxes, either 6.5ft, 8ft, 8.5ft or 9ft,

depending on wheelbase, which measured 115, 127 and 133in (2.9, 3.2 and 3.4m). The most popular combination of all remained the C10 with longer 127-in wheelbase and 8-ft (2.4-m) Fleetside box. An interesting addition was the 3/4-ton Longhorn, based on the 133-in chassis with an 8.5-ft box specifically designed for campers. That year Chevrolet sold nearly 21,000 Camper Special pickups and over 32,000 in 1972.

It wasn't a good year for Chevrolet, as it happens, the combined effects of a recession and a UAW strike aimed at General Motors seeing supremacy go to Ford, though

OPPOSITE and THIS PAGE
New squared-off lines greeted the 1960s.
This is a mildly customized 1962 Chevy 10.

ABOVE
1964 Chevrolet 20.

OPPOSITE
1967 Chevrolet 10.

Chevrolet would snatch it back the following year, when it produced over 739,000 trucks. In the meantime, the pickups received a new grille and the big 396 V8 was replaced by an even bigger 400 (actually 402ci/6588cc), though with no more power. Like its predecessor it remained a relative minority choice compared with the 250,000 customers specifying a 350-ci V8 in 1971, though was now more popular than the 292-ci six. Around 100,000 also ordered air conditioning, with over 200,000 opting for automatic transmission and/or power steering, while larger numbers than ever went for CST and Comfort & Convenience option packs.

Now into its final year, the fifth-generation post-war Chevrolet pickup carried on much as before, now with front disc brakes and new optional packages, including the Cheyenne and Highlander. Perhaps more

significant that year was the little LUV pickup. With ever-increasing numbers of imported mini-pickups sold in America each year, General Motors decided to enter this market itself, but like Ford, which sold a Mazda pickup as the Ford Courier, decided it was not worth building one on home ground. Instead, it took a 34.2 per cent stake in Isuzu Motors of Japan, and set about adapting its existing small pickup to comply with U.S. legislation.

The LUV (Light Utility Vehicle) resembled a miniaturized version of the full-sized trucks, which was quite an achievement, given that its major external

OPPOSITE
Despite the increasing popularity of the roomy Fleetside, many buyers still preferred the traditional Stepside.

LEFT
A 1965 Fleetside, demonstrating just how much extra load space it offered.

change was a Chevrolet grille. Based on a 102-in (2.6-m) wheelbase, the LUV had a 6-ft cargo box and was powered by an overhead-cam 111-ci (1819-cc) four-cylinder engine producing 80bhp. It may have

seemed unexciting compared with a full-sized V8 loaded with options, but there was still a market for mini-trucks such as this. Meanwhile, it had been quite a departure as far as Chevrolet was concerned.

Tricky Times
Chevrolet's line-up of light trucks now included the LUV and even a panel-van version of the Vega compact, but its bread-and-butter best-sellers remained the full-

FAR LEFT and BELOW
The 1964 Chevy was a working vehicle, but was now increasingly seen as leisure transport.

sized pickups, the two-wheel-drive C- and four-wheel-drive K-series. They all had new styling for 1973, which they shared with the Blazer, which was really a short-wheelbased, four-seater version of the light truck, not covered here, it being more of an SUV than a true pickup. More massive and squared-off than ever before, they presented a large egg-crate grille to the world, with a sculptured line running along the sides from nose to tail. The cab was wider than before, with instruments and controls arranged in a semi-circle around the driver. Wheelbases were up across the range, starting with 117.5in (3m) for the base $\frac{1}{2}$-ton C10 with 6.5ft load bed. Long-wheelbased C10s had

OPPOSITE and THIS PAGE
Welcome to the 1970s, and bigger more brutal styling than ever before, though they had a more car-like interior.

OPPOSITE
Oil crises may come and go, but Chevrolet went on building full-sized pickups like this C10.

PAGE 78
This Stepside is from a slightly earlier era.

PAGE 79
A 1970 Chevrolet C10 with some simple customizing.

long been the best-sellers, and these now offered 131.5in (3.3m) for an 8-ft bed, a chassis which was shared with the base 1-ton C30s. The ³/4-ton C20s came with a 127-in (3.2-m) wheelbase and 8-ft bed, and the entire range still had the choice of flush Fleetside or running-board Stepside boxes, the former by far the more popular by now.

As for engines, the long-serving 250-ci (4097-cc) six was still the base unit for C10s, rated at 100bhp under the new net measurement system. The optional 292-ci (4785-cc) six made that 120bhp/225lb ft, though at 115bhp/205lb ft the smallest 307-ci (5031-cc V8 was rated slightly lower. Buyers wanting extra power could opt for the popular 350-ci (5735-cc) V8 (155bhp/225lb ft) or a new big-cube option only offered on the C20 and C30, Chevrolet's 454-ci (7440-cc) eight, offering 240bhp and 355lb ft. Another new option was the Crew Cab, which cost $1,000 but could seat six and came with the longest of all wheelbases of 159.5 or 164.5in (4 or 4.2m) to retain an 8-ft bed for useful haulage capacity. This was joined by the 'Big Dooley' twin-wheel option for the C30s for 1974.

The pickup range was now bigger than ever, with a bewildering array of options. Quite apart from all the engine/transmission choices, the latter still including three- or four-speed manual as well as automatic transmission, there were the various trim levels. Taking 1975 as an example, these began with Custom Deluxe, which included a bench seat and plenty of brightwork. Next up was Scottsdale, costing $137 to $199 extra depending on the model. This added a wood-

grain trim, courtesy lamps, cloth upholstery and several other luxuries; if one could afford it, the Cheyenne trim from $237 extra gave one colour-keyed upholstery, plus the option of bucket seats, a cigarette lighter and extra sound insulation. Finally, the ultimate trim option for a 1975 pickup was Silverado, for which at least $312 could be added to the price. This had 7in (18cm) of seat padding, full instrumentation, wood-grain panels, storage pockets in the doors, carpeting, a headliner and extra sound insulation, plus of course plenty of exterior touches to make everyone aware that it was a top-notch pickup.

Meanwhile, the little LUV carried on, selling steadily and with few changes apart from the addition of a Mikado trim package (Chevrolet was clearly not trying to conceal the mini-truck's Japanese origins). From 1977 it was also offered in chassis-cab form to accommodate camper bodies, with a longer 118-in (3-m) wheelbase with a 7.5-ft bed from 1978. Four-wheel-drive was a new option for 1979, when 100,000 of these rebadged mini-pickups were sold, encouraging Chevrolet to press ahead with its own home-grown compact pickup.

In the meantime, the full-sized pickups had a new option – the Bonus Cab from 1976 – with the same six-seater interior as the Crew Cab, but with only two doors, and based on the same 164.5-in (4.2-m) wheelbase. The 402-ci (6588-cc) V8 was replaced by a new 400-ci (6555-cc) small-block of 175bhp/290lb ft, but the top power option remained the 240-bhp 454 V8. A new Sport option for 1977 pickups was a stripes-

only package, while the engine options were reshuffled with a new 305-ci (4998-cc) V8 at 130bhp and slightly extra power for the 250-ci (4097-cc) six and 454-ci (7440-cc) V8.

These were joined by General Motors' 350-ci (5735-cc) V8 diesel for 1978, an option on the ¹/2-ton C10. General Motors' Oldsmobile-built diesel had acquired something of a poor reputation in passenger cars at the time. It offered the promise of reasonable V8 performance coupled with diesel economy, but was really a hurried conversion of a gasoline engine and proved troublesome in service. However, it made more sense in the pickups, where drivers were less concerned with diesel noise or the ritual of cold-starting. In any case, General Motors did overcome the diesel's problems of reliability, and despite a substantial price premium it remained part of the pickup line to 1983, when it was replaced by a larger, new-generation V8 diesel.

There were no major changes for 1979 or '80, but 1981 was important for Chevrolet pickups nonetheless. The second oil crisis had hit the sales of pickups and big sedans especially hard. Not only were pickups often bought as second cars, making them a luxury that could be dispensed with when times were hard, but even the small ones tended to be less fuel-efficient than equivalent cars. The result? Pickup sales plummeted by 50 per cent in 1980, compared with the 1978 peak, and the road to recovery would be slow. Moreover, although Chevy sold over 400,000 pickups alone in the 1981 model year, it was now regularly taking second place to Ford.

OPPOSITE
*The 1968–72 El Camino was a great
success. This is an example from 1970.*

LEFT and BELOW
*A slightly customized C10 from 1980. This
was a bad year for Chevrolet pickups, when
sales plunged by 50 per cent.*

Against this background, the LUV was substantially revamped, with smoother styling and a new cab with more glass. A new interior brought more space and better appointments and while the latest LUV was lighter than the old, it had a greater payload and slightly longer wheelbase at 104.3in (2.6m). Better brakes, suspension, heating/ventilation and electronic ignition were other improvements, though the 111-ci (1819-cc) four-cylinder engine was otherwise unchanged.

The full-sized pickups also lost weight as Detroit and the American public took a renewed interest in fuel economy, the result of two fuel crises and the continuing encroachment of imported compacts. The

OPPOSITE
Full-sized pickups like this were still America's favourite working vehicles in spite of the price of fuel.

LEFT
1980 Chevrolet Silverado 30, with General Motors' own 6.2-litre V8 diesel engine.

saving was between 87 and 300lb (39 and 136kg), even though the same-sized cab and load bed were retained, and was due to details such as a lighter rear bumper or aluminium 4x4 transfer case. The 1981 pickups also shared a smoother, more aerodynamic, though still fairly bluff front

end with the Blazer. This was characterized by the optional twin headlights, stacked vertically. There were plenty of detail improvements/additions, such as low-drag disc brakes, cruise control and, on the 4x4s, quadruple-shock front suspension. A new 305-ci high-compression V8 sought to offer

good performance along with improved economy, with a 9.2:1 ratio and the advance of ESC (Electronic Spark Control). But if tradition was required then the big 454-ci V8 was still available, albeit reined back to 210bhp in an attempt to curb its unfashionable thirst.

ompact Recovery

or Chevrolet, 1982 was characterized by its covery from the disastrous beginnings of e decade, leading to the launch of its own ompact pickup, the S10. The successful UV had proved how popular a domestic-badged mini-pickup could be, and continued to sell steadily. There was a problem in that there was a large gap between the LUV and $\frac{1}{2}$-ton C10, which only a compact pickup could fill.

This the S10 did, styled as it was to resemble the full-sized trucks but with a wheelbase of 108 or 118in (2.7 or 3m), giving a load bed of 6ft or 7.5ft and payloads of 1,000 and 1,500lb (454 and 680kg) respectively. The standard power unit was a 119-ci (1950-cc) four, producing

OPPOSITE
A 1995 Chevy 1300 with extended cab

BELOW
1990s Chevrolet S10 LS

82bhp at 4,600rpm and 101lb ft at 3,000rpm, mated to a four-speed manual transmission. There was also a 173-ci (2835-cc) V6 of 110bhp and 148lb ft, the first time a V6 had been offered in any compact or mini-pickup. Three trim levels included standard, Sport and Durango, and there was an Indy 500 special in that first year.

Launched alongside a similarly compact Blazer, the S10 proved to be a roaring success, selling nearly 178,000 in its first year. There was no diesel option on it, but LUV buyers could choose a diesel 137-ci (2245-cc) unit of 58bhp and 92lb ft. The full-sized pickups also had a new diesel in the range as the old 350-ci V8 was dropped in favour of a Chevrolet-built 379-ci (6211-cc) V8. Available right across the range, the 350 having been offered only on the C10, it produced 130bhp and 240lb ft if one could afford the option cost of $1,173. This made it more than twice the price of the 454-ci gasoline V8, but the savings would in time have made up the difference for those with high mileage.

The S10 range was radically extended the following year, which turned out to be the final season for the LUV, which was effectively replaced by the S10. An Extended-Cab added 14.5in (37cm) to the length and four-wheel-drive was a new option virtually across the range. There was also a new, slightly larger 121-ci (1983-cc) four-cylinder engine offering just a little more horsepower than the base unit, and the LUV's 137-ci diesel also joined the line-up, though uprated to produce 62bhp and 96lb ft, while the 173-ci V6 remained the most

powerful option of all. In 1984 a sport suspension package was added with Bilstein gas-pressure shocks. The S10 had certainly fulfilled its early promise, selling nearly 180,000 in 1983 and almost 200,000 the following year.

Meanwhile, the full-sized pickups soldiered on with the venerable 250-ci (4097-cc) six their base engine, but was finally changed for 1985 with the new 262-ci (4293-cc) Vortec V6 with cast-iron cylinder block and 9.3:1 compression ratio. Power peaked at 155bhp at 4,000rpm and torque at 230lb ft at 2,400rpm. In addition to the base 119-ci (1950-cc) four, the S10 also had a new engine. This four-cylinder 151-ci (2474-cc) unit was fuel-injected to produce 92bhp and 132lb ft, and was standard on the 4x4 S10. Trim levels now included Standard, Durango, Tahoe and Sport. There was little change to the S10 or full-sized pickup for 1986, though all S10s now had fuel injection; it was the same story for 1987, which turned out to be the final year for the full-sized pickup which had first appeared back in 1973, making it the longest-lived of the post-war breed. There were some final improvements, however, notably in fuel injection and full engine management for all the gasoline V8s, which boosted power and efficiency. The aged 292-ci (4785-cc) straight-six was dropped, leaving the Vortec V6 as the only pickup without a V8 beneath its hood. As for the big-cubes, the 130-bhp 279-ci (4572-cc) diesel and 454-ci (7440-cc) 230-bhp gas V8s were still options.

The long-awaited replacement was officially a 1988 model, though it had been

launched in light-duty form as early as April 1987. It was certainly a case of evolution rather than revolution, both inside and out. There was nothing radical about the sixth-generation post-war Chevrolet pickup, and given its conservative marketplace, there was no need for it to be. In terms of the layout of the basic range, nothing had changed, with three payloads ($1/2$-ton R-1500, $3/4$-ton R-2500 and 1-ton R-3500) and four wheelbases (117.5, 131.5, 141.5, 164.5in/3, 3.3, 3.6, 4.2m). But there was a greater emphasis on convenience, with larger doors, lower step-up height and more space inside the cab. Extended-cab six-seaters were now available, not only on the heavy-duty pickups but also across the range, the whole cab/bed structure being double-walled and with great attention given to prevention of corrosion.

All of these pickups were flush-sided Fleetsides, apart from a solitary Sportside, only in short-wheelbased R-1500 form. Ironically, the Sportside styling, so outmoded in many ways, would acquire a sexy retro chic in the 1990s, 40 years after the Chevrolet Cameo made the flush-sided look fashionable. The Vortec V6 was still standard in the R-1500 and 2500, and was now an option in the S10 as well, but the 292-ci straight-six was making a comeback, now fuel-injected, in the extended-wheelbased R-3500. Three mid-sized V8s comprised one 305-ci (170bhp) and two 350s (190 and 210bhp) while the big 454 still headed the range. Buyers now also had a choice of diesels, 130- and 148-bhp versions of Chevrolet's own 379-ci (6211-cc) V8.

OPPOSITE
Pickups can be fun! This is a 1500 from the 1990s.

The new R-trucks enabled Chevrolet to make some inroads on Ford, currently holding top spot in truck sales. Chevrolet sold over 1.3 million trucks in the 1988 model year, over 500,000 of which were R-series pickups. In fact, throughout 1989 they were the best-selling of all the General Motors lines, now with the new-generation 4x4 K-series and 4x2 C as part of the range.

Trim levels were three: base Cheyenne, Scottsdale and Silverado, though a variation was the Fleetside Sport, sold alongside the 4x4 Sportside. Meanwhile, the S10 was benefiting from Back Country and, in a nod to the past, Cameo special editions.

The full-sized had its own special editions for 1990. The 454SS was billed as a performance option, fitting the 230-bhp

454-ci (7440-cc) V8 into the short-wheelbased C1500. In its latest injected form, the big V8 offered 385lb ft, and driving through a three-speed automatic made this SS for the 1990s a real muscle truck. With sports suspension and loaded with equipment, the SS looked good, though it was actually a slow seller when it was first announced. The other special for 1990 was

OPPOSITE and ABOVE
A late 1990s 1500 with four-wheel-drive, dual-purpose tyres and fibreglass accessories.

RIGHT and OPPOSITE
A 2000 Chevy Silverado 1500. More and
more pickups like this were being bought by
private buyers.

PAGE 92
Looks familiar? There's a clear Dodge Ram
influence in this 2004 crew cab.

PAGE 93
A 2003 S10 compact crew cab.

the C/K1500 Work Truck, a stripped-out low-priced variant aimed at business users and there was a similar S10 'EL'. The R designation had been dropped along the way, leaving the two-wheel-drive C and four-wheel-drive K, as had been the case in the 1970s.

There were few major changes for 1991, for either S10 or its big brothers, but the heavier-duty trucks now had the option of General Motors' latest electronically-controlled four-speed automatic transmission. The Work Truck and 454SS continued, and the no-frills EL S10 pickup could now be had with four-wheel-drive and the Vortec V6. Among the big trucks, the C/K3500 Crew Cab finally adopted the new-generation 1988 styling; until then it had carried on as the old model, but as this was one pickup that really did only sell to business users, the pressure to keep up with the latest look wasn't so great. Chevrolet finally offered a new diesel as well, a 400-ci (6555-cc) V8, turbocharged to produce 190bhp at 3,400rpm and 380lb ft at 1,700. It was only available on pickups of 8,600-lb (3900-kg) GVW and over, however, and the 130-bhp 379-ci diesel, still in non-turbo form, carried on.

These big diesels were really aimed at business users, but Chevrolet wasn't forgetting the leisure truckers, producing a new C1500 Sportside sport variant for 1993. This came with the top Silverado trim, alloy wheels and tinted glass. The price for the standard Sportside was $13,985 that year, a $500 premium over the equivalent Fleetside. Both of these models were available with

extended cabs, still with only two doors, as
was most of the S10 and C/K range.

The S/T10 had a serious makeover for
1994, making it roomier and more powerful
than before and, according to Chevrolet,
more comfortable and safe into the bargain.
Both 4x2 S10 and 4x4 T10 were similar to
their predecessors but with slightly
smoother, more aerodynamic styling and 20
per cent more glass. The base engine was
now a 133-ci (2179-cc) injected four of
118bhp and 130lb ft, while the V6 came
with four-wheel anti-lock brakes, the base
model having rear anti-lock only. There were
short- and long-box regular cab pickups,

plus an extended short-box and standard or
LS trim, while a 195-bhp Vortec V6 was
among the options. In contrast, the full-sized
pickups, from the C1500 Fleetside Work
Truck to the K3500 Crew Cab 'Big Dooley',
saw few changes that year or the next.

Into the 21st Century
Fast forward a decade or so and Chevrolet
was still making and selling a range of
pickups. There was now the Colorado, a
mid-sized machine that replaced the long-
running S10 in 2004, though by now it had
left its compact origins far behind. Prices
now started at $15,730, the range including

regular, extended or crew cab, powered by
the 175-bhp Vortec 2800 four or 220-bhp
Vortec 3500 in-line five. Transmission
was a five-speed manual or four-speed
Hydra-Matic.

The C/K full-sized mantle had been
donned by the Silverado, this too a
complete range of pickups – regular,
extended or crew cab with Fleetside or
Sportside boxes, offering from 43.5cu ft
(Sportside) to 70.7cu ft (Fleetside long-
box). No fewer than eight engines were
offered, starting with the now-familiar
Vortec 4300 V6 (195bhp) and including
285- and 295-bhp Vortec V8s plus the

OPPOSITE and LEFT
With the onset of the 1970s, El Camino turned into a muscle car that happened to have a load bed.

PAGE 98
Not many private owners would attempt this in their 2004 Silverado 2500 HD, but liked to know they could if they wanted to.

PAGE 99
2004 Silverado Performance.

ltimate 8100 power unit of 330bhp. There was also a diesel, the 300-bhp Duramax 6600 V8. Completing this 21st-century trio was the avalanche, an upmarket four-door that was more SUV than pickup, with prices starting at under $35,000 and a choice of 295- or 320-bhp Vortec V8s.

Only a trio was not quite true, for there was one more bona fide part of the Chevrolet line-up – the SSR. Part roadster, part pickup, this extraordinary hybrid first appeared at the 2000 North American Auto Show. Clearly a modern concept, complete with retro styling, it drew its inspiration from the 1953 Advance Design pickup, with a similar horizontal grille and rounded headlights and fenders. Of course, no 1953 pickup had a 390-bhp LS2 V8 or four-speed Hydra-Matic, or a six-speed manual option, though it could carry a little more than the 22.5cu ft promised by the $43,000 SSR's bijou load bed. It was not exactly a practical pickup, but the SSR did prove something – that Chevrolet had more than half a century of pickup heritage on which to draw.

El Camino

El Camino was one of Chevrolet's rare mistakes, at least in its first incarnation. Ever since Chevrolet sales first began to overtake those of Ford in 1928, when Henry switched from Model T to Model A production, General Motors' top-selling division had,

more often than not, held the upper hand. This went for pickups, too, as Chevrolet launched its all-new post-war light trucks a year ahead of Ford in 1947. Chrysler, Buick, Pontiac – none of them got a look-in as the battle for America's top spot, in both cars and trucks, was between Ford and Chevrolet, Chevrolet and Ford, to the exclusion of anyone else.

So when Ford launched its car/truck hybrid, the Ranchero, in 1957, Chevrolet got something of a fright. Industrial espionage usually gave it an idea what Ford was up to, but this time it failed. Even worse, people seemed to love the revolutionary Ranchero; it was suitable not only for gentleman farmers looking for something sleek to drive into town as well as haul hay, but also businesses delivering their goods in upmarket neighbourhoods. Consequently, in the first year, over 21,000 were sold. Dedicated to fighting Ford in every aspect of the market, Chevrolet needed a Ranchero of its own, and fast. But instead of its usual fast-moving sprint, the division took two years to come up with the El Camino, by which time it was arguably too late.

It seemed simple enough on paper. Ford had used a canny mix of existing components to create the Ranchero, including a two-door station wagon and the Skyliner convertible. Chevrolet also had a suitable two-door wagon, so it was simply a case of cutting off the roof behind the front seats and replacing it with a pickup bed.

And it would have been that simple, except that by the time the El Camino was ready for production, the two-door station wagon had been dropped. With fewer donated parts, many unique panels had to be especially tooled, including the quarter panels, upper door frames, the load bed and inner panelling, though the tailgate was borrowed from a four-door station wagon. In fact, just about everything rearward of the Impala-based front end was made specifically for the El Camino. That cost money, and meant that Chevrolet had to sell many Caminos to cover its costs.

It was built around a 119-in (3-m) wheelbase, the Impala front end accommodating a wide range of engines. The base 1180 model came with Chevrolet's 235-ci (3851-cc) six-cylinder engine of 135bhp, while the slightly upscaled 1280 brought the 283-ci (4637-cc) V8 which, in two-barrelled carburettor form, claimed 185bhp. It was also possible to specify the four-barrelled 283 for 230bhp, or if real horsepower was required, the division's beefy 348-ci (5703-cc) V8. This came with 305, 315 or 335bhp, depending on carburettor and compression which, in ultimate guise, meant an eye-popping 11.25:1 and no fewer than three carburettors to keep in tune. In theory, one could even order the 1959 El Camino with fuel injection, though there is nothing to suggest that anyone actually did.

The Camino came in standard Biscayne trim, which included a dull, grey vinyl interior and only one sun visor. However, there were plenty of extra options, including power steering and brakes, air conditioning, Posi-traction rear axle, tinted glass and power-operated windows. From the outside, however, the Camino still resembled the flamboyant, finned child of the fifties that it was, even without the additional options. With one of the high-horsepowered V8s in place, El Camino was certainly fast, though it was also softly sprung, the consensus at the time being that it felt more like a soft sedan than a true pickup, unlike the firmer Ranchero. But over 22,000 were sold in the first year, outstripping the Ranchero, so it looked as though 1957 hadn't mattered after all.

It all went sour in 1960, however. The first El Camino's styling had been pure 1950s, with its huge wings and cats-eye tail lights, but fashion was changing rapidly and American buyers were turning to compact cars and more conservative styling. Ford recognized the signs and dropped its original Ranchero in favour of one based on the smaller Falcon. Chevrolet did its best to tone down the garish El Camino, flattening off the fins and giving it a less flamboyant front end, but the basic body shape was unchanged in that it was still a big, heavy car, straight out of a previous era. Consequently, the situation with Ford was reversed: sales slid to just over 14,000, while those of the compact Ranchero soared to over 21,000.

Chevrolet realized that the first El Camino would never recapture its respectable first-year sales and dropped the car for 1961. Nor was there a new Camino to replace it, as Chevrolet's own compact, the Corvair, had a rear-mounted engine that made a pickup conversion impossible, while the conventional full-sized Chevys were just too big. There would be no El Caminos at all for the time being.

OPPOSITE
A 2004 Colorado with crew cab and the distinctive split grille of that year.

The show-stopping 2004 Colorado Cruz.

El Camino Makes a Comeback

But after three years it was back, and to such an extent that not only did it decisively overtake and outsell the Ranchero, it also outlived it as well. Chevrolet based the El Camino on its mid-sized Chevelle for the 1964 model year. This was a smart move: not only was the Chevelle a modern car with a wide choice of engines, it was also based on a 115-in (2.9-m) wheelbase – usefully more compact than the 119-in original but still large enough to offer a decent-sized load bed. The Chevelle also had a youthful, sporty image which fitted the El Camino, and the clean, square look that was currently popular.

Available in Standard and Custom trim, the Camino again came with a wide choice of options, including engines, and was described by Chevrolet as a 'personal pickup', broadening its appeal beyond business users. The standard power unit was a 194-ci (3179-cc) six of 120bhp and 177lb ft, but there was also a choice of two V8s. The familiar 283-ci unit was now in 195-bhp guise, with a Rochester two-barrelled carburettor, while the top-performance engine was Chevrolet's small-block 327-ci (5358-cc) with 250bhp and 350lb ft.

This guaranteed sprightly performance: in fact, the El Camino would acquire something of a reputation as a muscle truck, either with the optional four-speed manual transmission or the three-speed Hydra-Matic automatic that was offered from 1967. The standard six was enlarged to 230ci (3769cc) for 1966, producing 140bhp and with 220lb ft peaking at 1,600rpm. The Camino's place as a muscle truck was confirmed that year, when Chevrolet's big-block 396-ci (6489-cc) V8 became an option. As fitted to El Camino, this had a single four-barrelled carburettor and 11.25:1 compression, producing a monstrous 375bhp. It could also be had in less highly-strung 325- and 360-bhp forms, while the small-block 327 was still available, as was the 283.

However, only the top 396 would do where performance freaks were concerned, especially when it came with the SS package of blacked-out grille and bulging power hood. But what really attracted them to this hottest truck of its time was that it was cheaper to insure than the equivalent Chevelle SS sedan, simply because it was classed as a truck. With insurance rates

soaring on muscle cars, this was an important consideration, and many more El Caminos were sold for exactly that reason. Fleet buyers also took advantage of the same loophole, not because they wanted to tear up the tarmac with a 396SS, but simply for reasons of economy. Little wonder that sales of Chevrolet's pickup reached 30,000 a year between 1964 and '67, when the Ford Ranchero was making less than 20,000 annually. Chevrolet may have been tardy with the first El Camino, but by now this no longer mattered.

Chevrolet must have taken the concept of the muscle car to its heart, for the third-generation El Camino, launched in 1968, was not only longer, wider and lower than the old, but was more of a muscle car into the bargain. This was largely due to the 'flying buttress' B-pillar, raked rearwards to suggest the roofline of a sports coupé. Inside, one stepped down into an all-black interior that was comfortably enfolding, with bucket seats and full instrumentation in the SS.

El Camino now seemed to be a muscle car that happened to have a load bed instead of a rear seat. It is true that it was still possible to order one of the 'personal pickups' with a six-cylinder engine, upsized to 250ci (4097cc) for 1970, though most buyers went for one of the many V8s. The smallest 327-ci (5358-cc) came in 250-, 275- or 325-bhp forms, and the big 396 as 325-, 350- or 375-bhp. In 1970 the 396 was topped by a 454-ci (7440-cc) option, which in ultimate 11.0:1 compression form was credited with 450bhp and 475lb ft. It was now

the height of the muscle-car boom, and it was not to last much longer. But then, who thinks that the Ford SVT Lightning is a new idea?

In the meantime, supplementary 307-ci (5031-cc), 350-ci (5735-cc) and 402-ci (6588-cc) V8s now appeared and sales headed skywards. Over 40,000 flying-buttress Caminos were sold every year between 1968 and '71, exceeding 57,000 in 1972, its final year. It was the most successful El Camino yet, still outselling the Ranchero and spawning the almost identical GMC Sprint.

Muscle cars were forced to mend their ways in the early 1970s, which included El Camino. Increasing insurance premiums and accident rates, concerns about safety and emissions, all brought fundamental changes, the 1973 El Camino being no exception. But instead of downsizing its pickup, Chevrolet chose to take it upmarket, billing it as a luxury pickup rather than a sporty one.

The base engine was now a 307-ci V8, though a six returned in 1975 to improve fuel economy, and though it was still possible to have a 350- or 454-ci V8, these were in a low-compression, regular gas-compatible state of tune. Power ranged from 115bhp to 240bhp for 1973, though was now measured in net rather that gross figures, so the fall wasn't as great as it seemed.

Meanwhile, reasoning that drivers of the 1970s were more concerned with luxury than horsepower, Chevrolet equipped this bigger, heavier and more luxurious El Camino with a whole range of trim levels and option packs. The Standard and Custom, the latter soon renamed the Classic, were

supplemented by the Estate, with wood-grain side panels, the SS, now a sporty-looking cosmetic package, and the Conquista, with an optional Del Ray pack which included flared wheel arches, front spoiler and suitable decals. *PV4* magazine tested a 1974 El Camino against a same-year Ranchero and decided there was not a great deal to choose between them. Both test cars were fully loaded with options, the 454-ci Camino coming out $18 cheaper, slightly faster and marginally more thirsty, though as ever it was softer around bends. *PV4* concluded that both were equally comfortable, responsive and well-built.

But it still left the new El Camino bigger, heavier and slower than the old, though the public appeared to love it even so. Over 64,000 customers bought one of Chevrolet's car/trucks in 1973, which would remain its best model year ever. Sales never again reached that peak, slumping to 33,000 by 1975, though they did recover somewhat in 1976 and '77. The truth was that history was repeating itself. Just as the very first El Camino soon became out of tune with the times, the same thing was hapening again. There was no longer room for the heavyweight El Camino in a world where even the Ford Mustang had been radically downsized.

The new model was launched in 1978, over 600lb (270kg) lighter than its predecessor and almost a foot shorter. In spite of this, it had an extra inch of wheelbase at 117in (3m), and claimed better head-, hip- and legroom into the bargain, so was far more effective in terms of space.

The gasoline V6s proved more popular, and gradually increased in size through El Camino's final decade, reaching 262ci (4293cc) by the end of production.

As before, there was quite a sprinkling of trim levels. Alongside the standard El Camino from 1978 were the Super Sport (front spoiler, rally wheels, black detailing); the Royal Knight (presumably for Camino owners concerned with chivalry, castles and dragons); and the Conquista – the most popular – with contrasting colour on the centre of the body, hood and a lower tailgate.

The basic car was the same, whether drivers fancied themselves as racing drivers, medieval knights or Spanish conquistadors, and would remain in production for almost a decade. This downsized Camino sold at well over 50,000 annually in its first two years, through sales gradually declined in the 1980s. The rapidly growing market for SUVs was claiming the typical car/pickup buyer as its own and, distinctive as it was, El Camino was missing the rugged attraction of four-wheel-drive. The same was true of the GMC Caballero, identical in all but badge, which was also affected by dwindling sales in the 1980s. When General Motors sold less than 14,000 El Caminos in 1987 and less than 2,000 Caballeros, the end was clearly in sight. Production ceased at the end of that model year.

Chevrolet has kept on producing pickups and for 2010 lauched a new range of Colorado, Avalanche and Silverado models with various engine sizes. They also launched a Hybrid to bring them into the future of green motoring.

ABOVE
A 2004 Chevy Colorado LS SPO, accessorized up and ready to roll.

OPPOSITE:
The Silverado Hybrid was launched at the Chicago Motor show in 2009.

A six-cylinder base engine was reintroduced to these more modest dimensions, in this case a V6 of 200ci (3277cc). This was tuned more for torque than power, offering 160lb ft and 95bhp; but even taking into account the new measurement system it was probably the least powerful El Camino there had ever been. But the V8 options, of course, were still there, a 145-bhp 305-ci and 165-bhp 350. The 305 V8 would be available right up to the end of production in 1987, while various other eights came and went. There

was a smaller 267-ci (4375-cc) unit offered between 1979 and '82, and an interesting, though short-lived option was the 350-ci diesel Oldsmobile.

This offered the prospect of 105bhp and good torque combined with reasonable fuel economy. Unfortunately, the Olds diesel had been hurriedly converted from a gasoline V8 and proved unreliable and prone to poor starting in cold weather and blown head gaskets. After the first rush of enthusiasm, buyers lost interest, and El Camino's diesel option was dropped after a couple of years.

CHAPTER TWO
DODGE: THE RAM ROLLER COASTER

When John Dodge was asked why he and his brother Horace had decided to built their own car, after making a fortune supplying parts to Henry Ford, his reply was typically down to earth: 'Just think of all those Ford owners who will one day want to buy an automobile.' The Dodge brothers had grown rich in this line of business, and were well respected, but it was not enough. They were sick and tired of being 'carried around in Henry Ford's vest pocket'.

Born in the 1860s, Horace and John were self-made men. Their father may have owned a machine shop, but their background cwas far from privileged. Although they were born four years apart, the brothers could have been identical twins, both showing a similar aptitude for engineering (nurtured among their father's lathes) and destined to work together for their entire lives. They were shunned by Detroit society because of their humble beginnings, even after they had grown wealthy, but they got their revenge. Refused membership of the Detroit Country Club, they bought a plot of land next door, planning to build a huge house that would overlook the club's grounds and annoy the people who had shunned them.

However, that was all in the future whe they set up in business to make bicycles an car parts, but their real break came in 1901 when they moved to Detroit. Supplying components to the rapidly growing automobile industry, they soon gained a reputation for quality and technical innovation, and their list of clients included big names like Ransom Olds as well as Henry Ford.

But to escape from Henry's 'vest pocket', the brothers launched their own car in November 1914. Their good reputation ensured that everyone took notice, and whe it arrived, the Model 30-35 certainly didn't disappoint. It was the first mass-produced car with an all-steel body, plus a powerful four-cylinder engine and solid construction. The 212-ci (3474-cc) 35-bhp four was mated to a conventional three-speed transmission, justifying a higher price than the Ford Model T. Customers obviously approved, and the car was a hit, selling 45,000 in 1915 and over 70,000 the following year. Within three years of starting roduction, Dodge was the fourth biggest car maker in America.

At first, the brothers had no ambitions to build a truck, but history steered them in this direction. In 1916 General John Pershing had used a fleet of Dodges in his border skirmishes with the Mexican revolutionary, Pancho Villa, and was impressed by their roughness and durability. Still the brothers resisted all requests to build a light-truck based on their car, for the very good reason that they couldn't keep up with demand as it was. However, they couldn't ignore the U.S. Government, which ordered 20,000 ½-ton chassis, ambulances and cargo trucks. With production under way, building trucks for civilians was an obvious step to take.

The result was the screenside Commercial Car, a straight adaptation of the military ambulance, which went into production in October 1917. It wasn't a pickup, having a standard canopy and roll-down curtain-sides of oiled duck, but a truck it most certainly was. The entire front end was taken straight off the Model 30-35, but was reinforced by heavier springs and bigger 33 x 4-in (84 x 10-cm) tyres. The steering column was mounted at a steeper angle to maximize the load space, which measured 71in long by 43in wide (180 x 109cm).

At $885, the Dodge Commercial was twice the price of a Model T truck, but offered nearly twice the power and features like 12-volt starting/electrics. It could also carry a full 1,000lb (454kg) and came, of course, with the Dodge brothers' enviable reputation for durability, being, according to publicity, 'so efficient, so strikingly free

OPPOSITE and LEFT
By 1937, when this pickup was built, Dodge had been in the truck business for 20 years.

from need of repair, and so economical to run, that it constitutes a real asset to any business requiring delivery.' The Commercial was highly successful; along with a similar panel van, it helped Dodge to the number two position behind Ford.

Sadly, the brothers weren't able to enjoy this success for long. John died of influenza in early 1920, and a devastated Horace passed away in December. The widows of the two men now owned the company, though Frederick Haynes took over as president within months of Horace's death. Four years later, it was sold to a New York bank for the record-breaking sum of $146

million, underlining what a major enterprise Dodge had now become.

Without the brothers to guide it, the car side rather lost its way, but the trucks went from strength to strength as the standard screenside and panel van sold to satisfied customers. Some were sold in bare chassis form, to which aftermarket bodywork could be fitted.

Dodge's healthy truck business was at least partly due to an agreement with Graham Brothers trucks of Evansville, Indiana. Active from 1921, Graham built 1- and 1½-ton trucks, using Dodge engines, transmissions and other parts, to be sold

OPPOSITE and LEFT
A well-customized Dodge from 1937. The
company was now part of Chrysler, which
attracted more investment and higher sales.

exclusively through Dodge dealers. Since Graham could offer a whole variety of wheelbases and body styles, this strengthened the whole business, without damaging sales of Dodge's own 1/2-ton trucks.

The original screenside and panel trucks saw only minor changes in the early 1920s, as sales recovered from the slump of 1921.

But 1923 saw some real changes, when the trucks were upgraded to 3/4-ton, with a bigger radiator and slanting windshield, power still being provided by the 35-bhp 212-ci four. The following year, the wheelbase grew by two inches to 116in (2.9m), which increased the screenside's total capacity to 84cu ft. Dodge delivered over 20,000 of these 3/4-ton trucks that year,

if those with bare chassis were also included. Also that year, Graham Brothers became a division of Dodge, as the two companies grew ever closer, and Robert Graham was increasingly influential within the whole corporation, rising to director by 1925. Ray Graham was also on the board, and Joseph Graham became general manager, which explains why all Dodge trucks were

marketed and sold as Grahams in 1927 and '28, though the arrangement would not last long. In fact, the three Graham brothers withdrew from the whole enterprise in 1926, to set up Graham-Paige, but the division that bore their name continued as part of Dodge.

Dodge built its first closed-cab truck in 1926, which as the $3/4$-ton Express really qualifies as the company's first true pickup. This used the standard 116-in wheelbase, though a 140-in (3.5-m) chassis was also launched that year; in an apparently retrograde step, the trucks also changed from 12- to 6-volt electrics. By 1927, the $3/4$-ton bore a Graham badge, and the range ran to three Express pickups: $3/4$-ton/116-in wheelbase; 1-ton/126-in wheelbase; and 1-ton/137-in wheelbase. Thanks to Graham's body-building capacity, there were 15 models up to 1 ton, plus Graham's heavier-duty vehicles and buses, while Dodge also

OPPOSITE
A 1945 Dodge pickup with the bulbous look
that was carried over from 1941.

added commercial versions of its sedan, coupé and roadster to the line. All of this helped the company to become the third-biggest American truck manufacturer that year.

All of these trucks still used the faithful Dodge four, producing the same 35bhp, and had the familiar three-speed transmission. There were some significant changes for 1927, notably a stronger five-bearing crankshaft which made for smoother power delivery, plus a Morse chain drive to replace the timing gears and internal oil pump and a general rejigging of the ancillaries.

Goodbye Graham
There were few changes for 1928, though hydraulic brakes were a big step forward. All of the trucks were still badged as Grahams, and if it hadn't been for an important milestone in the company's history, the Dodge name would have faded away then and there. It didn't, thanks to Walter P. Chrysler.

Chrysler was determined to build an empire comparable to that of Ford or General Motors, and despite starting relatively late, this is exactly what he did. He had great experience of the motor industry, having worked for Buick and Willys. He had also transformed the Maxwell Corporation into Chrysler, and by 1928 had launched Plymouth as a low-cost competitor to Ford.

But Chrysler/Plymouth was still relatively puny, and needed to grow quickly to match its bigger rivals. That was where Dodge came in. The truck-maker was several times the size of little Chrysler, and had a

good network of dealers, but with the Dodges and Grahams gone needed someone with drive and determination to take it forward. So in July 1928 Dodge became part of Chrysler, and within months the Graham badge had been dropped; from now on, all Dodge trucks would carry its own name.

New trucks had already been planned for the 1929 model year, which according to the Dodge system began in April 1928. The 212-ci four, five-bearing crank and all, was dropped in favour of a 208-ci (3408-cc) L-head six from the Dodge Victory Six car. With a seven-bearing crank and compression ratio of 5.18:1, it produced 63bhp. There was a new $1/2$-ton truck, the 110-in (2.8-m) wheelbase Merchant's Express, though this came only in panel van or chassis forms. Then came a new $3/4$-ton DA-120 (120-in/3-m wheelbase) offered in Express and stakeside form, among others, and the 1-ton DA-130 (130-in/3.3-m) with a similar choice of bodies, and there was a 140-in (3.5-m) 1-ton as well.

All of these had been planned before the takeover, but Chrysler's influence was clearer in the new $1/2$-ton Merchant's Express for 1929, using a Plymouth four of 175ci (2868cc) and 45bhp. Once again, there was no pickup, but any aftermarket body could be bolted onto the chassis. At $545, this took Dodge into a lower-priced class of truck and closer to Ford. The same year, Chrysler introduced the Fargo badge on some trucks, though only for export – a name that would survive until 1972.

The four-cylinder Merchant's Express and $3/4$- and 1-ton sixes continued into 1930,

the bigger models with longer wheelbases. For 1931, the $1/2$-ton's price was slashed by $110 in an effort to win sales during the savage Depression. Dodge also added a six-cylinder variant, the F-10, using a 60-bhp 190-ci (3113-cc) unit that also delivered 120lb ft, while the basic four, now upgraded to 196ci (3212cc) and 48bhp continued, while prices for pickups ran to a competitive $644 for the four, $744 for the six. There were more price cuts for 1932, the four-cylinder pickup reduced to $584, while the six-cylinder 124-in wheelbase cost $730, cheaper than the 1931 $1/2$-ton six. Despite Dodge's best efforts, sales slumped to less than 9,000, half what they had been the previous year, but the company was already planning its first post-Depression truck.

According to author Don Bunn, it was Walter Chrysler himself who insisted on maintaining research and development through the darkest Depression years. This persistence paid off in January 1933, when a new range of Dodge trucks was announced. They brought a new touch of glamour to the line-up, based on equivalent Dodge cars with raked, V-shaped radiators and rounded fenders that hid the chassis. Unlike Ford and Chevrolet, Dodge used engines from within the corporate diaspora and for 1933 the new $1/2$-ton range was powered by Plymouth's L-head six, which now delivered 70bhp at 3,600rpm and 130lb ft at 1,200. They used Dodge car chassis and were the final Dodge trucks to do so. Bare chassis and sedan delivery variants were launched in January 1933 with the Commercial Express pickup following a couple of months later. This was

OPPOSITE and LEFT
Like other manufacturers of pickups, Dodge
concentrated on producing military vehicles
during the Second World War. These are
1944 weapons carriers.

built on a 111.25in (2.8-m) wheelbase and offered a load bed 63in long, 45.75in wide and 15.5in deep. It was of all-steel construction at a time when most pickup beds had wooden floors. A longer 119-in (3-m) wheelbase version was also offered, but only in chassis or van forms, while the 109-in ¹/2-tons continued. There were also bigger pickups based on a 131-in (3.3-m) wheelbase, rated at ³/4 to 1 ton.

The new range was hugely successful, and sales rocketed by over 300 per cent, in a year when the truck industry as a whole was growing by a 'mere' 36 per cent. Sales of over 28,000 were enough for Dodge to regain third position in the truck market; the following year over 48,000 trucks were sold, confirming Dodge as one of the leading manufacturers.

Now named the KC-series, the ¹/2-ton trucks were barely changed into 1935, when

RIGHT and OPPOSITE
Experience in four-wheel-drive and high-volume truck production would stand Dodge in good stead once the war was over.

RIGHT and OPPOSITE
Experience in four-wheel-drive and high-volume truck production would stand Dodge in good stead once the war was over.

the ³/4- and 1-ton KH-series was greatly expanded with the option of 136-, 148- or 161-in wheelbases. These were not new either, but derated versions of the bigger 1¹/2-ton trucks already produced by Dodge.

Smaller wheels and tyres, plus lighter springs and axles, made them lighter-duty, and they used the same engine as the KC – Plymouth's L-head six – which had now been uprated to 201ci (3294cc). It was also

given a full-height water jacket. With a 5.8:1 compression ratio, power was unchanged at 70bhp, but torque was increased slightly to 138lb ft. All Dodge trucks (including the 3- to 4-tonners) now had six cylinders; the L-

head unit in particular would prove to be adaptable and long-lived, powering Dodge pickups right up to 1960.

Meanwhile, 1935 was another good year for Dodge, with sales up 27 per cent to well over 60,000 as the truck market completed its recovery during 1931–32. Business was now so good that Dodge began building trucks in Los Angeles and Canada in addition to the factory at Hamtramck, Michigan.

But under the Chrysler regime, there appeared to be no room for complacency, and for 1936 Dodge announced another new line-up. The Commercial series of LC ½-tonners looked quite different from the old ones, with a concave front grille and horizontal vents in the hood. All of them used a 116-in (2. 9-m) wheelbase (replacing the previous choice of two), and featured 'Fore-Point' weight distribution. This was marketing speak for the good engineering practice of moving cab and power unit further forward in the chassis, spreading the load towards the front axle and giving more room for a longer load bed.

The 201-ci L-head was unchanged, but now sat on Chrysler's three-point rubber mounting system, while the suspension benefited from another corporate development – Amola steel for the springs. The chassis itself was a double-drop truck type with five substantial cross members instead of the car chassis that Dodge 1/2-tonners previously used. Despite costing a modest $500 in pickup form, the LC was well-equipped, with ammeter, speedometer, fuel gauge, oil pressure and temperature gauges, a glove compartment and vacuum-powered windshield wiper. It even had a height-adjustable steering wheel, and the cab doors were now front-hinged.

The LE 3/4-ton trucks shared many of the same improvements, such as Fore-Point, Amola steel springs and the full instrumentation. The difference was that they came in a choice of three wheelbases – 129in, 136in and 162in – though a pickup was only offered with the middle length. A long-wheelbased stakeside cost $759 (only $20 more than the 136-in model), while the 136-in pickup came in at $739.

After such far-reaching changes, 1937 was quieter, though the familiar six was enlarged to 218ci (3572cc), which boosted power to 75bhp and torque to 155lb ft. The

RIGHT and OPPOSITE
Two-tone paintwork gives this 1946 truck a
smart appearance.

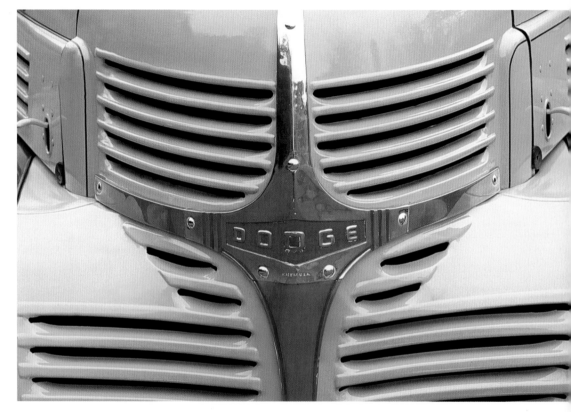

only other change to the 1/2-ton was the
prefix MC, but the bigger trucks saw bigger
changes. As well as the upsized six, they
now shared styling with the 1/2-ton, and were
more of a genuine halfway house between
the light truck and the big 1 1/2-tonner.
Before, they had been a derated big truck,

but now Dodge referred to the 3/4- and 1-ton
as its 'in-between' trucks. There were two
wheelbases offered on this MD/ME-series:
120in, able to accomodate a 7-ft load bed,
and 136in for a 9-ft bed. At the same time,
Plymouth began selling pickups, though
these were really Dodges dressed up as

Plymouths, and sold for a few dollars less.

Nineteen-thirty-seven was not a good
year for Dodge, and sales dropped by nearly
a quarter, which saw the division slip to
fourth place in the U.S. truck ratings. Worse
was to come in 1938, when sales plummeted
by nearly half. It was, of course, a bad year

for the industry in general, a sting in the tail of the Depression, but Dodge suffered more than the average, though it did manage to maintain its fourth place. The trucks were barely changed that year, apart from a new grille which resembled that of the Dodge car line-up, while the ¹/₂-ton was now dubbed RC and the bigger trucks RD. Something else that hadn't changed was the long list of

options available on all the Dodge trucks. Take the ¹/₂-ton. One could pay $8.50 extra for a chrome bumper or $2.75 for plated headlights; while four-speed transmission was $25 and sun visors a couple of dollars each. There were no fewer than three different governers from which to choose, starting at $4. But the reality behind the 1938 Dodge pickups was that they hadn't

changed, and for the very good reason that divisional engineers were perfecting something new for 1939.

Art Deco Truck
Dodge named 1939 the 'year of the truck', and its completely redesigned TC series ¹/₂-ton the 'truck of the year', for which there was good reason. For a start, the new for

1939 trucks were being made in a brand-new $6 million factory in Warren, Michigan. This was designed specifically for building trucks – nothing else – and at the time was the largest plant of its kind in the world. Dodge trucks are built there to this day.

As for the TC, this had the new Art Deco styling, being applied to everything from trucks to toasters at the time, which lent a new streamlined grace. The windshield was split in two, and V-shaped to look aerodynamic; there were 'speed lines' on the rear of the fenders and a new front end finally left the 1930s radiator grille behind, adopting fender-mounted headlights. Beneath this streamlined exterior, the 1939 TC actually had less power than previously, reverting to the 201-ci (3294-cc) L-head six of 70bhp/148lb ft. The ³/4- and 1-ton TDs retained the 218-ci (3372-cc) six, now with 77bhp and 158lb ft. They also shared the new styling of the TC, the sheet metal being actually the same, with a 120-in wheelbase on the ³/4-ton TD15 pickup and a 7.5-ft load bed. As for the 1-ton, there was a choice of 120-in or 133-in wheelbase, the latter with a 9-ft bed. The ¹/2-ton's bed, incidentally, was now wooden with steel rubbing strips, instead of the all-steel construction which Dodge had pioneered.

With a new, forward-looking line-up, and the truck market in general bouncing back from the gloom of 1938, Dodge could hardly fail to do well in '39. And it did, with sales climbing by almost 43 per cent to over 88,000, while another 19,000 trucks were exported. However, this was not enough to regain the coveted third position, and Dodge

RIGHT and OPPOSITE
There was a plain cab for the driver of a
1946 pickup, though it was quite well-
equipped by the standards of the day. There
was also a useful load space.

mained in fourth. But that year, in another example of forward planning, the company offered a diesel option on its heavy-duty trucks, with an engine designed and developed in-house. However, it would be many years before light-duty Dodges could be diesel- powered.

Had Dodge made a mistake in saddling the 1/2-ton TC with the smaller 201-ci six? It certainly seemed that way, as the main change for the 1940 VC was to up the power of this long-running motor to 79bhp peaking at 3,000rpm, with torque rising to 154lb ft at 1,200. Other changes were minor, and included sealed-beam headlights and a 35-amp generator, plus right- and left-threaded wheel retaining bolts on the appropriate sides to prevent them from working loose. The 3/4- and 1-ton trucks received more power as well and the 218-ci (3572-cc) L-head six was boosted to 82bhp at 3,000rpm and 166lb ft; the compression ratio was 6.5:1. They had the same updated electrics as the VC, while wheelbase and body options were the same as the previous year.

The military was already gearing up, even before America's formal entry into the Second World War, and Dodge supplied over 20,000 1/2-tonners in 1940 alone, adding to the 54,000-odd civilian sales that year. Between 1942 and '45, of course, the new truck factory in Michigan would be totally devoted to war work, but that hadn't happened yet. For the time being, civilian pickups were still being produced into the 1941 model year, though changes were few as military contracts began to take up more company time. Power was boosted again on

the 1/2-ton, now prefixed 'WC' due to a new high-lift cam: in fact, at 82.5bhp the 201-ci six now made as much power as the previous year's 218, with peak torque of 160lb ft. To keep ahead, the 218 six in the bigger trucks was also given a boost to 85bhp and 170lb ft. Other than that, it was business as usual, and civilian sales increased again to almost 63,000. But Dodge's truck factory actually produced another 100,000 on top of that, underlining how important military contracts now were.

The division's marketeers made full use of this association. 'Dodge Marches with the Nation', went the publicity in the fall of 1942. 'Again the scene has shifted from the highways of America to the battle fronts of the world. Again Dodge Dependability of peace-time translates itself into the precision craftsmanship of war. And again the word comes back from the final testing grounds of warfare that Dodge Craftsmanship is Dependable under the most grueling extremes of service.'

By that time, civilian production had ceased, actually ending in April 1942, though '42 model-year trucks were produced for eight months. The 1/2-ton WC finally regained the 218-ci L-head six, which now offered 95bhp and 172lb ft, and was shared with the 3/4-ton WD. The WC also had a stronger chassis and clutch housing for these last few months, and a more efficient radiator. Finally, the WD20/21 1-ton trucks adopted a new 230-ci (3769-cc) L-head six-cylinder engine of 105bhp and 184lb ft. But it was still possible to order Deluxe cab equipment, even as war loomed, which

brought air-foam seat and back cushions with leather upholstery, passenger's armrest, an electric windshield wiper, an interior light, a sun visor and chrome trim around the windshield – all for an extra $25.

A Head Start

Dodge had a proud boast after the end of the Second World War. Only two hours after the final military truck had rolled off the production line, it claimed the factory's readiness to mass-produce civilian trucks. Of course, it did have something of a head start, having carried on limited civilian truck production right through the war. Numbers were tiny compared with military production (only nine were built in 1943, though there were nearly 8,000 in '44) and the trucks were unchanged '42 models and built only for civilians in essential occupations.

So it is not so surprising that when it received the green light for civilian production, Dodge was able to crank up to speed immediately, and take full advantage of a market that had been starved of new trucks for over three years. It didn't set any production records, at a little under 145,000 in 1946, but civilian sales reached a new high, with 96,490 Dodge trucks finding buyers in the 12 months from December 1945. This was up by 53 per cent compared with 1941, though the industry on average failed to match the pre-war figure.

Of course, the trucks were almost identical to those offered before America entered the war, due to the speed with which Dodge switched to civilian production. The 1/2-ton WC received heavier-duty steering

OPPOSITE
1950 Dodge Power Wagon. This civilianized version of the respected army truck would remain in production for many years.

OPPOSITE

Dodge Power Wagons were often used by utility companies and other fleet operators. This one has a crane attachment.

gear, axle shafts and differential, but there were no other mechanical changes. An intriguing feature was an air-filled seat cushion, which the driver could adjust by means of a control valve to accommodate his weight. The 3/4- and 1-ton trucks were also barely changed, though there was one new model – the Power Wagon. This may not have conformed to everyone's idea of a pickup, but such a long-running truck, having been offered in America right up to 1968, is worthy of mention. The Power Wagon was really a civilianized version of the wartime four-wheel-drive 3/4-ton truck, and was now aimed at farmers, with power take-offs, full off-road capability and a four-speed transmission with two-speed transfer case. Power came from the same 230-ci (3769-cc) six as in the regular 1-ton trucks, and the Power Wagon was offered as chassis-cab or pickup-style Express. It cost nearly $600 more than the equivalent 1-ton on account of its special features.

There were no changes for 1947, with the pre-war designed 1/2-ton WC, 3/4-ton WD15 and 1-ton WD20/21 continuing on, though prices greatly increased. The WC pickup, with 116-in wheelbase and 6.5-ft load bed, now came in at $989, or $121 more than the previous year's identical truck. The 3/4-ton pickup (7.5-ft bed) cost $1,096, or $1,162 in 1-ton form, with the 126-in wheelbase version at $1,187. Not cheap by any means, but they would begin to look like bargains compared with the brand-new range of 1948, as post-war inflation, materials shortages, plus the fact that America's truck industry could

sell everything it made, began to take effect.

In the space of six months, all of America's major truck-makers launched their new post-war line-ups. Chevrolet and GMC stole a march in June 1947, Dodge followed in December, and Ford in January '49. So despite their head start into civilian production, Dodge wasn't particularly early when it launched the new Series B. However, author Don Bunn argues that the B-Series Dodges were 'by far the finest and most advanced pickups of their day'.

First off, the styling, even by the standards of these post-war period, was quite advanced. The full-width grille and the way the front fenders blended back into the doors were more early 1950s than late '40s. Dodge described the all-new cab as the 'Pilot House', in which the driver sat high, while visibility was further improved by a higher and wider windshield and windows than on other pickups. A combined heater/defroster/ventilation system was standard. The Pilot House came with a choice of Standard, Deluxe or Custom trim, the Deluxe simply having added vent wings in the cab doors and rear quarter windows for $25. The Custom package was more comprehensive, with these two items plus deluxe seat cushion, interior light, left armrest, twin sun visors and electric wipers, which added $46 to the price.

Beneath the bodywork the B-series also showed original thinking. Dodge engineers moved the engine forward and the front wheels back, placing more payload onto the front axle; this was the 1930s Fore-Point principle, which allowed more payload

without a heavier rear axle and springs, but here combined with a shorter wheelbase that made the truck more manoeuvrable. Despite the shorter wheelbase, moreover, there was no loss of cab-to-rear-axle length, so load beds were no shorter than before. Manoeuvrability was also improved by cross-steering and a wider front tread, which allowed a 37-degree turn in either direction, while the design of the steering gear reduced kickback.

Thanks to the clever chassis layout, the 108-in wheelbased 1/2-ton could carry the same 6.5-ft load bed as the old truck, though the cargo box was wider and over 5in deeper, giving 40 per cent more space overall. Front and rear axles had a greater load capacity, the front springs were longer and the brakes were bigger and more efficient than before.

What didn't change was the running gear – the engine, clutch, transmission and rear axle. The 1/2- and 3/4-ton B-series offered the familiar 218-ci L-head six in 95-bhp form, while the heavier-duty 1-ton packed the bigger 230-ci (3769-cc), with 102bhp and 184lb ft. The line-up was broadly the same. Pickups were available as follows: 1/2-ton, 108-in (2.7-m) wheelbase, 6.5-ft (1.98-m) bed, $1,263; 3/4-ton, 116-in (2.9-m) wheelbase, 7.5-ft (2.3-m) bed, $1,371; 1-ton 116-in wheelbase, 7.5-ft bed, $1,435; 1-ton, 126-in (3.2-m) wheelbase, 9-ft bed (2.7-m), $1,465.

Dodge sold around 114,000 trucks in 1948, nearly 119,000 in '49, which set more records for the division but was still behind Ford and Chevrolet. Dodge made no

ignificant changes to the pickups for 1949, and even the new features for 1950 would not have caused palpitations at General Motors or Ford. Bonded brake linings were now fitted across the range and the parking brake and the three-speed gearshift were moved to the steering column. As far as pickup beds were concerned, there was a new ½-ton pickup with lower 17-in (43-cm) sides. The original 22.4-in sides were still available, the two boxes referred to as 'lowsides' and 'highsides'. Finally, all light trucks, including the pickups, now had the option of Fluid Drive transmission, which had previously only been offered in the Route-Van.

Sales were down to less than 100,000 that year, partly because of a three-month

strike early in 1950. In fact Dodge, which had begun the post-war era with such optimism, would find itself losing ground and market share as the 1950s wore on, trailing Ford and Chevy by a wider margin each year. It was a feature of the company's history that repeated itself more than once – boom followed by stagnation.

The B-series was given a mid-life facelift for 1951 with a new rectangular grille with two large horizontal bars replacing the three stacked bars. There were more prominent parking lights, and the dashboard was improved by moving the instruments in front of the driver where previously they had been centrally placed. There were trim and colour improvements inside the cab, too, and a horn ring and

indicator switch on the steering wheel. Some think there was a higher compression ratio and more power, but there is no evidence of this. New Oriflow shocks made for a smoother ride and there were other minor improvements like anodized brake cylinders.

The lowside pickup was now standard, with highsides optional, and for $5 one could have the cargo box painted Amour Yellow or Dodge Truck Red to match the cab. Normally the boxes were black whatever colour one chose for the cab, but a more cheerful occasional option was the Spring Special. To kickstart sales in the new year, the Spring Special Dodges had attractive two-tone paint jobs, blending box, cab and front end. They looked neat, but failed to have an effect on Dodge sales,

OPPOSITE and THIS PAGE
'Job-Rated' was a new name for a new range of pickups launched in 1949, complete with 'Pilot House' cab.

OPPOSITE
Same model, but what a difference a
radical lowering of the chassis makes.

LEFT
A 1952 B-series, with the new rectangular
grille offered from 1951.

across the wide open plains of the Midwest in summer could be dazzling to the eye.

Also for the first time, buyers had the option of a long-wheelbased, high capacity 1/2-ton pickup. This combined the 1/2-ton's underpinnings and payload with the 116-in wheelbase and 7.5-ft highsided cargo box of the 3/4-ton. Designed for operators hauling light but bulky loads, it was offered at $1,379, a modest $35 premium over the standard short wheelbase.

Alongside these major changes were

OPPOSITE and THIS PAGE
A 1952 Dodge in period dress, still powered by the L-head six-cylinder engine.

hich were still sluggish despite a rapidly rowing market. They did increase to over 06,000 for 1951, but dropped back slightly e year after, way below the peaks of 947–49. When one considers that in 1951 ord sold 180,000 trucks and Chevrolet over 50,000, then the position of Dodge can be en in perspective.

Nineteen-fifty-three was the final year r the B-series pickups, but Dodge made ore changes than ever before. The long-erving L-head six-cylinder engines were

unchanged in 218-ci and 230-ci forms, but automatic transmission was a new option – in fact it was a first in the industry. The 'Truck-O-Matic' was a similar unit to the one used in Chrysler and De Soto cars, and was a $110 option on all the trucks. Who could have forseen that within a few years an automatic would be one of the most popular options on light trucks. Another innovation was tinted glass ($12 extra), which was not an early way of tempting buyers but a recognition that driving a truck

A one-piece windshield for 1954 helped to keep Dodge up to date, as did the option of a V8 engine.

new, bigger rear fenders for the pickups, which would be used on Dodges right up to 1985. Dual tail lights were now fitted, and certain cab options such as armrests and sun visors were colour-co-ordinated. All of the 1953 improvements were applied across the range: 1/2-ton 108-in/116-in wheelbase, 3/4-ton 116-in wheelbase and 1-ton 116-in/126-in wheelbase. But despite the improvements, it was another bad year for Dodge. Sales plunged by over 19 per cent as the overall truck market continued to grow, causing the division to slip from third to fifth place in the ratings.

Running on the Spot
What Dodge lacked was a little excitement in its light trucks, but that arrived for 1954 with the V8. Available right across the range, it was named 'Power Dome' (engineering copy writers worked overtime in those days), a thoroughly modern 241-ci (3949-cc) overhead-valve unit with 7.5:1 compression ratio and hydraulic valve lifters. It offered 45 per cent more power than the old 218-ci (3572-cc) six, with 145bhp at 4,200rpm and 214lb ft of torque peaking at 2,400rpm.

This was enough to make the little Dodge the most powerful light truck on the market, and the division sought to publicize the fact by driving a 1/2-ton V8 continuously for 50 days at the Chrysler Proving Ground. It covered 50,198 miles (80784km), setting a new world endurance record. Later, the AAA certified the V8's fuel economy at 22.2mpg, so it wasn't particularly thirsty either. Chrysler, of course, was establishing its own V8 reputation with the legendary hemi V8 in

some of its cars, the deep-breathing hemispherical combustion chambers producing unrivalled power and efficiency. A hemi was fitted to the 1 1/2-ton and over heavy-duty trucks, though not to the light-duty pickups.

The 1954 light trucks were instantly recognizable, due to modern new cab styling with a big one-piece curved windshield, a much larger area of glass and a fresh look. The whole cab was mounted lower for easier entry and exit, and the chassis was also new, with great attention paid to the turning radius; the original shorter-wheelbased B-series had earned Dodge trucks a good reputation for manoeuvrability, and this was reinforced in the new C-series. There was no change to the basic range of 6.5-, 7.5- and 9-ft cargo boxes in the 1/2-ton, 3/4-ton and 1-ton trucks, and the 7.5-ft big-capacity 1/2-ton also continued.

That V8 option cost an extra $120, though the faithful sixes carried on, with more power squeezed from them that year: higher compressions delivered 100bhp/177lb ft from the smaller 218-ci six and 110bhp/194lb ft from the bigger 230-ci one.

But in spite of the V8, the new cab and other innovations, Dodge fared worse than ever in 1954. A recession following the end of the Korean War did not help matters, neither did cut-throat competition from Ford and Chevrolet. Whatever the root cause, Dodge sales slumped to a little over 60,000 that year, which amounted to 7.3 per cent of the American truck market. Dodge hadn't had such a small slice of the pie for many a year.

Dodge sent a significant memo to its dealers as they prepared for the 1955 model year, advising them that 1954 C-series trucks delivered from November '54 could be counted as '55s, which was a sure sign that production had run ahead of demand during 1954. Or it may only have been a ploy to keep the production lines flowing, as the new for 1955 C-series pickups weren't actually launched until April of that year.

The Pilot House cab was given extra glass, with a wraparound windshield and a rear window the width of the cab to improve visibility, while two-tone paint and new bright upholstery colours cheered things up inside and out. Buyers now had a choice of Custom or Custom Regal cabs, though it also offered a special entry-level version of the basic 1/2-ton pickup, offered in lowside form only for $1,446 or $86 cheaper than the standard model.

Mechanical changes were few but significant as the 218-ci L-head six was finally pensioned off and the 230-ci, now boosted to 111bhp and 201lb ft, became the standard motor on all light trucks. Meanwhile, the V8 was given extra cubic inches, and as a 259-ci (4244-cc) engine now offered 169bhp at 4,400rpm and 243lb ft at 2,400, though the V8 pickup's status as the most powerful light truck on the market had been shortlived as a power race began to gather speed. The Truck-O-Matic also joined the great options list in the sky, replaced by Chrysler's more modern Powerflite transmission.

Sales recovered a little that year but fell back again to less than 60,000 in 1956, when

here were no changes of note to the pickup.
Dodge's main focus of attention that year
was the Town Wagon (a passenger version of
the ¹/₂-ton panel van) and slotting more
powerful V8s into the heavy-duty trucks, an
industry-wide trend encouraged by the
spread of freeways across America.

Still, the pickups did get plenty of notice
the following year with a new front end –
the 'Forward Look' – which saw the fender
line extended forward and fronted by hooded
headlights, while a new rear-hinged hood
could open to 90 degrees for full
accessibility to the engine. Considering the
flamboyance of the late 1950s, this was
rather mild, but the new Sweptside pickup
really entered into the spirit of the age.
Chevrolet's Cameo pickup, together with
Ford's Styleside and car-based Ranchero,
had demonstrated there was a demand for a
flashy light truck that would be as happy
transporting antiques as it would bales of
straw on the farm, and the Sweptside was
Dodge's response. Dodge Suburban rear
fenders provided sculpted sides and tailfins,
were set off by two-tone paintwork. It was
based on the 116-in 'long box' ¹/₂-ton and all
came with Custom cab trim. At $1,614, the
Sweptside actually cost slightly less than the
standard ¹/₂-ton with the 7.5-ft bed, but not
many were sold, though it made a good
collector's item.

The Sweptside and new front end were
only a part of a whole raft of changes to the
1957 pickups as Dodge tried to recover lost
sales. All light trucks were renumbered that
year as the D100 ¹/₂-ton, D200 ³/₄-ton and
D300 1-ton, and all were given 12-volt

OPPOSITE and LEFT
Even workaday Power Wagons are restored
these days. This is a model from 1956.

electrics. Four-wheel-drive was a new option for the ½- and ¾-ton, billed W100 and W200 respectively. Offered across the range of body styles, these had a two-range transfer box and high ground clearance like the 1-ton Power Wagon. To keep abreast of the power race, the V8 was uprated again, this time to 315ci (5162cc) with an 8.5:1 compression ratio; this exceeded 200bhp for the first time – 204bhp,

to be exact – with 290lb ft. This was the largest V8 offered in any light truck, so it was not for nothing that the publicity of the time referred to them as 'Power Giants'.

Sadly, this was to no avail as sales fell a further 14 per cent to less than 50,000. Dodge was now languishing in fifth place, with a mere seven per cent of market share. But it persevered and launched yet another restyle

for 1958, this time with quadruple headlights, full-width hood and new grille. Apart from rerated springs on the D100 to improve ride quality, there were very few other changes for what was now known as the L-series. Colour that year included Klondike Yellow and Alaska White, plus two-tones with a Sahara beige top. The range had now expanded to 228 different trucks up to 1 ton, despite

A two-wheel-drive D100 from the early 1960s. The W100 was the 4x4 variant.

nich Dodge production fell to the lowest
vel since the Second World War. Sales
opped by over 20 per cent.

Until now, the befinned Sweptside apart,
odge was without a flush-sided pickup to
challenge those of Ford and General Motors,
which was rectified in 1959, when the
Sweptline arrived, with straight flush sides
and extra capacity. It was workmanlike and
had no fins, selling for $16 more than the
standard pickup, which continued as the
Utiline. Four-wheel-drive W-series pickups
came as Utilines only, but the rest had the
choice of both styles.

Other updates, for what turned out to be

BELOW LEFT
Awaiting restoration? It is touch and go
whether or not this late-1960s pickup will
be saved.

PAGES 142 and 143
A 1971 pickup with the classic customizing
cues fashionable at the time.

the penultimate year for this generation of trucks, included an hydraulic clutch, instruments placed in front of the driver and a marginal capacity boost to the V8. This now measured 318ci (5211cc) though power and torque were unchanged. The 230-ci (3769-cc) six did get more power, however, with 120bhp and 202lb ft, while 1-ton W300 4x4s used a 251-ci (4113-cc) version of 125bhp/216lb ft. This was a better year for Dodge, after a depressing 1958, with sales up an upbeat 40 per cent, though as the whole market was recovering actual market share was down to 5.5 per cent. Neither did the gloom lift with the decade, for sales fell again in 1960 despite more spent on advertising. The slogan for 1960 was, 'You Can Depend on Dodge to Save You Money in Trucks'.

Prelude to Profit

There was nothing new for 1960, betraying the fact that Dodge had an all-new truck on the way. When it arrived in October, the new for 1961 truck – the Dodge Dart – heralded a change in design philosophy. The 1948 truck's short wheelbase and high manoeuvrability was sacrificed for a more conventional layout, with wheelbases up by at least 6in (15cm) right across the range. The styling was entirely new, of course, leading the 1960s trend towards a squared-off look with slab sides. Both Utiline and Sweptline pickup boxes continued, the latter 4in wider than before, and with 10 per cent more cubic capacity.

By now the chassis was stronger and more massive, with wider and longer leaf springs at both ends of the truck to smooth out the ride and improve handling. A dropped centre in the chassis allowed easier access to a lower cab, which was also several inches wider.

The biggest news was that Dodge finally bade farewell to the L-head six (though it did linger in the 1-ton W300), its place taken by the new overhead-valve slant-six that had made its debut in Chrysler's compact, the Valiant. In the pickups, it came in 170-ci (2786-cc) form and 101bhp/136lb ft, though only in the light-duty ½-tonners) or 225ci (3687cc) with 140bhp and 201lb ft. Of course, this wouldn't have been a Dodge pickup without a V8 option, and the 318-ci (5211-cc) unit was carried over, though slightly derated at 200bhp/286lb ft. All of them came equipped with alternator electrics before either Ford or Chevrolet made the transition.

The new trucks seemed just the thing to tackle a new decade, though Dodge sales actually dropped again that first year. However, they finally began the long haul back to respectability in 1962, as sales increased to 59,000 or so. As the 1960s wore on, Dodge would command an increasing share of the rapidly expanding light truck market, the post-war jinx having finally been broken. It is interesting that this success was achieved without annual model changes. Instead, Dodge simply introduced changes as and when it was ready.

So the new Crewcab was launched halfway through the 1962 model year. Like similar pickups it could seat six, and was mounted on a 146-in (3.7-m) extended

wheelbase. The base was the ³/4-ton D200, with a 6.5-ft (2-m) cargo box offered in Utiline or Sweptline styles. The 4x2 range now ran from the D100 Utiline at $1,809 to the D300 Utiline at over $2,100, though there was still no Sweptside box for the 1-tonner. Four-wheel-drives were still offered in the W100/200/300-series, though the 1-ton 300 now adopted the new slant-six, albeit in 'heavy-duty' form. Transmission options remained three-speed manual (heavy-duty or extra heavy-duty), four-speed manual or the three-speed Loadflite automatic with pushbutton controls.

Dodge was gaining quite a reputation among the muscle-car enthusiasts, thanks to the legendary hemi V8 and the lower-cost Big Wedge. Some of this muscle found its way into the pickup line during the 1960s, notably in the big-block 426-ci (6981-cc) power unit. This was quite a beast, with a 10.3:1 compression ratio and four-barrelled carburettor, which added up to 365bhp at 4,800rpm and 470lb ft at 3,200rpm. It could only be had in tandem with a whole list of mandatory options: power brakes and rear axle struts attempted to keep all that power in check and the Loadflite automatic was compulsory as well, along with power steering and cosmetic features like a tachometer and plenty of extra brightwork. This made the 426 an expensive option, and few buyers actually ordered it. It was also only offered for two years, but did indicate the way the pickup market was heading, as well as confirming Dodge's position as the maker of hot-rod trucks.

The big-block V8 was only available along with the Custom Sport Special package, which Dodge offered on pickups from 1964. Aimed at leisure users, this added bucket seats, a centre console, twin sun visors, armrests and carpeting, plus extra stripes and chrome embellishments on the outside. Of buyers who chose it, most went for the 225-ci (3687-cc) slant-six or 318 V8, rather than the full-house 426. There were few other changes to the conventional pickups that year as Dodge concentrated on the new compact forward-control A100, which came as pickup, panel van or wagon.

Like similar trucks from Ford (Econoline) and Chevy (Corvair 95) it borrowed heavily from the equivalent compact sedan and was aimed to combat the popular VW Transporter. The A100 wasn't wildly successful, accounting for only 3 per cent of compact truck sales, but did offer the option

OPPOSITE and BELOW
The Ram badge and hood mascot have long been symbolic of Dodge. This is an example from the 1980s.

f a 273-ci (4474-cc) V8, which was unique n a compact truck. The performance image as further boosted by drag racer Bill Golden, who built a hemi-powered A100 that ould perform power-wheelies on command. As a six-cylinder or V8 truck, the A100 was art of the Dodge line-up until 1970.

The conventional pickups were given heir share of the limelight in spring 1965, when single headlights heralded several changes to the load beds. The 122-in wheelbase was stretched to 128in (3.25m), which allowed the fitting of an 8-ft (2.4-m) Utiline box. Sweptline boxes were now double-walled and had an optional full-length moulding, while all the pickups had a new rear end with a wider, vertical tailgate. A vertical rear assisted the fitting of slide-on camper units, which was a rapidly expanding market at the time. With the new rear end, the sweptlines in particular looked clean and tidy, with flat-topped wheel arches in the cargo box. Dodge was still having a good decade. Sales increased 19 per cent in 1965, which turned out to be the division's best year since 1949, with over 119,000 buyers signing a cheque at their Dodge dealership. Not only that, but the division finally climbed out of fifth place back into fourth.

After all the hard work of 1965, 1966 was a quiet year. Buyers could choose from nine Utiline pickups and seven Sweptsides, both styles offered on the D200 4x2 Crewcab in its 146-in wheelbase, though only the Utiline in the 4x4 version. The utilitarian ex-army Power Wagon incidentally, was still on sale, though now nearing the end of its life. This too came as a Utiline pickup, on its unique 126-in wheelbase, at $3,555. It was also the only Dodge to carry on using the elderly L-head six, now in 125-bhp 250-ci (4097-cc) form.

Increasing numbers of buyers were willing to pay extra for a V8, as the decade continued. When Dodge had first introduced the option back in 1954, it was a minority fitment, but now the tables were turned. Over half the customers for 3/4-ton D200s took the V8 route in 1966 as well as nearly half buying long-wheelbased D100s. Only in the light-duty short-wheelbased D100s were V8s a distinct minority.

This growing thirst for power encouraged Dodge to offer another muscle engine. For 1967, a 383-ci (6276-cc) V8 replaced the big 426. It was slightly tamer, with fewer cubic inches, a 9.2:1 compression ratio and 258bhp/375lb ft (though some say 323lb ft). However, it was a great deal of power and torque for a light truck, especially the short-wheelbased D100. At the same time, the 318-ci (5211-cc) V8 was uprated to 210bhp and 280lb ft, while the base motor for all the pickups was the 225-ci (3687-cc) slant-six. Dodge was apparently determined to capture as much as it could of the booming recreational market, offering a camper special as well extra power options. It even developed a four-speed transmission specifically for campers, with a relatively high third gear, which became an option on all the pickups.

Another pickup aimed at weekend users and campers was the Adventurer launched in 1968. This replaced the Custom Sports Special and was a plusher version of the same thing, with a vinyl roof and colour-keyed carpets as well as the bucket seats. 'Dodge Adventurer,' went the double-page colour advertisement, 'the pickup that leads a double life … Adventurer is a handsome devil. Almost too handsome to be called a pickup … Don't buy a pickup you'll want to put in a barn with the livestock. Go Adventurer and travel first class.'

As 1969 came and went, Dodge must have been well satisfied with the decade. Not only had it kept pace with an expanding market, it also commanded an increasing share of it, and new sales records were set in both 1968 and '69, over 177,000 Dodge trucks finding buyers in the final year of the decade. The only change that year was Cushioned Beam front suspension, which saw the addition of an anti-roll bar to the I-beam front axle; unlike some of its rivals, Dodge clearly didn't yet believe in independent front ends for light trucks, which didn't seem to worry the buying public one jot.

Sales were still healthy during 1970 and '71, even though the basic truck was now ten years old. However, there were some useful changes to the 1970 trucks behind the new grille. Four-wheel-drive W100 and W200 pickups could now be had with Loadflite automatic transmission for the first time, and new three-speed full synchromesh was standard on all 1/2- and 3/4-ton models. To make life easier for campers, the tailgate could be removed or replaced quickly by one person to ease the fitment of a camper unit, which was an industry first. Camper Special pickups now had an electrical hookup between the camper unit and the truck,

OPPOSITE
The Power Wagon badge was later applied to smaller trucks such as this 1980s pickup.

and a 25-gallon fuel tank was standard.

For 1971, the final year of the D-series pickups, the changes were more in the model range than in the mechanics. No-frills economy models are usually seen as a feature of the later 1970s, but Dodge offered one this year, the 114-in (2.9-m) wheelbase Sweptline Special, with a 198-ci (3245-cc) slant-six, three-speed manual transmission, basic trim and new options. At the other end of the scale, the popular Adventurer blossomed into three variations. The base package consisted of brightwork and mouldings only; next up, the new Adventurer Sport added yet more exterior

OPPOSITE and BELOW
A U.K.-registered Dodge from 1980, when full-sized pickups were out of favour, though Dodge's little Mitsubishi-based D50 was holding up well.

OPPOSITE
Proof that even modern pickups sometimes
work for a living. The 1996 Dodge Ram in
towing mode.

LEFT
The new-generation Ram transformed
Dodge's fortunes in the 1990s.

decoration like a Delta hood ornament.
Finally, the Adventurer SE (available only
on 128-in wheelbased Sweptsides) had all
of this plus applications of wood to the
lower body sides.

Happy Campers
Avoiding annual model changes and
keeping the same truck in production for
ten years served Dodge well in the 1960s.
So it maintained the same philosophy in the
1970s, when a new generation of Dodge
light trucks was announced. The new line
would prove wildly successful: in 1972, its
first year, Dodge found its market share
rocketing to over 13 per cent, which is
more than double that of the dark days of
the late 1950s, mindful that the truck

market had greatly expanded by this time.

The new for 1972 truck had a boxy,
almost timeless look, with little in the way
of character; but beneath the skin it had
been designed to appeal both to business
users and weekenders. First off, it was
bigger all round, with wheelbases increased
by up to 5in (13cm). The doors were
bigger, giving easier access to a larger cab

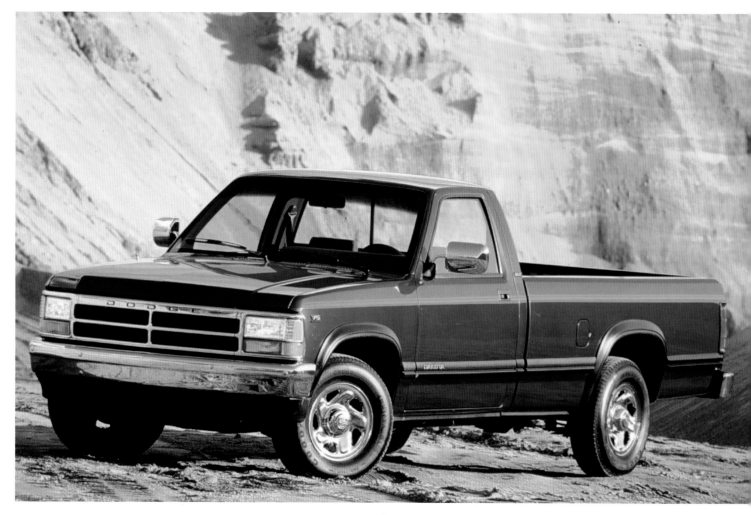

with bigger windows and windshield, the
se of curved side windows adding 4in
10cm) of shoulder width. The cab was more
ivilized, with a car-type dashboard and
xtra sound insulation, with new options like
ruise control and integral air conditioning.

Even more significant, in the pursuit of a
more car-like ride and handling, was the

final adoption of coil-sprung independent
front suspension on the two-wheel-drive
trucks, as well as wider treads front and rear,
and bigger brakes. The 4x4s were altogether
more workaday, retaining the I-beam front
axle and leaf springs together with beefier
clutch and brakes.

Engine choices still began with the

225-ci (3687-cc) slant-six, seen in a pickup
more than ten years earlier, with the 150 net
bhp 318-ci (5211-cc) V8 optional right
across the range. The 383-ci (6276-cc) V8
was dropped and replaced by a 360-ci
(5899-cc) unit of 180 net bhp and 295lb ft,
while a 320-lb ft 400-ci (6555-cc) V8 of 200
net bhp was also available, but only on the

OPPOSITE
A 1996 Dodge Dakota. This is a lighter,
more economical alternative to the Ram.

BELOW LEFT
Dodges have always been favourites with
campers. This is a Ram 3500 with
removable camper unit.

RIGHT and OPPOSITE
*The ultimate muscle pickup? A 1998 Dodge
Magnum V10.*

two-wheel-drives. In some ways, the line-up
was the same as ever: 1/2-ton D100 (115-in
wheelbase); 1/2-ton D100 (131in); 3/4-ton
D200 (131in); 3/4-ton crew cabs; 1-ton D300
(135in); and the W-series 4x4s. Camping
Special packages served the ever increasing
recreational market with appropriate
electrics, and Dodge pretty well had the
market in these sewn up, supplying 85 per
cent of the chassis. Utiline and Sweptside
pickups were throughout, with the Crew Cab
in 149- or 164-in wheelbases.

Dodge had spent $50 million designing
this new truck line-up and it had all been
worthwhile. In the first year, sales leaped to
over 260,000, up by nearly two-thirds on
1971.

There was another innovation for 1973 –
the Club Cab. It was a simple idea, but its
subsequent success confirmed what a good
one it was. Extending the cab rearwards by
18-in (46cm) provided enough weatherproof
space for tools, camping equipment or even
two extra passengers, as long as they didn't
mind using the little fold-down jump seats.
Another side window was part of the Club
Cab package, giving better visibility; the
option was available on the D100 133-in
wheelbase (giving a 6.5 ft loadbed), the
149-in (for an 8-ft bed) or the D200 (same
wheelbase and bed length). Whether or not it
was due to the Club Cab, this was another
record year for Dodge, with over 330,000
trucks sold, though the market was
expanding so fast that market share actually
slipped a little.

No one in the truck business could claim
to be clairvoyant, so it wasn't really Dodge's

fault that in August 1973, only months
before the first fuel crisis struck, that it
introduced the Ramcharger SUV (based
directly on the D-series trucks) and the
biggest ever gasoline V8 option on a pickup.
So it was hit especially hard by rising gas
prices: sales fell and many buyers switched
to the slant-six in preference to one of the
V8s. As for the pickups, there was little new
that year, though the popular Club Cab
option was extended to the 4x4 W-series.
The 440-ci (7210-cc) V8 that replaced the
400 offered 230 net bhp and 350lb ft,
provided one could afford the fuel bills.

The odd thing was how quickly
everyone seemed to forget. As the queues
disappeared and gas supplies got back to
normal, people went straight back to ticking

the V8 option box. Nineteen-seventy-five
proved to be Dodge's second best production
year in history, and that was despite pulling
out of the heavy-duty truck market
altogether. Less than 16 per cent of Dodge
truck buyers insisted on buying a six, and
reflecting the increasing interest in 4x4s,
Dodge gave the W-series pickups full-time
four-wheel-drive and reworked suspension
for a less jarring ride, which is where
experience of the SUV Ramcharger paid off
The recovery continued in 1976, with sales
up 43 per cent. It was almost as if the fuel
crisis had never occurred.

During the 1960s, camper trailers and
other weekend leisure tools had been the
coming thing. Now in the mid-1970s came
the era of custom trucks, whether as vans,

ckups or four-wheel-drives. All the manufacturers responded to this trend with their own factory customs, and Dodge was no exception. The 1977 Warlock was based on the D100 or W100 Utiline and came ready to cruise, with gold trim, gold wheels and oak side boards. Colours included Sunfire Metallic and Bright Red, while black bucket seats were standard. The Warlock could be equipped with any engine from the Dodge pickup range, from the 225-ci slant-six to the

440-ci V8. The six now became the Super Six, with an extra ten horsepower, thanks to a two-barrelled carburettor, while an overdrive four-speed transmission was also offered to anyone concerned about fuel economy. Other factory customs were the D100 True Spirit and Power Wagon W100.

Perhaps the most famous of all Dodge factory customs was the Li'l Red Express Truck of 1978. Now this was altogether more serious than those paint 'n' stripe specials and

certainly had a thorough cosmetic treatment: Canyon Red paint job, oak bed trim, chrome side steps and mag alloy wheels (7in front, 8in rear) with tyres to match. But it also had a modified E59 police V8 under the hood. Based around the standard 360-ci (5899-cc) unit, this had a Thermoquad carburettor and a particularly hot camshaft straight out of the late 1960s. Officially, Chrysler declined to rate the engine, but its output was thought to be around 220bhp.

OPPOSITE
1998 Dodge Magnum V10.

BELOW
A late 1990s Dodge Ram 2500 with Club Cab.

Chrome highlights set the Quad Cab 2500 off to advantage.

The LRT also took advantage of new emissions laws that year, which were less tight for trucks of more than 6,000-lb (2720-kg) GVW, which is why it got away with two chromed vertical exhaust stacks without catalytic converters. The same thinking lay behind the new D150 pickup launched that year. Officially this was a heavy-duty version of the 1/2-ton D100, though it was really only a means of getting around the legislation, the new pickup tipping in at just over the 6,000-lb mark. Another sign of the times was Dodge's first diesel option on its light trucks. It was actually a Mitsubishi unit, a straight-six of 243ci (3982cc) that delivered 103bhp and had a smaller appetite for juice than any of the V8s. It came with two 12-volt batteries to master the 20:1 compression on cold mornings, and was available on the D/W150 and D/W200 pickups.

There was something about Dodge. When the truck market did well, Dodge soared; when it was in trouble, Dodge seemed to suffer more than most. Take 1979, for example, when the second fuel crisis struck. Gas queues and rising prices once again hit sales of 4x4s and big pickups and vans, the light trucks that Dodge so depended on. Sales of pickups plummeted by 30 per cent that year, after a record 1978, and the demand for recreational vehicle chassis (of which Dodge was the leading supplier) virtually ceased.

Fortunately, Dodge did do something in line with the times, launching the mini-pickup D50. This was actually a rebadged Mitsubishi, Ford and Chevy having already

demonstrated that disguised Japanese pickups could be popular with American buyers, and the D50 was no exception. Rated at 1/4-ton, it had a 6.5-ft cargo box and could carry up to 1,400lb (635kg). Four-cylinder engines of 122ci (1999cc) or 156ci (2556cc) drove through four- or five-speed manual gearboxes or an automatic.

Meanwhile, the full-sized pickups received a new grille with twin or quad rectangular headlights, while there was a fuel-economy version of the D100, equipped with a single-barrelled 225-ci (3687-cc) six, radial tyres and torque converter lockup. The 'adult toys' custom trucks also carried on for another year, though the Li'l Red Express Truck came in more sanitized form in what was its final year.

Dodge must have thanked providence for the little D50, for it was the only pickup with sales heading in the right direction in 1980. The full-sizers plunged by 60 per cent that year and one factory was closed, while another converted to produce Chrysler's front-drive K-car. The only changes to the D50 were a couple of new colours, but that didn't matter – it was in demand. The full-sized D100 was dropped, leaving the D150 as the lead-in full-sized pickup, now with a four-speed overdrive transmission to boost economy. The W-series switched to part-time four-wheel-drive for the same reason, a four-speed transmission replacing the three-speeder. By this time, the biggest V8s – the 400 and 440 – had been dropped, leaving the 160-bhp 360 V8 the largest on offer.

Back to the Future
Nineteen-eighty-one was a low point for Dodge, with just over 170,000 trucks sold. Even the little D50 had lost its shine (down to around 25,000), though Dodge sought to widen its appeal that year by renaming it the Ram 50 and offering it in Custom, Royal or Sport trim levels. The full-sized pickups had more aerodynamic styling that year, and despite falling sales still came in a range of formats, including conventional, Crew Cab or Club Cab (the latter with 34cu ft of storage space), Sweptline or Utiline cargo boxes and 225-ci six or 318-ci (5211-cc) V8 power units. The basic range was as follows: 1/2-ton D150 (in four wheelbases); 3/4-ton D250 (three wheelbases); and 1-ton D350 (three wheelbases). There were four-wheel-drive equivalents of each one, still named the W-series. Dodge also reinvented its Ram symbol, which dated back to 1933, and used the name to emphasize the toughness of its trucks. It had been dropped in the mid-1950s, but with Chrysler under the invigorating leadership of Lee Iacocca, who had been brought in to save the corporation from bankruptcy, it was back.

Dodge never built an equivalent of the car-based Ford Ranchero or Chevrolet El Camino, but it came closest with the 1982 Rampage mini-pickup. This was based on the front-wheel-drive Dodge Omni, its front end taken from the 024 coupé. Power came from the coupé's 135-ci (2212-cc) overhead-cam four, producing 84bhp. A four-speed High Line and five-speed Sport completed the line, the latter with black detailing, 14-in alloy wheels, Rallye instruments and loud

A 2003 Ram 1500 with Quad Cab, the six-seat Club Cab but with four doors.

graphics. Neither was a serious workhorse, but the Rampage could carry 1,100lb and its roomy cab impressed the road testers of the time. With more cab space and slightly quicker acceleration, the Rampage made a good home-grown alternative to the VW Rabbit. But the buying public didn't agree, and fewer than 30,000 were sold in three years, after which time the Rampage was dropped.

The Mitsubishi-based Ram 50 did better, with over 34,000 sold in 1982 alone. It now came in three guises: Custom, Royal (with deluxe trim) and Sport (bucket seats, extra instruments, wide wheels). Engine choices were unchanged, but the mini-Ram did have the option of four-wheel-drive, which took the price of the Sport to over $9,000. With four-wheel-drive, it adopted the Power Ram badge as the full-sized pickups had before. These now offered Royal and Royal SE trim packages as well as options including a complete wrecking truck and snow plough. In a gesture towards fuel economy, a 'Miser' model was new for 1982, with four-speed overdrive transmission and a price nearly $900 less than that of the cheapest two-wheel-drive D150. It was available on the 115- and 131-in wheelbases, with 6.5- or 8-ft Sweptline rear ends. So popular was the Miser that it became a permanent part of the range, precipitating the return of the D100 in 1984.

There were few changes to any of the pickups in 1983, and the D100's rebirth wasn't the big news it seemed, with all the familiar components on offer. Dodge was concentrating on the new mini-van Caravan,

which stole a march on the opposition and gave the company a real boost. As for the D100, it shared the same wheelbase and cargo box options as the D150, plus the base 225-ci (3687-cc) slant-six engine, the only difference of note being a payload that was around 1,000lb less. The real point of the reborn D100 was that it gave Dodge a full-sized price leader; in short-wheelbased form with a 6.5-ft bed, it cost only $6,403 – over $600 less than the Ram 50 Sport.

Dodge's mini-pickup received a facelift for 1985. It was nothing major, however, only a new grille and the same choice of Custom, Royal or Sport, with two- or four-wheel-drive. Meanwhile, the full-sized line-up was being slimmed down. The Club Cab, Crew Cab and Utiline were all dropped within the space of a couple of years, and by now were looking undeniably outdated, well into their second decade and with no replacement on the horizon. They did get a facelift for 1986, with a new more simple grille, but sales were still plummeting, dropping below 100,000. They seemed to be in danger of being caught up by the Ram 50, which achieved over 76,000 that year.

Dodge capitalized on the fact by reworking the Ram 50 more thoroughly the following year. It was bigger all round, with two wheelbase choices (105.5in and 116.5in), new panels and larger cabs. Naturally, the cargo boxes were also bigger, now measuring 6 or 7.3ft, depending on the wheelbase. The four-cylinder engines were unchanged, but the new mini-pickup (if it could still be classed as such) looked chunkier and more aggressive than before. It

would be part of the Dodge line-up well into the 1990s.

But the big news for 1987 was Dodge's new mid-sized pickup, the Dakota. Claimed to be America's first truck of this size, it slotted in between the 50 and full-sized, and came in 112- and 124-in wheelbases, in two- or four-wheel-drive and with the choice of five-speed manual or three-speed automatic transmissions. Base engine in the 4x2 was Chrysler's 135-ci (2212-cc) four (the very same that had powered the Rampage), with a new 239-ci (3916-cc) V6 an option. The new motor had been derived from the familiar 318-ci (5211-cc) V8, and delivered 125bhp and 195lb ft. It was standard in the 4x4 Dakota. At first, trim levels were base, SE and LE but Dodge later added a lead-in Dakota S to undercut the Chevrolet S10.

The new V6 found its way into the full-sized pickups the following year, when the ancient slant-six was finally dropped, while their V8s received throttle-body fuel injection. But the full-sizers were in danger of fading away. From the start, they were outsold by the Dakota, which was quite a landmark, the first time since the Second World War that the full-sized pickups had failed to be Dodge's best selling light trucks. Overweight, outdated and out of fashion, the full-sized Dodges looked as if they were heading for the graveyard.

But they were saved. Late in 1988, Dodge management announced that the big pickups would finally have a diesel option, and not any old diesel either. Maybe it was lessons learned from the Oldsmobile diesel a decade earlier, but whatever the reason, it

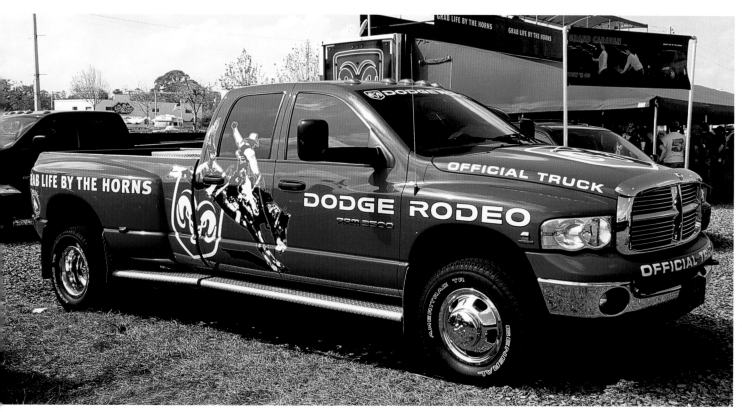

ecided to buy in a genuine Cummins
ngine. It was hugely expensive, adding up
$4,000 to the price of any truck to which
was fitted, but the 359-ci (5883-cc) turbo-
esel straight-six turned out to be the
aviour of the line. Its secret weapon was
00lb ft at only 1,700rpm, which made it

ideal for towing vehicles. The Cummins
name, the feel of this big six and even the
way it looked beneath the hood, all added to
its big-rig credibility. So as well as being a
truly useful workhorse, the Cummins option
gave some street cred to the entire line-up. It
was, unlike any diesel-powered Ford, Chevy

or anything else, the Real Thing. Dodge sold
17,000 of them in the first year, taking
orders for 10,000 more, though Cummins'
production lines were at pains to keep up
with the demand. By 1993, over 50,000 had
found homes.

Another bright spot of 1989 was the

OPPOSITE
2003 Dodge Ram HD with Quad Cab.

ABOVE
2004 Dodge Ram 3500 Rodeo.

Shelby Dakota. There were signs that performance was coming back into fashion, and though these Shelbys weren't muscle trucks, power coming from the standard 318-ci (5211-cc) V8, they did carry that magical name and looked the part; 1,500 were built that year.

The Club Cab returned for 1990, the full-sized version now built in Mexico, while the Dakota added its own, adding 18in (46cm) to the cab length, with two folding jump seats

like the original. Despite the Dakota's success (over 72,000 were sold that year) the Ram 50 continued as Dodge's entry-level pickup, though it had engine upgrades for 1990. The 156-ci (2556-cc) four became the base unit, with a new Mitsubishi-built optional 184-ci (3015-cc), which increased the towing limit to 3,500lb (1588kg). Thanks to Cummins, and the return of the Club Cab, full-sized sales were back to six figures in 1990, an improvement of 10 per cent. They declined

again in '91, though this was a poor year for the whole industry. The Cummins turbo diesel was now intercooled as well, though quoted outputs were unchanged, and the Dakota received a V8 option for the first time.

But where engines were concerned, the big news came for 1992, when the re-engineered Magnum V6s and V8s were fitted to all Dakotas and full-sized pickups. Entry-level Dakotas were still four-cylinder-powered, but with the Magnum V6 under the

OPPOSITE
2004 Dodge Monster Truck.

BELOW
2003 Dodge Ram 2500.

ood they offered 180bhp and 225lb ft. Opt
or the 318-ci V8, with 230bhp/295lb ft, and
he less than full-sized Dakota was
ransformed into a performance truck.
tandard on the 1-ton D350, and optional on
he 1/2- and 3/4-tonner was the 360-ci
5899-cc) V8 with 190bhp and 295lb ft,
hough this hadn't had the Magnum

treatment yet. When it did, for 1993, outputs
were up to 230bhp and 325lb ft. All of these
fuel-injected engines were thoroughly
reworked versions of the long-serving
overhead-valve units, though they did the
business just the same. The Magnum 360 V8
marked the extent of the changes for 1993,
as the full-sized pickups entered their final

and 22nd year of production. They had seen
two fuel crises, surviving the ups, downs and
rebounds. But this time, with the small Ram
50 dropped, the Dakota edging up into V8
territory and sales of bigger pickups on the
up, the time was right for a brand-new full-
sized pickup, which is exactly what
happened – and how!

OPPOSITE
A customized Dodge Ram.

BELOW
2003 Dodge Ram 1500.

Ram Revolution

Every manufacturer has a milestone product and some have several. But Dodge has only one candidate – the 1994 Dodge Ram. Single-handedly, it transformed Dodge from rowdy to daring, more than doubling the division's share of the full-sized pickup market and establishing the basis of a whole decade of profitably. But it nearly didn't happen.

Back in 1987, Dodge accepted that it needed to replace the full-sized D/W pickups, and sooner rather than later. At the time, conventional wisdom within the industry held that buyers of pickups were a conservative bunch and that if anything too radical was tried, it would scare them off. That's why every big pickup on the American market looked much the same, a brick-like box, with only a few rounded edges here and there to suggest it was aerodynamic. Dodge hadn't done too badly with this philosophy over the years, which was reflected in the prototype Phoenix pickup shown to customer clinics in late 1987. Summed up, comments included, '...well, it's OK, sort of'. It was this lukewarm response that spurred Chrysler to take a chance and design something radical.

The Ram was the result, code named T-300 in prototype form. This time the reactions were less equivocal. Less than half of those questioned really liked the distinctive new pickup, some didn't like it all, but no one could ignore it. This was the response that Dodge needed, and four years later, after an investment of $1.2 billion, the radical truck was launched, making a huge impression.

The front end, with its unashamedly retro hood rising above the fenders, was completely unique, allied to a meaty, aggressive look that the buying public and motoring press just loved. Not that there was anything very radical beneath the skin, but all the right ingredients were there. A strong, stiff chassis supported a wide track, with independent coil-sprung suspension plus 60-in leaf springs at the rear. Payload models were $1/2$-ton 1500, $3/4$-ton 2500 and 1-ton 3500, with wheelbases of 119 and 135in (3- and 3.5-m), plus 6.5- and 8-ft (2- and 2.4-m) cargo boxes to suit. The new Ram cab not only looked distinctive, it was also roomier than any of the opposition, with a 40-20-40 split seat and an upscaled Laramie SLT trim option providing more luxuries than ever before.

Engine-wise, there was less to shout about, at least at first, the familiar Magnums having been carried over. The 239-ci (3916-cc) V6 now offered 175bhp and 230lb ft, while the optional 318-ci (5211-cc) V8 made 220bhp/300lb ft. Standard on the big 3500, and optional on the others, was the 360-ci (5899-cc) V8, with 230bhp/330lb ft. And of course, the totemic Cummins turbo-

OPPOSITE
2005 Dodge Ram Power Wagon. U.S. manufacturers were greatly affected by the power of nostalgia and the resurrection of authentic old names.

BELOW
2005 Dodge Ram 2500 Regular, a basic working pickup, which some still were.

*A Dodge Dakota Quad Cab for 2005, with
new front end and flared wheel arches.*

intercooled diesel was still on the options
list, now offering 175bhp/420lb ft with a
manual transmission.

So far so good, except that Ford and
Chevy both had much bigger V8s. With
brutal performance back in fashion, the 360
was beginning to look a little puny, so
Dodge decided to leapfrog the opposition
with something quite different – a V10. It
actually arrived in the spring of 1994, a few

months after the main Ram launch, but the
effect was just as overwhelming. With 488ci
(7997cc), this new monster engine gave
Dodge the biggest, most powerful gasoline
pickup on the market, with the added kudos
of ten cylinders. Power came to 300bhp at
4,000rpm and 450lb ft at 2,400. There could
have been more, but there was doubt that the
standard transmissions would take the strain.
The V10 wasn't actually that new, owing

much to the existing V8s and sharing many
parts with them. With its cast-iron cylinder-
block, it weighed 800lb (365kg), but then in
a market where biggest was once again best
it was probably considered a good thing.
Incidentally, an all-aluminium version was
built for the Viper sports car, which actually
went into production before the Ram.

This double whammy of the radical-
looking Ram, followed by the monster V10,

produced the impact Dodge needed, though for some, the Ram V10 was even more out of tune with its times than the old brick-like pickups had been – anyone would think that America wasn't dependent on imported oil, and that global warming was mere science fiction. But the pickup-buying public didn't care about any of that. The Ram was big and macho and tough, and within two years it had muscled its way into America's ten top-selling vehicles, outnumbering many a sensible sedan. A V10 Club Cab was voted *4-Wheel & Off-Road* magazine's 4x4 of the Year.

Dodge quickly built on this success with a Club Cab for 1995, which added 20in (51cm) to the cab length and a wide bench seat in the back, which officially meant seating for six, though eight could be squeezed in if they were good friends. It was vital to the Ram's market, and once the Club was on stream, it made up 60 per cent of total production. Most of these were sold as private transport. Of the standard cabs, 72 per cent went to private customers, 15 per cent to the commercial/retail sector and only 13 per cent to big fleets.

Whoever was buying it, there was such a demand that Dodge's production lines couldn't keep pace. Over 230,000 pickups

LEFT and ABOVE
A 2006 Dodge Mega. Is it a truck or is it a luxury car with a load bed?

Dodge Ram from the mid-2000s with a retro look and UK plates.

were produced in the first year and the first 12 month's allocation of Club Cabs sold out in eight weeks! Consequently, another plant in Mexico was switched to Ram production, and when it also failed to cope, the former minivan factory in St. Louis, Missouri, was converted as well, giving a total capacity of 450,000 a year.

Meanwhile, a Camper Package was reintroduced for the 2500 and 3500 pickups in 1996. As Americans returned to their profligate ways, as far as gas consumption was concerned, it was plain that the RV market was due for a revival. Racing was back in vogue, too, and after Dodge Rams were used as trackside support at the Indianapolis 500, a line of Indy 500 Special Editions was offered, based on the ½-ton 1500 in dark blue. In September 1996 a Cummins-powered Ram set a new diesel speed record on the Bonneville Salt Flats in Utah, at 141.256mph (227.32km/h). It wasn't exactly stock-racing, either. The turbo-intercooled diesel had been race-tuned to 450bhp and 890lb ft, substantially adding to the growing Ram legend.

So successful was the Ram that few could have been surprised when the latest Dakota was launched for 1997 as a 'baby Ram'. It was styled to look like a smaller version of the real thing, with the same imposing front end and wide, squat stance. Engines and transmissions were largely carried over from the original Dakota, but that didn't matter, as the new one was able to offer the Ram experience to a new sector of the market. Prices started at $13,235 for the 150-ci (2458-cc) four-powered 4x2 SBx, and Dodge sold over 130,000 new-style Dakotas in the first year. To put this in perspective, over 350,000 full-sized Rams found buyers in 1997, which was a slight drop on the year before.

The Ram Sport was a mild appearance package on the 1500 pickup, but more serious was the SS/T (Super Sport Truck) announced for 1997, which came in red, green or black with wide dual silver stripes, 17-in wheels and a sports tuned exhaust. The standard power unit was the 245bhp 360-ci (5899-cc) Magnum, and if that wasn't enough, a Mopar R/T Performance package

ded another 45bhp, enough for 0–60mph
–100km/h) in 7.2 seconds and a 15.6-
cond quarter-mile.

The Club Cab played a vital part in the
am's success, but another variation was
fered for 1998 – the Quad Cab. It was
ally the six-seater Club but with four
ors, albeit with a difference. Instead of the
ur conventional doors of a crew cab, the
uad Cab's rear pair were rear-hinged, and
th no B-pillar, gave unrivalled access to
e rear bench seat. Without a B-pillar, the
b had to be considerably strengthened,
hile the front belts were seat-mounted to
ep them out of the way. The rear bench
so folded up to create extra stowage room.
iving the Ram this unique feature,
ossessed by no other pickup on the market,
derlined that Dodge was on one of its
ward rolls throughout the late 1990s.

Also new for 1998 was an upgrade of
e venerable Cummins diesel. It was
tually a new engine, despite sharing the
59-ci (5883-cc) capacity and straight-six
yout with the old engine. Now with four
lves per cylinder and high-pressure
ectronic injection, plus manual
ansmission, outputs rose to 230bhp at
700rpm and 450lb ft at 1,600rpm, while, as
ver, automatic transmission had to make do
ith slightly less power and torque. It was
ow nearly 10 years since the original
ummins had injected new life into Dodge's
d-generation pickup, and it was clearly
ere to stay. That year, Dodge sold more
ams than ever – 410,130, to be exact,
ough to make it the fourth best-selling
hicle of any type in America. To put

2500 model with Hemi engine from 2007.

another way: for every old-generation pickup
sold in the late 1980s, Dodge was selling
five Rams.

There were no major new features for
1999, apart from a power increase on the
V10 to 310bhp, but a notable show truck
appeared in the form of the Power Wagon
Concept. It was clearly inspired by the post-
war Power Wagon which Dodge built in
small numbers right up to 1968. With a host
of styling cues borrowed from the 1946
original, it also used an authentically
muscular 442-ci (7243-cc) Detroit diesel of

250bhp and 450lb ft. The press loved it, but
the 1999 Power Wagon never got beyond the
concept stage.

One of the reasons for using the Detroit
diesel was to demonstrate that a modern
diesel engine could be just as clean as a
gasoline unit, and for 2000 Dodge announced
another update to its own Cummins option.
Now named the Torque Master High Output,
the 359-ci (5883-cc) Cummins produced
slightly more power (245bhp) than its
predecessor, and a monstrous 505lb ft.
Breaking the 500-lb ft barrier was highly

ymbolic, as torque figures were becoming as otemic for big pickups as horsepower had een for the muscle cars of the 1960s.

Whether or not the private owner really eeded 505lb ft was highly questionable, but he fact that it was a highly-effective narketing tool against Ford and Chevrolet, vhich couldn't match it, was never in doubt. Dodge's standard transmissions couldn't ope with these sorts of figures, so the new iesel was only offered with a substantial New Venture six-speed manual gearbox. Driving through this, and a 4.10 rear axle, a Cummins-powered Ram 3500 4x2 could tow p to 15,150lb (6875kg).

By 2002, the Dakota was still offering he authentic baby-Ram experience, and it vas to Dodge's credit that it had kept an ntry-level four-cylinder engine instead of aking the Dakota relentlessly upmarket. Not hat it was cheap by any means, at $14,610 or the base regular cab 4x2, but it was over 2,000 less than the least expensive full- ized Ram. The range was now huge, with uad Cab and Club Cab versions included, s well as four-wheel-drive and a choice of rim extending to base, STX, SLT and Sport. And if four cylinders weren't enough, then here were some familiar options, now with xtra power: 239-ci (3916-cc) V6 (175bhp); 87-ci (4703-cc) V8 (235bhp/295lb ft); and 60-ci (5899-cc) V8 (250bhp/345lb ft).

This was an important year for the Ram, vhich saw many changes, including revised tyling (though it was still very much a am), more space in the cab (the cargo box vas shortened by 3in to make room) and ide air bags. All three payloads offered a

choice of ST or SLT trim, and power options included the lead-in V6, two V8s, the ever-present Cummins diesel, and of course the V10.

As for the V10: it's a fair bet that as soon as the Dodge Viper was launched, with its aluminium 500-bhp version of the Ram's ultimate engine, quite a few enthusiasts began to fantasize on how a 500-bhp Ram pickup would feel. They got their chance to find out in 2003, with the Ram SRT-10.

Ten years before, it would have seemed something only to dream about: a road-legal, fully-cataliticized light truck, with 500bhp and 525lb ft, the performance of a sports car and the outline of a regular pickup – there for the taking, as long as there was $45,000 burning a hole in one's pocket!

The SRT's secret was that it borrowed heavily from the Viper, not only the aluminium version of the V10 in full sports-car tune, but also the all-wheel disc brakes and the six-speed manual gearbox. The Ram's suspension was lowered all round and Bilstein shocks were fitted. In fact, there were five of them, the extra Bilstein bolted in between chassis and rear axle to prevent too much hopping around under fast getaways. And given a sufficiently skilful driver, the following were possible: Dodge claimed 0–60mph in 5 seconds, 0–100 and back to zero in 18 seconds, plus a top speed of 150mph (240km/h). The company had been determined to out-muscle Ford's SVT Lightning truck, and it had succeeded. Some preferred the SVT's lighter, sharper feel, while others claimed the SRT's greater weight and size didn't matter, given the

instant grunt emanating from its non-supercharged engine. A case of horses for courses, perhaps?

But to end the Dodge pickup story with the SRT would somehow not be fitting. It had been an engineering achievement in its own right, but at the end of the day, this 150-mph pickup was merely a toy for the rich. More relevant to most buyers was the latest Cummins diesel, announced in mid-2004 as an option on the 2500 and 3500 Rams. These heavier-duty pickups made up one-third of all Ram sales, and nearly three-quarters of their customers opted for the Cummins diesel. By now, Dodge had overtaken General Motors to capture 28 per cent of the diesel heavy-duty pickup market, with only Ford selling more.

2013 models have revised engine and transmission options. The PowerTech 3.7L V6 is discontinued, and the PowerTech 4.7L V8 equipped with the 6-speed 65RFE Automatic takes its place as the new base engine, still producing 310 bhp (230 kW) and 330 lb·ft (450 N·m). New to the lineup is Chrysler's corporate 3.6L Pentastar V6, coupled to the new ZF 8-speed Torqueflite8 Automatic. It achieves best in class V6 power, and best in class fuel efficiency and makes 305 bhp (227 kW) and 269 lb·ft (365 N·m). The Pentastar/ZF 8-speed is a $1000 dollar option. Due to a new electric power steering system, the 5.7L HEMI V8 no longer has a power steering pump, and gains 5 horsepower, now making 395 bhp (295 kW) and 407 lb·ft (552 N·m). It is still available with the 65RFE 6-speed Automatic, having the new 8-speed Torqueflite8 Automatic as an extra cost option

OPPOSITE
Dodge Ram 2009/2010 at off road impact show, still producing a winner.

CHAPTER THREE
FORD: EFFIE & LIZZIE

In many ways, Henry Ford was the perfect man to build America's definitive pickup. He had no desire to build the fastest car in the world, the most exclusive or most exotic, but the cheapest. His cars were working tools: not pretty, but simple, tough and reliable, and the man in the street could afford them. And there was something else. Henry came from farming stock, his father having arrived on a boat from Ireland in 1863 to escape the potato famine, and he understood the drudgery of work on a small farm. Ironically, he would later develop a keen nostalgia for America's fast-disappearing, rural way of life, which his own Model T played a part in destroying.

Henry determined to advance the mechanization of American farms, and began experimenting with tractors as early as 1906, well before the Fordson Model F appeared in 1917. The Fordson F, of course, was the Model T of tractors and a boon to thousands of small farmers. But the ubiquitous Ford pickup arguably played as great a role as the Fordson tractor in bringing American farmers into the machine age. Here was a workhorse that could haul grain and supplies as well as double as rudimentary family transport.

Pickups may not have been the first thing on Henry's mind, but they changed the American landscape as surely as the Model T car and Model F tractor.

The first ever factory-built Ford pickup didn't officially appear until 1925, but such vehicles existed long before that; cars were often supplied in chassis form, allowing customers to fit whatever body they chose – often a basic flatbed or wooden-sided pickup box. Henry's early experiments with cars are well known and bear some examination here.

Despite his farming background, the

oung Ford showed no inclination to emulate his father, developing his talent for engineering by joining the Edison Illuminating Co. instead, and in his spare time building what he referred to as a quadricycle in a workshop behind his house. It was a simple two-cylinder machine, even a little crude, but it worked, and Henry sold it, going on to design more sophisticated examples. By now he had financial backing, and as chief engineer of the Detroit Automobile Co. built a Delivery Wagon, which was sold to a local company. Alas, Henry quarrelled with his backers and resigned, setting up the Henry Ford Company in 1901. Here he built racing cars, including the record-breaking 999. Once again, however, disagreements with financiers brought the project to an end.

The breakthrough came in 1903, when Alexander Young Malcomson, a local coal merchant, agreed to bankroll Henry's third venture. This time, the venture was successful, and the two-cylinder Model A, built mostly of bought-in parts, was soon in series production. There was no commercial version, but there is photographic evidence that they were fitted with aftermarket commercial bodies. The factory did offer its own Delivery Van from 1905, but this was a panel van rather than a pickup. Mass-production hadn't yet arrived, but the Model A and its successors were reliable and relatively cheap. The four-cylinder Model N that followed in 1907 was even more affordable, and Ford produced a brand-new chassis for $600, to which any commercial body could be bolted, many becoming

179

flatbed trucks.

When the legendary Model T was launched in October 1908, Ford was already a major force in automobile manufacture. There was nothing radical about the Model T, though its 178-ci (2917-cc) four-cylinder engine did have a detachable cylinder head. There was two-speed epicyclical transmission, a Ford favourite since the early days, based on a strong chassis with an I-beam front axle and transverse leaf springs front and rear. That, of course, provides a fine basis for a working truck; like its predecessors, the T could be delivered in chassis form, ready for immediate conversion.

Over 10,000 Model Ts were built in the first year, but production skyrocketed from 1913, when Ford's massive new factory, complete with moving production lines, came on stream at Highland Park, near Detroit. In the first year of mass-production, a staggering 200,000 vehicles left the factory, while 300,000 Ts were built the following year, the figure being not far short of three-quarters of a million by 1916. Costs were progressively lowered and Henry cut the price of the Model T to match. That year, the basic chassis was priced at only $325, ready for conversion.

Meanwhile, there were short-lived attempts to offer a pickup-style Model T direct from the factory. The Commercial Roadster was announced in 1912, with a removable rumble seat to liberate the load space and a one-piece dashboard. Plainly not a success, it was dropped later the same year. In 1913, Ford built just over 500 Model T

OPPOSITE and LEFT
The 1925 Model TT. This was the heavier-duty version of the standard ¹/₂-ton Model T.

BELOW
1929 Ford AA six-wheeler.

OPPOSITE
'Henry's made a lady out of Lizzie' –
the 1929 Ford Model A pickup.

Delivery Cars, which featured a standard T front end, complete with folding roof, with an open wooden box behind. Advertised as 'tougher than an Army mule and cheaper than a team of horses', it was listed at $625 but failed to catch on and like the Commercial Roadster lasted less than a year.

In the meantime, the Model T chassis was being sold in large numbers to body-builders who would work on them themselves. A wide variety of bodies were available from concerns such as the Columbia Body Company of Detroit or the Union Truck Manufacturing Company of

New York. Some of these were fitted by body-builders, others by Ford dealers. However, in 1916 there was a change of policy, when Ford dealers were forbidden to lengthen the Model T chassis to accommodate longer bodies.

The reason became clear the following

year when Ford announced the TT, a 1-ton version of the Model T chassis with a wheelbase lengthened by 2ft (0.6m). Mechanically, it was very similar to the standard Model T, and used the now-familiar 178-ci four-cylinder engine of 20bhp. The chassis itself was strengthened and the Model TT was also given a worm-driven rear axle, solid rubber tyres and a dual braking system. Like the Model T, it was offered in chassis form, though the factory price was now $600 rather than $325, reflecting its heavier-duty specification. By 1919, 100,000 1-ton Fords had left Highland Park. As with the T, a wide variety of commercial bodies was available, including a tipper, but the closest thing to a pickup was the express truck, which could be had with or without a closed cab. Production of the chassis rose rapidly, with over 120,000 produced between August 1919 and August 1920 alone.

Production continued along these lines until 1923, by which time the bare TT chassis was priced at $380 and the Model T at $235. In October of that year, Ford announced it was going to produce its own truck bodywork for fitting by dealers. The first was the all-steel Express, built by Budd Body as well as by Ford itself, while in January 1924 the company unveiled its own 'C-cab' for fitting to the truck chassis. Until then, Model T and TT chassis had been pared to the bone, having no driver's seat, let alone a cab.

But this arrangement didn't last, and in April 1925 Ford announced its first factory-built pickup. Officially, the model was a 'Model T runabout with pickup body'. It consisted of a cargo box with adjustable tailgate and four stake pockets – not especially long at 56in (1.4m), but over 40in (1m) wide and a useful 13in (33cm) deep. The chassis on which it sat was adapted with heavy-duty springs and 8- x 1.19-in rear drum brakes. The TT was also given a commercial variant, in this case an 8-ft (2.4-m) platform stake body with 12- x 2-in rear drums and optional closed cab. Both trucks had a long list of options, including electric starter and lights, other body variations and a windshield wiper. Ready to work and painted Commercial Green, the Model T pickup cost $281 f.o.b. (freight on board) Detroit, though existing T owners could buy the cargo box separately for $25. This could be classed a retro-fit in modern terms and 75,000 were sold through dealerships in 1926.

The Model T pickup was most successful, selling over 33,000 in its first year. In fact, it was clear that it was what most commercial customers had been waiting for, as Ford sold only a little over 6,500 Model T bare chassis that year. By contrast, nearly a quarter of a million TT chassis were built.

The pickup's price leaped to $366 in 1926, which reflected the fact that several options – starter, electric lights and demountable tyres – were now standard, though balloon tyres (standard on the TT from mid-year) were extra. There were bigger brakes, now approaching TT dimensions, and revised fenders, springs and front spindles. Power was finally listed at 22bhp, slightly up on what had gone before.

But the Model T and TT commercials were short-lived, simply because they had come late in the life of Henry's most famous car of all. Nineteen-twenty-seven would be their final year, the new Model A taking over the following year. In the meantime, the only notable change was that pickups could now be had in a choice of four colours: black, blue, brown and the original Commercial Green. Fenders and details were still black, however, whatever colour was selected, so some things never changed.

A Model A for a New Era

Few people dared to argue with Henry Ford. By now, his son Edsel may have been president of the entire Ford enterprise, but Henry still had the final say on just about everything, which would continue until 1945, when Henry's grandson, Henry Ford II, took command of the tottering empire. Disagreeing with Henry could mean instant dismissal, but some still did, and that included Edsel, who was worried, as the 1920s wore on, that the faithful Model T was looking undeniably old-fashioned. It may have been cheap, but the new six-cylinder Chevrolets were now offering more power, three-speed transmission and a choice of bright colours. But an increasingly recalcitrant Henry refused to believe that the T was anything less than perfect: look at the millions of Americans who had them – surely they couldn't all be wrong?

But as Chevrolet began to narrow Ford's lead, which would have been unthinkable in

RIGHT and OPPOSITE
RIGHT and OPPOSITE
The Model A has been a natural candidate
for the hot-rod treatment over the decades.
This is a pickup from 1929.

he glory days of the Model T, even Henry had to admit it was time for a change. In May 1927, Ford announced that the T production lines were being halted in preparation for an all-new model, though it wasn't ready quite yet. In fact, it was seven months before the new Model A was finally unveiled, which made it even more exciting when it finally arrived. Crowds formed outside Ford showrooms and mounted police were called in to keep order. The company received half a million advance orders.

As it happened, the Model A was by no means radical, but it was up to date by the standards of December 1928, and thus a huge advance on the T. And it was entirely new. Bolted into the new chassis was a 200-

OPPOSITE
A fully-restored 1930 Ford Model A pickup.

BELOW
1933 Ford pickup with V8 power.

(3277-cc) L-head four-cylinder engine. With 4.22:1 compression and 40bhp at 2200rpm, it was neither exotic nor overpowered, though it did offer nearly double the horsepower of the Model T. It was mated to a conventional three-speed sliding-gear transmission, the floor shift working in an H-pattern: the T's old tree-pedal, two-speed epicyclical transmission may have been easy to use, but fewer than ever drivers were familiar with it, and in the age-old numbers game, three speeds were surely better than two. Few would argue that four-wheel brakes were better than two; these the Model A had, still not hydraulic, however, and were a bone of contention within Ford. There was, of course, a choice of colours, and it was generally agreed that the Model A looked rather more attractive than the family Tin Lizzie.

So what did all this mean as far as the light-duty Ford pickup was concerned? Unlike the Model T, the A had a commercial variant from the word go. It was mechanically identical to the car, based on the same chassis, engine and transmission, though the pickup box had actually been carried over unchanged from the 1927 T. As before, this had a wooden load bed with metal runners, now painted in the body colour. The actual wood varied, but included beech, birch, oak, pine and maple. Colour choices were down to two – Rock Moss Green and, needless to say, black. Another way in which it differed from the T was that until August 1928 it was only available as an open cab, with a non-retractable soft-top of canvas and mica providing protection from

the elements, though a closed steel cab, the bodywork by Briggs Manufacturing, was offered from August for an extra $50. Despite its mid-year appearance, sales soon overtook those of the open-cab, and over 47,000 were sold in 1928. Standard equipment, whatever cab was chosen, included a six-volt electric system with starter, a hand-operated windshield wiper, a tool kit and fender-mounted spare wheel. And in an uncharacteristic concern for driver comfort, Ford provided a comfortable seat covered in artificial leather.

The Model A pickup was rated as a $1/2$-tonner, but a higher payload version was offered alongside it from the start, though the Model AA was rated at $1^1/2$ tons, significantly heavier-duty than the 1-ton Model TT it replaced. Like the A, it used the passenger car's transmission and L-head four, though some may have noticed that the headlight and radiator shells were painted black instead of plated, as on the Model A pickup. Under the skin, there were extensive changes. The Model A chassis was extended with a 131.5-in (3.3-m) wheelbase and suitably strengthened. A heavier-duty front spring was complemented by 13- or 16-in rear leaf springs, while the driveline was also beefier and had a two-piece drive shaft. The front brakes remained the same as those of the passenger Model A, but two 14-in drums to the rear, larger radius rods, a bigger worm-gear rear axle, 20-in welded-steel spoke wheels and truck-type high-pressure tyres completed the AA's specification.

All this cost more dollars than the $1/2$-ton pickup: in bare chassis form the AA was

listed at $460 compared with $325 for the lighter-duty A. This was the cheapest way to buy a AA: it also came in chassis-cab form, Express (pickup), panel van, platform, stakeside and Dual High forms. By far the biggest seller was the bare chassis, indicating that most AA buyers had their own bodywork fitted, though Ford did sell over 21,000 AA platform trucks in 1928 and over 18,000 Dual Highs.

In typical Ford fashion, Model A production was rapidly increased as time went on, and 1929 would see well over 100,000 pickups built, split about two to one in favour of the closed cab, and with Ford offering more body styles than before. There were few changes in this second year of production, though the A pickup did look snazzier by now, especially when it was a soft-top roadster pickup with whitewall tyres, brighter trim and an extended range of colours, including L'Anse Dark Green and Gunmetal Blue. The steering wheel was now black instead of red. The AA had few changes early in the year, apart from the five-hole discs that replaced the spoked wheels in February 1929. But in October there were several significant improvements, when a four-speed gearbox became standard, as was a spiral-bevelled rear axle, 14-in front drum brakes and beefed-up front suspension. Like the A, it was now leaving the Ford production lines in large numbers; in fact, over 300,000 were built that year, just over half of which were in bare chassis form.

The Depression was on the horizon but no one seems to have told Ford planners, who introduced yet more bright colours for

OPPOSITE
This stakeside Ford pickup has been customized by its British owner.

OPPOSITE
Mild rather than wild. A tastefully
transformed pickup from the early 1930s.

1930, among them Pegelax Orange, Blue Rock Green and Rubellite Red. It seemed to be heralding a general facelift for the Model A, with bigger tyres, wider fenders and a deeper radiator shell. All pickups now had roadster or open-cab-style doors, now with exterior handles, while the open cab itself had a fold-flat windshield, the screen of the closed cab pivoting open to provide ventilation, while a soft panel in the roof provided even more air. Meanwhile, the heavier-duty AA had the same styling update as the smaller trucks.

But in spite of the Pegelax Orange, America's rapidly sliding economy saw sales of trucks begin to decline in 1930, and Model A pickup production fell to just under 90,000, the vast majority of which were closed cabs, while Model AA production more than halved compared with its peak in 1929.

Ford hadn't had to deal with something like this in years and the company renewed its efforts to tempt buyers. Ford trucks came in a choice of 38 colours for 1931, and a new, high-capacity pickup was launched with a bigger box offering 22.2cu ft of load space, which was 28 per cent more than the standard pickup. It had a 16-gauge steel floor over a hardwood base. Also new was the Deluxe pickup, a fancy variation on the basic workhorse, with wood-lined cargo box, chrome-plated brass rails along the sides and standard cowl lamps. Its appearance was striking, though with less than 300 actually made that year, it did little to help Ford's recovery and Model A sales ended up slightly down, at a little over 158,000.

But the Model A was already on borrowed time in that it would never match the longevity and record-breaking sales of its predecessor. Meanwhile, back in Dearborn, Henry Ford realized that his cars and trucks needed a boost to keep them abreast with the competition, which meant more power and more cylinders. But simply to match the six-cylinder cars from General Motors wasn't enough for Henry and he decided to leapfrog them once and for all with the world's first affordable V8: the famous flathead also made it into the 1932 light trucks as America's first ever V8-powered pickup.

It would power Ford cars and trucks for the next 21 years. However, there was nothing actually new about V8s: Cadillac had offered one as early as 1915 – but never before had they been at mass-production prices. On paper, the V8's power and torque were not stratospheric, at 65bhp and 114lb ft, neither was it a big engine by American standards at 221ci (3621cc). It also suffered teething troubles, with failures in the piston and cylinder block following the engine's premature introduction. But these were rectified, and the sheer novelty of a cheap V8 attracted customers back to Ford in 1932.

Pickups were not given the V8 until later in the year, having been based on the new Model B18 from the start, with the same modern front-end styling and a body 10in (25cm) longer than before, though the wheelbase was only 3in (8cm) longer. For those who mistrusted V8s, Ford continued to offer a basic four-cylinder Model B with an uprated version of the familiar 200-ci L-head four, now producing 50bhp at 2,000rpm and

90lb ft at 1,500rpm. This saved $50 on the V8 and offered nearly as much torque, so as far as hard-headed businessmen were concerned it was probably the better buy. A heavier-duty Model BB came in both four-cylinder and V8 forms and there was a deluxe variation which added $30 to the BB's price. But it was not easy to get hold of one in 1932, whatever truck one ordered. Due to the upheaval caused by the V8's introduction, and the fact that the Depression was now at its most profound, truck production dwindled that year to only 1,395 Model B fours and V8s.

Ford cars and the Sedan Delivery panel van were updated the following year as the sleek-looking Model 46, but the pickups continued much as before, with only a sloping radiator giving them a more streamlined appearance. More to the point for most buyers was the 112-in (2.8-m) wheelbase, still with a choice of open or closed cabs and with the 50-bhp four-cylinder engine as the base power unit. As for the flathead V8, its early problems having been rectified, power was boosted to 75bhp at 3,800rpm, though torque was unchanged at 114lb ft, while aluminium cylinder heads, improved cooling and ignition, plus a higher compression ratio, delivered the goods. This was all well and good, but production figures for 1933 do not appear to be available, suggesting that truck production was still in the doldrums.

There was yet more power from the V8 for 1934, thanks to a Detroit Lubricator or Stromberg two-barrelled carburettor, now up to 85bhp at 3,800rpm. Buyers of that year's

Model 46 trucks still had the 50-bhp four-cylinder option, which remained $50 cheaper, despite it being its final year. The 112-in wheelbase allowed a pickup box 44in wide and almost 70in long (1.2 x 1.8m), with a steel floor over a hardwood base, while sockets on the end of the flared sides allowed stakes or advertising boards to be fitted. As

well as bidding farewell to the four-cylinder engine, 1934 also proved the final year for the open-top pickup, whose sales had dwindled substantially. Overall, however, sales were up, and Ford announced that it had produced 191,861 trucks in the 1934 model year, placing it second only to Dodge.

The ¹/₂-ton pickup was updated as the

Model 50 the following year, now only in 85-bhp V8 form. It looked quite graceful and was a far cry from the early gawky Model T pickups, with sloping radiator and valanced fenders like the Ford sedans. Moreover, it was of all-steel construction, and mounting the engine 8in (20cm) further forward shifted the payload forward as well,

OPPOSITE
By the mid 1930s a Ford pickup with chrome radiator trim and wooden stakesides was quite a stylish machine.

ABOVE
1930s Ford tanker.

195

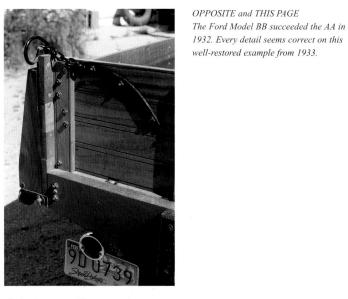

OPPOSITE and THIS PAGE
The Ford Model BB succeeded the AA in
1932. Every detail seems correct on this
well-restored example from 1933.

eliminating some of the rear overhang.
Meanwhile, the 1¹/₂-ton BB had become the
Model 51, based on its original 131.5-in
(3.3-m) wheelbase or a longer 157-in (4-m)
version. There were few changes for 1936,
though buyers were again given more
choice, the deluxe pickup having returned
together with a vast range of options,
including dual windshield wipers, spotlight
and stainless-steel hubcaps. Of all the Ford
light trucks, the standard pickup was by far
the most popular that year, with over 49,000
sold. Nothing else came even remotely close.

There were more significant changes for
1937, with a new smaller V8 of 135ci
(2212cc) joining the original. With 60bhp,

OPPOSITE and LEFT
A V8 option turned 1930s Ford pickups into
virtual production-line hot rods, possibly
inspiring later generations of hot-rodders.

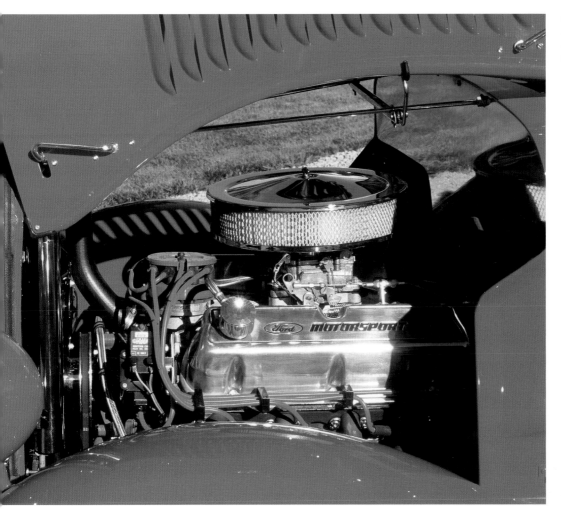

OPPOSITE and LEFT
Ford's flathead V8 proved most responsive to tuning, another attraction where hot-rodders were concerned.

is was significantly less powerful than the
21-ci (3621-cc) flathead, now producing
9bhp, though it would be offered up to
940. More shortlived was the Coupé-
xpress, basically a Ford coupé with an odd-
ooking pickup box protruding from the
unk. It was intended for business travellers
d Ford dropped the idea after a year, even
ough Chevrolet persevered with its own
milar model. The standard pickup was not
ven the faired-in headlights of the Ford
dans, though it did have a two-piece
indshield, while the heavy-duty Model 51
as replaced by the 1-ton 75, though only
ith the 60-bhp baby V8.

There was yet more new styling the
llowing year, the pickups gaining a
lbous front grille and horizontal hood
uvres. As ever, there was a wide range of
odies on offer, alongside the standard
ckup, including a platform truck, stakeside
d chassis-cab, all of them with a choice of
e 60- or 90-bhp V8s, though some sources
st the bigger V8 as still offering 85bhp.
ow designated the Model 81C (90bhp) or
2C (60bhp), all of these 1/2-ton variations
ere offered alongside the 1-ton 81Y
90bhp) and 82Y (60bhp), both with a 122-in
-m) wheelbase and a similar choice of
ody styles. These all continued into 1939
ith few changes, though a '9' suffix was
dded to the model number. In addition,
ere was a new 3/4-ton version, the 92D,
esigned for bulkier loads and based on the
me 122-in wheelbase as before.

According to historian, John Gunnell,
e 1940 Ford pickups are considered by
me to be the best-looking ever made. They

were certainly up-to-the-minute, having
faired-in headlights like the Ford sedans,
while the cab was also altered to make it
more like a car. Otherwise, the pickups
continued in 1/2-, 3/4- or 1-ton forms, with the
60- or 85-bhp V8 beneath the hood, a
slightly lowered compression ratio having
made the 90-hp flathead a thing of the past.

By 1941, Ford was more concerned with
potential military contracts, especially for
the new 1/4-ton reconnaissance vehicle,
referred to as the 'GP'. It didn't get the
contract, but the name stuck, turning into
'Jeep' along the way. Unusually, there were
few style revisions as far as the civilian
pickups were concerned, but a complete
range of engines was now available, with
1/2-, 3/4- and 1-ton trucks offered with four
different power units. First off was a 120-ci
(1966-cc) L-head four-cylinder, a true
economy option with a single-barrelled
carburettor and 30bhp. Ford's first six-
cylinder pickups were powered by an L-head
six of 226ci (3703cc) and 90bhp at 3,300rpm
with 180lb ft at 1,800rpm, making it the
torquiest of the group. For buyers still
insisting on a V8, there was the existing 85-
bhp unit, plus a slightly larger 239-ci (3916-
cc) version of the same flathead with 95bhp.

There was more power the following
year, when the two V8s were uprated to
90bhp (221ci/3621cc) and 100bhp (239ci).
The four and six were unchanged and once
again a full options list was offered on all
Ford pickups, which now had new full-width
front-end styling with a distinctive
'waterfall' grille. However, this came to an
abrupt halt in February 1942, when

America's involvement in the war brought
civilian truck production to an end and it
would be more than three years before
production resumed.

When it did, in 1945, the trucks were
barely changed, though the four- and six-
cylinder options had gone, leaving only the
100-bhp 239-ci V8 in both 1/2- and 1-ton
forms. The former, with a 114-in (2.9-m)
wheelbase, came as pickup or stakeside, and
the 134-in (3.4-m) wheelbase 1-ton as a
stakeside only. There was little change for
1946, though the name was changed to
reflect the bed length (6.5ft on the 1/2-ton, 8ft
on the 1-ton) and the 226-ci (3703-cc) L-
head six returned. The six was an interesting
alternative in that, on paper, it gave away
only 10bhp to the V8 with the same 180lb ft.
The difference was that its torque peaked at
1,200rpm against 2,000rpm, so it was
probably more suitable for towing or heavy-
duty tasks, albeit with the V8's speed. But
whatever engine it had, Ford's light truck
was now getting old, something that became
especially obvious after Chevrolet launched
its new truck in 1947. Luckily, Ford's
answer was not long in coming.

The F-Series
There is no doubt that the Ford F-series is
the Model T of trucking. This is a pickup
that has been in production for over 50
years, outselling not only the Model T but
also the VW Beetle, and by the end of the
20th century, 26 million had rolled off the
production lines. In 2001, the F-series
celebrated its 25th anniversary as America's
best-selling truck, by which time it had been

RIGHT
Ford pickups often doubled as basic family transport, and some still do.

OPPOSITE
Faired-in headlights distinguish this as one of the good-looking 1940 Fords.

the most successful vehicle of any type, car or truck, for 20 years. It was an astonishing achievement.

Yet in 1947, when the F-series was designed, things were not so rosy for Ford, and the company was losing a million dollars a day. It fact it was in virtual collapse as Henry Ford II and his team of whizz-kids sought to regain control of the tottering empire. Ex-Bendix man, Ernie Breech, was brought in to plan a new car line-up for 1949. In the meantime, Ford trucks were left to lag behind Chevrolet, which had renewed its line of light trucks in 1947.

Ford needed to emulate Chevrolet's bo post-war styling, and even thought of dropping the famous flathead V8, mainly because Chevrolet was doing so well sellin

y a six. Fortunately for the F-series, the
mpany's new product planning department
anaged to persuade the management that a
8 was what made Ford distinctive, not to
ention the fact that new automated
achinery meant it cost only $16 extra to

make. The flathead V8, so central to the
early F-series, stayed.

In fact, several items from the old trucks
remained, notably the 90-bhp six as well as
the 100, also the load bed. But some things
did change, most obviously the modern

styling, and a one-piece windshield and
horizontal grille with built-in headlights
were added. These set off the new cab,
which was wider and higher than before,
with comfortable features such as three-way
air control, a coach-type seat – adjustable

OPPOSITE and ABOVE
Customizing takes many forms, and the
1940 Ford lends itself to the process
especially well.

OPPOSITE and LEFT
A 1940 Ford in a rural setting. It came with
a choice of 60- or 85-bhp V8s, plus $^1/_2$-, $^3/_4$-
or 1-ton payloads.

ore and aft – a sun visor and ashtray, while
Magic Air heater and defroster was an
option. Noise and vibration were reduced by
rubber-mounting the cab, but it was possibly
an exaggeration to describe it as the 'Million
Dollar Cab'.

The F-series actually constituted a whole
range, though we are only concerned with
the lighter-duty variants. These were the 1/2-
ton F-1, the 3/4-ton F-2, the 3/4-ton heavy-
duty F-3 and the 1-ton F-4, all offered with
either six-cylinder or V8 power. Wheelbases
measured 114, 122 and 134in respectively,
and pickup prices ranged from $1,144 for
the F-1 to $1,578 for the stakeside F-4. And
there were other options besides Magic Air,
including a four-speed transmission, 6.50 x
16 six-ply tyres, a heavy-duty radiator, and
even a radio and 'Spiralounge' seat for the
Million Dollar Cab.

'Star-spangled new!', gushed the full-
colour advertisements. 'Excitingly
MODERN! Strikingly DIFFERENT! …
New Million Dollar Truck Cab! … 3 New
Truck Engines! … Over 139 New Models!'
Ford trucks were 'bonus-built' to last longer,
the publicity claiming a ten-year life, which
is nothing special now, but was quite
something for a hard-worked pickup back in
1948. It was hard-sell but necessary if Ford
was to overtake Chevrolet as America's best-
selling truck. If it failed, it wouldn't be for
want of trying, as the F-series went into
production at 16 plants across the U.S.A.
and Canada. Between them, 300,000 Ford
trucks were produced in 1948, an 18 per cent
increase over the previous year. Ford hadn't
overtaken Chevrolet yet, though that would

come, but there was no doubt that the F-
series trucks had arrived and they were a hit.

Well, maybe 'hit' is also an
exaggeration, or it must have seemed so to
Ford in 1949, when sales slipped to a mere
227,531, way below the 1947 figure, let
alone that for 1948. Not that the company as
a whole was suffering, with car sales
heading for the stratosphere, but it was clear
that the success of the light trucks couldn't
be taken for granted. There were very few
changes to the still-new F-series that year,
and precious little for 1950, though Ford
claimed the entire F-series now spanned 175
engine/model combinations, of which the
light pickups were only a small part. In spite
of there being nothing new in the pickup
line, sales bounced right back again, with
nearly 359,000 sold that year, mostly due to
booming sales of the 1/2-tonners, which were
benefiting from the fact that newly
prosperous farmers were acquiring their first
post-war truck and military demand had
been stimulated by the Korean War. And
while the faithful V8 may have been a
flathead rather than one of the hot new
overhead-valves, it still made Ford's Effie
the only lightweight pickup with an option,
which counted for much.

The F-series was given a facelift for
1951, the original five horizontal bars having
been replaced by one massive one supported
by three similarly chunky uprights. There
were new colours, with Vermilion, Meadow
Green and Silvertone Gray among the seven
options. The standard cab now had 5-Star
trim, while the 5-Star Extra package added
headlining, more soundproofing and seat

padding, two-tone trim, extra brightwork,
armrests, door locks, sun visors, a locking
glove compartment, an interior light and
twin horns. There were also technical
advances, such as a vacuum ignition advance
device called Power Pilot, plus beefed-up
transmission and brakes. The basic range of
six-cylinder V8 F-1, -2, -3 and -4 was still
there, though sales took a downturn due to
restrictions on materials placed by the
government's National Production Authority,
whose job it was to ensure that the war
machine was kept supplied, even at the
expense of civilian production.

There was big news for 1952 when the
faithful L-head six was finally pensioned off,
replaced by the overhead-valve Cost Clipper
Six. Although smaller than the L-head at
215ci (3523cc), it was significantly more
powerful, with 101bhp at 3,500rpm, while
torque was slightly improved at 185lb ft.
Once again, the Ford six had a nice shallow
torque curve, peaking between 1,300 and
1,700rpm. Ford claimed 14 per cent better
fuel economy from this higher-compression,
more efficient engine. To maintain its power
advantage, and justify the extra $35 paid by
the customer, the flathead V8 was boosted to
106bhp and 194lb ft, due to a higher 6.8:1
compression ratio. Once again, production
was restricted by shortages and a steel strike
mid-year, while Ford's share of the truck
market slipped below 20 per cent.

According to some sources, Ford spent
$30 million developing its new range of
trucks for 1953. Some say it was more than
$50 million but, whatever the case, there is
no doubt that the new F-100 represented a

OPPOSITE
*The 1948 Ford F-1 – the start of a new era
for Ford pickups, and a highly successful
one at that.*

211

major relaunch. Although the 101-bhp six and 106-bhp V8 were carried over, just about everything else was in some way changed. A new chassis moved the front wheels 4in (10cm) further back, improving the turning circle and shifting the load centre further forward, making for better weight distribution. By now there was greater emphasis on the driver, with a larger, roomier cab with curved one-piece windshield, 55 per cent larger than before, plus bigger windows to the side and rear. A piece of cultural history was born when the open side windows were now low enough to rest an arm on when driving, giving rise to the classic pose of pickup drivers! More leg and headroom contributed to comfort, while the old 5-Star Extra cab became 'Driverized' with many of the same features.

There were new transmissions, too: a synchromesh three-speed, three-speed plus overdrive and a four-speed. More important, however, was the option of Fordomatic auto transmission on the 1/2-ton truck, which incidentally became the F-100, now with 110-in wheelbase, while the 3/4-ton F-2 and F-3 were both replaced by the F-250 with a shorter 118-in (3-m) wheelbase. The 1-ton was now named F-350, again losing 4in of wheelbase to bring it to 130in (3.3m). Different brakes and springs offered different payload options, of which there were five. And while the F-100 may have lost some wheelbase, its pickup box was lengthened to compensate, now measuring 6.5ft and 20in deep to give 45cu ft in all.

The new F-100-series was described in these terms: 'Ford Economy Trucks ... offer

OPPOSITE and LEFT
The 1949 Ford F-1, with new 'Million Dollar Truck Cab' and over 139 new models.

OPPOSITE
The ¹/2-ton F-1 was the best-seller, and
helped to restore Ford's post-war fortunes.

LEFT
Ford's F-series also extended to big trucks.
This is the 1951 Ford F-8 Big Job.

ver 190 completely new models … all
aded with TIME SAVING features to get
obs done fast. 5 great power plants;
ORDOMATIC and Overdrive available in
alf tonners; Synchro-Silent transmissions
hroughout.' Someone must have been
mpressed, as Ford sold over 317,000 trucks
1953, enough to give it a 26 per cent

share of the market.

This was topped the following year by a
best-ever 29 per cent, though strong sales of
Ford's medium- and heavy-duty trucks were
largely responsible. Not that the F-100 didn't
offer something new for 1954. As well as an
odd-looking grille, which only lasted a year,
it also marked the final departure of the

flathead V8, its place taken by an all-new
overhead-valve V8 called the Power King.
With a short stroke, overhead valves and
higher compression, it revved more freely
and produced more power, namely 130bhp at
4,200rpm plus 214lb ft. It also measured
exactly the same size (239ci/3916cc) as the
old flathead, though that was a coincidence.

BELOW
1951 F-1 pickup.

OPPOSITE
The ³/4-ton version of the 1952 F-2.

Meanwhile, the Cost Clipper Six was upsized to 223ci (3654cc), now producing 115bhp at 3,900rpm and 194lb ft. Both gave a greater margin of performance in a faster-paced world, while the Fordomatic option was now extended to the F-250 and F-350.

But the little F-100 was the most successful of Ford's extensive range of trucks, which extended to the F-900 'Big Job' and accounted for a good 40 per cent of the total in 1955. Of these, the pickup was far and away the most popular, with almost

125,000 finding homes that year. It underlined how important the pickup market was in America, then as now; there had always been an F-100 panel van, but it sold in small numbers compared with the pickup. There were no major changes that year,

hough the Power King and Clipper gained a ouple of horsepower apiece, neither were here any in 1956, which was the last year of he F-100 series.

What did change in that final year was he cab, which now came with a wraparound vindshield, a similar rear window joining he options list. The deluxe cab had become the Custom in 1955, with foam-rubber seating, extra sound insulation and trim, while extra could still be paid for the Magic Air heater. Ford also emphasized the wide doors of the 1956 pickup – 'almost a yard wide'. On the exterior of the cab, 12-volt electrics were a worthwhile improvement, and there was the option of a new 8-ft load bed for the F-100 – the Express. All the pickups now had 15-in wheels instead of 16. Meanwhile, Chevrolet had equipped its pickups with an overhead-valve V8, so Ford simply had to counter this with extra power. The Clipper Six now had an 8.3:1 compression and 139bhp at 4,200rpm, plus 207lb ft available between 1,800 and

OPPOSITE
The F-100, new for 1953 and a major advance.

BELOW
An F-606 tipper of the 1950s.

OPPOSITE
*The F-100 brought a new chassis and new
cab and transmissions, the whole range
costing Ford over $30 million to develop.*

2,700rpm. The Power King V8 had the same
higher compression, plus better cooling and
other improvements, while capacity was
boosted to 272ci (4457cc): this bigger Power
King came in 171- or 181-bhp form, the
latter for heavy-duty twin-wheeled F-350s,
and gave a striking power to weight ratio in
the little 1/2-ton F-100.

The Flamboyant Fifties
The first F-100 series had been deservedly
popular, helping Ford trucks to a best-ever
sales record in 1956 of over 420,000 units.
But in the fast-moving late-1950s, it was
beginning to show its age and its clear links
with the 1948 F-1. So 1957 saw a new look,
with integral front fenders, full-width grille
and a big glassy cab. Under the hood, the
Clipper Six and Power King continued, but
there were changes in the load bed, where a
new Styleside imitated the flush sides of the
Chevrolet Cameo, which had been
introduced the previous year. But there was a
big difference between them: Chevrolet had
priced the Cameo as an upmarket special
truck, but Ford charged exactly the same for
the Styleside as the more traditional-looking
Flareside. The result was that customers
chose the roomier, cleaner-looking Ford
Styleside by a factor of five to one,
outselling the Cameo by 30 to one.

Otherwise, the new generation of Ford
pickups was based on a familiar format, with
1/2-ton F-100, 3/4-ton F-250 and 1-ton F-350,
and standard or Custom cabs. A new feature
was the addition of a lower GVW version of
each, the F-110, F-260 and F-360. In fact, by
adding the engine choices, a list of 30

pickups was produced! It was much the
same line-up for 1958, though all the
pickups now had dual headlights, the 272-ci
Power King having been gradually
supplanted by a 292-ci (4785-cc) version,
which delivered 186bhp and 279lb ft. More
important for the year after were Ford's first
factory-built four-wheel-drive trucks. For
years, 4x4 specialist Marmon-Herrington
had been converting Fords to this format, but
the rapid growth of the market encouraged
Ford to bring them in-house: for 1959 the F-
100 and -250 118-in wheelbased pickups had
a four-wheel-drive option, with a two-range
transmission as part of the deal. They were
the first of a long line of Ford 4x4 pickups.

The 4x4 option was extended to F-250
stakeside and platform trucks for 1960,
along with many detail changes, such as a
new grille, improved brakes and internal
changes to the 292-ci V8 intended to
improve fuel economy.

Stylish as they were, these pickups with
their twin headlights had clearly outgrown
the 1950s and customers were now
demanding something new. So 1961 saw a
new chassis providing longer wheelbases
than before. A completely restyled body, of
which the cab was an integral part, revealed
a simpler, more squared-off appearance, with
a plain grille and bigger windshield. Engines
and transmissions were carried over from
1960, and load beds offered a wider tailgate,
but otherwise came in the same lengths of
6.5ft (F-100), 8ft (F-250) and 9ft (F-350).
Alongside these revamped traditional
pickups was the new Econoline range, a cab-
over-engine design that included its own

pickup and was clearly inspired by the
successful VW Transporter, as too was
Chevrolet's Corvair 95.

'Ford's full-time economy only starts
with low price!,' went the advertisement for
1962. 'Save on gas … save on oil … save o
tires … every day you drive!' Behind the
hype, however, very little had changed,
though Ford did reintroduce the Styleside
with a separate cab and load bed, having
discovered that not everyone liked the 1961
integral cab/bed. It now offered both, and th
model lists grew accordingly. No wonder the
publicity of the time boasted of the 'Biggest
pickup line in Ford history'. Nineteen-sixty-
three was another quiet year, despite the fac
that Ford built over 315,000 trucks. The
integral cab/bed was dropped for 1964, but
new separate Styleside now came in 6.5- or
8-ft lengths on the F-100 and F-250, or 9ft
on the 1-ton F-350, though the narrower old
fashioned Flareside, with its hardwood floor
was still available. Remember the Cost
Clipper Six? This had since been renamed
the 'Mileage Maker' and was supplanted by
a 262-ci 152-bhp version: the 292-ci V8 was
still an option for those seeking power and t
hell with the gas bills, though it had been
derated to 160bhp. Also new that year were
three option packages to make the F-100 or
F-250 pickups more suitable for a slide-on
camper unit, a growth market for Americans
venturing into the great outdoors at
weekends but without discomfort. Heavy-
duty shocks, clutch, tyres and electrics – all
were fitted for the rigours of a few days
camping in the national parks.

America's brief flirtation with compact

OPPOSITE and LEFT
A 1955 F-100 with the V8 option, though
buyers could still order their new pickup
with the cheaper, slightly less powerful six.

ars and fuel economy was now history, and Ford pickups were given a line-up of more powerful engines for 1965. There were two sixes – 240ci (3933cc) and 300ci (4916cc), Ford claiming that the latter had the legs of many V8s, which offered 150 and 170bhp respectively. Naturally, there was also a V8, a 352-ci (5768-cc) unit with two-barrelled carburettor and 208bhp, plus 315lb ft peaking at 2,400rpm. Whichever engine was chosen, it was mounted on the F-100 and 250 on a new independent coil-sprung suspension system, bringing ride and handling closer to the standards of a car, while the heavier-duty F-350 and all 4x4

pickups kept the old beam front axle and leaf springs. However, they adopted the Bronco's coil-sprung monobeam front end the following year, while new for 1966 was the Ranger cab option, which saw bucket seats and colour-keyed carpets in the fashion of the day.

Did someone mention Bronco? Ford's contribution to the lightweight 4x4 market was usually in the form of a four-seater hardtop – an early SUV – but for the first few years it came in pickup form as well, though unlike the International Scout, the format was dropped as the Bronco left its origins as a working vehicle far behind.

The pickup was on the same short wheelbase as the other Broncos and was able to carry a modest 32cu ft on its stubby load bed, but it could be had with four-wheel-drive, the standard motor being Ford's 105-bhp 170-ci (2786-cc) six. Incidentally, the Bronco pickup's official description was 'sport utility', which was ironic given that it was the most work-orientated Bronco of all. Rated as a 1/2-ton, it saw no major changes through the late-1960s/early-'70s, apart from an optional V8, and was dropped in 1972.

Ford's F-series pickups were restyled yet again for 1967, with a slab-sided, boxy look

OPPOSITE and THIS PAGE
1956 F-100. This was the final year for the original F-100, now with a wraparound windshield and larger rear window.

RIGHT and OPPOSITE
*1956 F-100. Twelve-volt electrics were
another worthwhile improvement that year.*

given to the new cab and matching Styleside box. Even the standard cab was well-equipped and more car-like than before, with Custom and Ranger upgrades still available. Two-wheel-drive and 4x4 pickups now used the same wheelbase lengths, and the F-350 was given independent front suspension. But the engine line-up was the same as before – consisting of the 240-ci and 300-ci sixes, plus a 352-ci V8 – with three- or four-speed manual and the Cruise-O-Matic automatic transmissions. But in spite of the new

models – the Bronco, Econoline and Ranchero – the full-sized F-series pickups remained Ford's bread and butter, with over 220,000 F-100s alone sold that year.

There were few changes for 1968, but the pickups received Ford's big-block 390-ci (6391-cc) V8 the following year. With a 10.5:1 compression ratio and four-barrelled carburettor, it offered 335bhp and 427lb ft, making it the meatiest F-series yet, while the standard engine was still the 240-ci (3933-cc) six of 150bhp. In fact, V8s were

still favourites with buyers of Ford light trucks, outnumbering the sixes by nearly three to one. Over 600,000 light trucks were sold that year, giving Ford a 32.6 per cent share of the market. A cheaper V8 option arrived for 1970 in the form of a 215-bhp 360-ci (5899-cc), though the muscular 390 was still available, and the line-up was augmented by a 190-bhp 330-ci (5408-cc) V8 the following year.

Important for 1972 was the Courier, Ford's answer to the flood of imported mini-

OPPOSITE and LEFT
1963 F-100 Flareside. This cost the same
as the more capacious Styleside.

pickups which had been proving so popular with American buyers. It wasn't actually a Ford at all, but a rebadged and trimmed Mazda pickup. This didn't seem to bother the buying public, however, as the four-cylinder 110-ci (1802-cc) Courier was the

right truck at the right time and sold in large numbers. Ford expected the 72-bhp Courier to sell to a younger, better-educated market than its full-sized pickups. It did, and the Mazda-made Courier became part of the Ford U.S. lineup for ten years. Meanwhile,

the traditional trucks were given a new grille for 1972, plus an apparent plunge in power, as horsepower was expressed in net terms rather than gross. Otherwise they were little changed, still consisting of the 1/2-ton F-100, 3/4-ton F-250 and 1-ton F-350 with Styleside

231

1963 F-100. This was still the basic ¹/₂-ton pickup, offered alongside the ³/₄-ton F-250 and 1-ton F-350.

and Flareside boxes, which, despite the public's enthusiasm for mini-trucks were more popular than ever. Ford sold nearly 430,000 F-100s in 1973, over 180,000 250s and a little over 54,000 350s. They remained the backbone of the light truck range.

Developed for 1974 was the Supercab, Ford's term for an extended cab, offered with the choice of a full-width rear seat or two facing jump seats that could be folded out of the way for extra loads. The Supercab had its own stiffer chassis and there was a crew cab option as well. As concerns about fuel economy began to surface once again, the 390-ci V8 option was dropped, and the 143-bhp (net) 360 was now the biggest cube.

There was a mild facelift in 1976, when the single headlights were recessed into a new front grille, while a new option of a cargo box arrived in the form of the 6.5-ft Flareside, with hardwood floor and 90 per cent flareboards. This was the shortest bed available, as the basic F-100 now offered 6.75ft, with an 8-ft option, also used in the

A 1960s F-100 Styleside. Pickup beds were 6.5, 8 or 9ft in length.

higher GVW F-150, and 9ft in the F-350. The engine range now consisted of 240-ci (3933-cc) and 300-ci (4916-cc) sixes, with V8s of 302ci (4949cc) and 360ci (5899cc). The F-150, incidentally, was described as a heavy-duty 1/2-tonner, with a payload 505–930lb (275–425kg) greater than that of the F-100. Another mild restyle followed in

1978, when the F-150 became the best-seller at over 420,000 units, which was half of all the full-sized pickups. In fact, the two together made up two-thirds of Ford's entire output of light trucks that year, which exceeded 1.2 million. The Courier and Bronco sold around 70,000 units each, so the full-sized trucks were in a different league.

Ford had finally overtaken Chevrolet in overall truck sales though it still maintained its lead as far as light trucks were concerned.

Rectangular headlights appeared in 1979, but otherwise the pickups were little changed. The base power unit was now the 300-ci six, and a 351-ci (5752-cc) unit joined the V8 line-up, replacing the 360,

233

OPPOSITE and LEFT
Flareside (opposite) and Styleside F-100s
from the 1960s. The names didn't change,
though the trucks did.

producing 156bhp (net) in the F-250 and 62lb ft in two-barrelled carburettor form.

New for the Eighties

The full-sized Ford pickups had by now taken on a dinosaur-like quality that seemed out of step with the times after two fuel crises and the growth of the mini-truck, but they remained Ford's best-selling light truck and by a huge margin. The American public was still in love with traditional pickups, whether for work or leisure, so there was no drastic downsizing or radical changes to the latest example announced for 1980, only more of the same.

There was a new grille, and Styleside models were given wraparound tail lights, while the Supercabs received a new twin-window treatment. A redesigned interior with new seats gave 10 per cent more legroom and aerodynamic detailing was

OPPOSITE
Slide-on camper units were popular, but an alternative was the bolt-on hardtop, as in this 1965 pickup.

ABOVE
1966 F-100 Flareside.

aimed to reduce drag by up to 13 per cent in the highway (Ford may have been concerned with fuel economy after all!). As before, the range consisted of F-100, F-150, F-250 and F-350, with Flareside and Styleside boxes of 6.5ft, 6.75ft and 8ft. The shortest wheelbase was 117in (3m), the longest 155in (3.9m), the 300-ci six continuing as the base power unit, with V8 options of up to 351ci/5752cc (156bhp).

The Courier, now into its eighth year, was barely changed from its original four-cylinder form, but still sold steadily, having been given the option of Ford's own ohc 140-ci (2294-cc) four from 1981. This turned out to be its final full year, it having been replaced by the Ranger in early 1982, though as an '83 model. This stayed true to its original concept, offering the choice of 122-ci/1999-cc (72-bhp) or 140-ci (79-bhp) fours, the latter standard on the four-wheel-drive version. In fact, the Ranger was a 'range' in itself, having been given the option of two wheelbases (108 or 114in), with short- or long-pickup beds to suit. As well as the base engines, there was an optional 82-bhp version of the ohc 140-ci unit, and – a first in any Ford pickup – a 135-ci (2212-cc) diesel of 59bhp. It was clear that the Ranger was not only for leisure but also for work. Like the full-sized F-100, it was rated as a 1/2-tonner, though at $6,289 for the short-bed 4x2, it wasn't that much cheaper. That year, the F-series also acquired its first diesel option, but only in the heavy-duty F-350. At 420ci (6882cc), and 170bhp and 315lb ft, it was the beefiest engine available in any of the F-series trucks at the time.

The Ranger was a little too close to the F-100 for comfort, so the latter was dropped in 1984, leaving the F-150 as Ford's base full-sized pickup, while the Ranger range was expanded with a stripped-out 'S' model. The Ranger lost its diesel option the following year, but a gasoline V6 of 170ci (2786cc) offered 115bhp. Not so for the big F-series, whose 420-ci V8 diesel was now available on the F-250 as well. This was only one of a multiplicity of F-series engines that year and stretched to 14 options. The Ranger's diesel option returned for 1986, now turbocharged to extract 86bhp from its 143ci (2343cc). Fancier trim packages were added as the 1980s progressed, with the High Rider 4x4 offered from 1987 but only with the high-level STX trim. This included a bed-mounted light bar, a front brush bar and a handling package. Ranger XLTs were more cosmetic, with two-tone paint, with a sportier GT joining the range for 1988. The Ranger was now America's best-selling compact pickup.

Perhaps more significant for 1987 was the fact that the F-series had reached its half-century, which Ford celebrated with revised styling and rear-wheel anti-lock brakes, the first on an American pickup. They were standard on every new F-series, along with an updated interior, power steering, power brakes and fuel injection. As ever, there was a bewildering list of options from which to choose, but Ford sought to simplify matters by grouping some together, which also saved the customer money: thus the 1987 F-series came in three trim levels, Custom, XL and XLT Lariat. Injection took the elderly 300-ci

(4916-cc) six up to 145bhp, with 185bhp/270lb ft from the optional 302 V8. The following year, the V8 diesel was upgraded to a Navistar V8 of 444ci (7276cc), with 180bhp and 345lb ft, though only on the F-350.

The Ranger was restyled for 1989 though the load bed was unchanged, but cab and front-end were new, giving the Ranger more of a family resemblance to the F-series. Inside, it had a similar contoured dashboard, while the base 140-ci (2294-cc) four now had twin-plug ignition. Trim levels were still S, S Plus, Custom, GT, XLT and STX, and Ford was right to offer such a choice as the Ranger was hugely successful. The F-series was still Ford's best-selling truck, not to mention the most popular pickup of any type, but nearly a quarter-million Rangers were sold that year as well.

The early 1990s were quiet times for both Ranger and F-series pickups. There was an electronic automatic transmission for the F-150 in 1990, a bigger 245-ci (4015-cc) V6 for the Ranger in 1992, plus a biggest-ever V8 for the F-350. Measuring 460ci (7538cc), it offered 230bhp at a relaxed 3,600rpm and 390lb ft at 2,200. There was bigger news in 1993, when Ford quietly offered a new option on the F-150 – the Lightning. Offered only on the 4x2 Styleside, it came with a 240-bhp fuel-injected V8 of 351ci (5752cc), plus an overdrive automatic transmission. It was Ford's first muscle truck, the first, as it happened, of a long line.

Ford chose to keep quiet about the Lightning, however, and it wasn't advertised for 1994, even though it was still available.

OPPOSITE
A 1970 pickup with Sport Custom trim to attract the growing numbers of customers for leisure trucks.

f more interest to working pickup users
hat year were the new Navistar diesels for
he F-250 Heavy Duty and 350, which still
ame with a solid front axle with leaf
prings. The 444-ci (7276-cc) Navistar V8
was offered in naturally aspirated or
urbocharged form, though the latter was
sted as only slightly more powerful at
90bhp, though it was capable of mustering

360lb ft at 1,400rpm.

But most exciting for 1997 was the fact
that the 1980 F-series was finally replaced
by something far more radical. In F-150
form, it was actually launched in January
1996 as a 1997 model, though the old model
carried on for some time in the heavier-duty
line-up. The rounded, aerodynamic look of
the new Fs caused quite a stir at the time,

being a real departure from the traditional
house-brick look of the American pickup.
Despite the controversial styling, the public
loved the new F-150, and demand
outstripped supply for most of the first year.
It was also new under the skin, with a new
SLA independent front suspension and
overhead-cam V6 and V8 engines from
Ford's Triton range. The base unit was now a

ABOVE
A 1990s Ranger XLT – Ford's more
compact pickup.

OPPOSITE
Ford F-150 Lariat. 1998 was the second
year for the new-generation F-series.

256-ci (4195-cc) 160-bhp V6, with 281-ci/4605-cc (220bhp) and 330-ci/5408-cc (235bhp/330lb ft) V8s optional.

The Ranger acquired a smoother, more aerodynamic snout the following year, though not as radical as the F's, along with a new 153-ci (2507-cc) four as the base power

unit, replacing the faithful 140. V6s of 182ci (2982cc) or 245ci (4015cc) were optional, as was a 90-bhp electric motor on the Ranger EV, yet another departure for Ford.

The original F-150 Lightning hot rod had only lasted a couple of years, but it returned for 1999 in the new-shape F-series.

It was even quicker than before, the 330-ci V8 having been supercharged for 360bhp and an astounding 440lb ft for true supercar performance. Business users were probably more interested in the dual-fuel version of the same engine, which could run on either gasoline or the cheaper CNG, and was an

OPPOSITE
The F-100 and F-150 were always the big
sellers, but there was still a place for the
heavier-duty pickups, such as this hardtop
F-350 XLT.

LEFT
An extended-cab F-250 from the early
1990s.

option on all F-150s, apart from the Lightning, of course. They would probably also have appreciated the new Super Duty F-250 and 350, both aimed specifically at the over-8,500-lb (3855-kg) GVW market. These were not simply heavy-duty spring-and-shock jobs, having their own body panels and massive front grille, and they gradually replaced the standard F-250 and 350. Highlight of the range, if one liked big motors, was the 275-bhp/410-lb ft V10 of 415ci (6801cc), and the 444-ci (7276-cc) Navistar V8 turbo for those who preferred diesel.

Special editions had long been a part of the Ford 4x4 story, but now the 4x2 pickup was combined with the Harley-Davidson F-150 for 2000. With black paintwork, black

FAR LEFT and LEFT
1994 Ford F-150 Lightning, something of a legend in its own lifetime. One of the first muscle trucks, it could muster 240bhp.

OPPOSITE
The 2002 Ford Ranger, more of a working pickup than some of the fancier full-sized trucks.

LEFT
A 2004 F-150, having recently celebrated 25 years at the top of the best-seller list.

RIGHT
Harley-Davidson special editions proved
popular, this being a 2006 F-150.

OPPOSITE
The Lightning returned as a permanent part
of the range: this is a 2004 F-150 SVT
Lightning.

ABOVE: Over the years Ford pickups got larger and larger, this is a F-650 from 2007.

RIGHT: Still in the showroom, a special 2010 edition F-150 Platinum.

leather and chrome wheels, it was plainly not a working truck, but highlighted the fact that both riders of Harleys and pickups were part of the same American blue-collar dream. The 281-ci (4605-cc) V8 was standard, though Ford claimed its exhaust note had been tuned to give it an authentic Harley V-twin rumble! So popular was this special edition, that Ford carried the Harley pickup

into 2002, alongside a new King Ranch limited-run model. As for the Ranger, that continued to sell well, year in, year out, with the engine again increased with the Explorer SUV's 207-bhp 245-ci (4015-cc) V6 as an option, though the 153-ci (2507-cc) four was still the base motor. In 2002 a new FX4 variant came with off-road extras such as BF Goodrich all-terrain tyres, skid plates,

limited-slip differential and Bilstein shocks.

The Ranger had certainly done Ford proud, but few would deny that the F-series was still the definitive Ford pickup. As it headed into the 21st century, it could celebrate over 50 years of production, 25 of which had been as the best-selling pickup of all. And while it could still be had in basic F-150 form, pickup lovers all over the world were more interested in the SVT Lightning, still the world's fastest truck, with a top speed of over 140mph (225km/h) and acceleration that wouldn't shame a Ferrari. Meanwhile, the F-350 Tonka Concept hinted at what the next F-series would be like, with a massive chrome grille hiding Ford's latest Power Stroke turbo-diesel V8, complete with 600lb ft driving through a five-speed automatic transmission.

The question is, would Henry Ford have approved of Effie's runaway success? Of the numbers built, yes, but of its development as a lifestyle accessory, probably not. That was not the Henry Ford way.

Ranchero

To think of Ford as an innovator doesn't seem quite right. For years, General Motors in general and Chevrolet in particular were seen as such. From the early days, General Motors consistently beat Ford to market with a choice of colours, independent front suspension and an overhead-valve V8. So it must have been a sweet moment for Dearborn when the 1957 Ford Ranchero was hailed as the industry's first-ever sedan pickup, two years before Chevrolet rather belatedly launched its response – El Camino

Actually, the idea wasn't that new. Ford had already built nearly 300 pickups based on the Model A Deluxe as early as 1931, though this was a special order for General Electric and a few other particular customers, and once completed, Ford's first car-based pickup was no more. Chevrolet built the Expeditor, a coupé with a small load bed replacing the trunk, from 1937, while Terraplane, Nash, Hudson and Studebaker all offered sedan pickups as well. But by the late 1940s all of these had fizzled out, and it seemed as though the sedan pickup was a pre-war idea that, for the American market at least, had had its day. Pickups were regarded simply as rugged, hard-riding workaday vehicles: the 1955–56 Chevrolet Cameo may have been given a fancy trim, but it lagged behind the sedans of the time.

Meanwhile, Ford had won leadership of the market in station wagons from Plymouth and Chevrolet, with a new line of all-metal two-door wagons. These were perfect as bases on which to build a sedan pickup, and Ford stylists produced three such prototypes in 1956. All were rejected by the company's infamous bean-counters, who calculated that sales would never justify the costs. But that wasn't the end of the story. For 1957, the Ford line-up, which was substantially new for that year, was headed by the glamorous Skyliner convertible. Using Skyliner parts suddenly made a sedan pickup make economic sense, and the new Ford Ranchero for 1957 was born. It was based on the Ranch Wagon, with a 116-in wheelbase, plus Skyliner parts, the only components unique

to the Ranchero being an inner tailgate stamping, a box liner and a back panel to close in the cab. This significantly reduced costs, enabling the basic six-cylinder pickup to be offered at only $2,073. But despite constraints of cost, the Ranchero was undeniably handsome for its day, looking every inch the work wagon with sedan comfort thrown in.

From the beginning, there were two levels of trim – Standard and Custom – together with a full range of options. Master Guide power steering, Sure-Stop power brakes, air conditioning, power seats – the list went on, all emphasizing the fact that the Ranchero was based on a sedan rather than a truck; as if that were not enough, buyers could also choose from the full range of Ford sedan engines.

These kicked off with a 144-bhp 223-ci (3654-cc) straight-six, followed by 272-ci/4457-cc (190bhp) and 292-ci/4785-cc (212bhp) V8s, both with two-barrelled carburettors. It was even possible to order a Ranchero with the Thunderbird's full-power four-barrel 312, offering 245bhp. Of course, it could never be as hard-working as a proper pickup – the load bed measured 32.4cu ft and the capacity was 1,190lb (540kg) – but the Ranchero still caused quite a stir. Here was a pickup that could be used for lighter jobs around the farm but would not look out of place in town on a Saturday night. Ford also targeted the growing breed of small businesses in the service industries – TV repairmen, decorators and owners of antique shops – who needed a pickup but appreciated the

Ranchero's classy appearance.

It was a success, and over 21,700 Rancheros were sold in the first year, other buyers favouring the more expensive Custom. Ford's rivals had been caught on the hop, since they had nothing similar to offer. Dodge managed to produce the Sweptside 100 pickup by mid-year, but it was merely a standard pickup with station-wagon rear fenders attached. Chevrolet did the job more thoroughly, however, with the Impala-based El Camino, but that didn't appear until 1959.

Not that 1958 was a good year in which to be launching new cars, a recession having put a major dent in car sales for the first time in over a decade. The Ranchero suffered along with everything else, and just under 10,000 were sold, the Custom again selling better than the Standard, which was in spite of the addition of the new 352-ci (5768-cc) Interceptor V8 and three-speed Cruise-O-Matic transmission. Sales recovered in 1959 but not by very much at a little over 14,000.

Because of what had happened the previous year, Ford dropped the slow-selling base Ranchero, leaving the Custom to carry on alone, still with straight-six and V8 options In any case, it now had a rival in El Camino, though the consensus was that the softly-sprung Chevrolet was more of a cosmetic pickup than the Ford original. Not that the Ranchero had been deprived of beautification, having been given Galaxie trim and a whole range of colours which included two-tones, such as Fawn Tan with Tahitian Gold.

OPPOSITE
The Ranchero was Ford's new idea for 1957, being a car-based pickup.

Downsizing

Nineteen-fifty-eight was a disastrous year when only two areas of the market were showing success – small imported trucks and compact sedans. America was going through a short-lived but intense compact-car boom, so it made sense that the next Ranchero would go the same way. In fact, so did just about everyone else: Chevrolet was contemplating a pickup version of the Chevy II, Rambler had built prototype compact flatbeds, and Studebaker was preparing a Lark-based truck. Meanwhile, Datsun had launched its little 1/4-ton pickup and VW was already selling thousands of Transporter vans and flatbeds a year. Little wonder then, that the 1960 Ranchero, based on the new compact Falcon, lost inches, pounds and excess fat. The Falcon, a sensible, economical sedan, the brainchild of the logical Robert McNamara, made an excellent pickup base. It was lightweight and economical and capable of up to 30mpg, which was most impressive for the time, neither was it underpowered, the 144-ci (2360-cc) six-cylinder engine offering 90bhp and up to 90mph (145km/h). Best of all, in a newly competitive market, at $1,887 the new Ranchero was cheaper than the old full-sized model and had fewer of its luxury options. However, buyers didn't seem to mind, and over 21,000 of the compact pickups were sold in the first year.

Sales fell marginally in 1961, despite the new option of a 101-bhp 170-ci (2786-cc) straight-six. El Camino had gone but there was new competition from Chevrolet's new Corvair-based 95 pickup. The VW Transporter was selling as fast as ever, and buyers looking for an alternative 1/2-ton truck could always opt for Ford's own Econoline, which was also based on the Falcon but without the sedan front end. Sales held up for 1962 – still over 20,000 – but there was increasing pressure to make the Ranchero bigger again as America's compact-car revolution began to run out of steam. In the end, 1963 saw a compromise, in that the Ranchero kept its Falcon base but adopted the intermediate Fairlane's 164-bhp V8 as an option. Sales dropped slightly, to a little over 18,500, and again the following year to 17,000 or so. Not only was the Ranchero seen as too small, but El Camino was also back, now in chunkier intermediate form; Chevrolet sold over 36,000 of them in 1964, leaving the Ford for dead. But Ford failed to retaliate for 1965, though the Ranchero was restyled and lost its Falcon badge. It was also given more power, with options including a 120-bhp 200-ci (3277-cc) straight-six and a 225-bhp 289-ci (4736-cc) V8. Sales improved a little, to over 19,000, but it was clear that the days of the compact pickup were numbered.

The change finally came in 1966, when the Ranchero was switched to an intermediate Fairlane base. This had several advantages. The market was already heading in this direction, in fact its arch-rival, El Camino, already had. It also meant that the Ranchero could be equipped with Ford's big-block 390-ci (6391-cc) V8. *Motor Trend* tested a Ranchero 390 and concluded that it was 'an almost bewildering array of compromises that come off beautifully'. In Ranchero tradition, it had firm rear suspension to cope with the payload, and a softer front end for a comfortable ride, which led to interesting handling characteristics. All in all, however, *Motor Trend* thought it worked well. The 390 V8 came with a two-barrelled carburettor, so it was punchy, with 270bhp and a quarter-mile time of 17.0 seconds while being less of a gas-guzzler than it might otherwise have been. Finally, the Ranchero was once again offered with luxury touches such as built-in air conditioning.

There were three levels of trim for 1967 – base, Ranchero 500 and 500/XL, and Ford began to target women in its advertising, having realized that pickups were often bought by couples for whom load-carrying was of lesser importance than status and ease of driving. 'Yes, ladies, the Fairlane Rancheros are trucks, but, just between us, they're your kind of trucks.' The concept of the pickup as a stylish personal car is often seen as a phenomenon of the 1980s, but Ford had been there 20 years earlier. Despite the extra features, the big-cube power and the luxury interior of the 500/XL, Ford saw no increase in Ranchero sales. In 1967, the mid-range 500 was the most popular model, followed by the base pickup (5,856 sold) and the luxury XL at less than 2,000. The following year, the Ranchero again grew bigger, along with the Fairlane, with an extra 4in (10cm) of wheelbase, though none of this benefited the load bed. Ford's 302-ci (4949-cc)V8 joined the options, though it wasn't available until 1969, and the upscale 500/XL was replaced

by the sportier-sounding GT with standard bucket seats, as Ford tried to attract a few muscle-car sales.

That was echoed by the muscular-looking Ranchero Scrambler, a show special that did the rounds that year. It was followed by a new range of V8s for 1969: the 351-ci unit and the ultimate 428 in two-barrel or four-barrel forms. Other features, characteristic of performance cars, such as low-profile tyres and close-ratio four-speed transmissions, nudged the Ranchero into muscle-car territory, though the base model still came with a straight-six, now of 250ci. The Rio Grande was a special-edition GT with plenty of fashionable black detailing, plus Magnum 500 wheels.

In fact, it seemed as though the Ranchero was moving ever further away from the original concept of a practical pickup with sedan comfort. Ford now had an eye on the booming recreational market, so when the Ranchero was upsized again for 1970, longer, wider and lower than before, the load bed was no bigger. As well as the base, 500 and GT, there was a new Squire, with fake wood-grain side panels, and optional trailer packages were aimed more at weekenders than Monday–Friday commuters. 'Tow a boat – tow a tent-trailer – tow a snowmobile!' went the publicity. 'Tailor the Ranchero to your mood – luxury-performance-play!' The GT could be had with hood scoop, tachometer and Ford's ultimate muscle-car motor, the 429 Cobra Jet Ram Air. But none of this appeared to be expanding the Ranchero's market, only changing it, and just over 21,600 were sold

in 1970. Sales did improve the following year, however, the mid-range Ranchero 500 still being the best-seller, followed by the base pickup, the GT and Squire in that order.

If there was any doubt as to the direction in which the Ranchero was heading, it was dispelled for 1972, when the new Torino-based pickup was launched. It looked more of a muscle car than ever, with its steeply raked windshield, wide track and sculptured side panels. Haulers would have been pleased that, for once, the larger overall size brought a bigger load bed, now 6.75ft long. All-round coil-sprung suspension was another worthwhile improvement and while the base model was dropped, buyers didn't seem to mind, for over 23,000 Ranchero 500s alone were sold that year, not to mention over 12,600 GTs and over 4,000 Squires. Moreover, the 1973 fuel crisis hadn't hit the Ranchero very hard and sales were up again that year. Like the Mustang, Ford's sedan pickup was seen as a relatively modest car, so many owners of larger cars traded them in. Not that they needed to relinquish their V8: for 1974 the six-cylinder Ranchero was actually deleted and the 351 V8 was now the base power plant. Did anyone buy the Ranchero as a working pickup any more? If so, they wouldn't have been tempted by the luxurious Brougham interior package, or by the choice of 17 different exterior colours, four interiors, with co-ordinated instrument panel and black, white, blue, green, brown, tan or gold vinyl roof.

In fact, this period would be the pickup's best ever, with over 43,000 Rancheros sold

in 1973, though it was to be a high point never achieved again. The shock of the first fuel crisis seemed to be taking its toll as premium gas became increasingly hard to find and new emissions laws began to bite. On top of that, economic forces were putting pressure on car sales, so it wasn't surprising that less than 15,000 Rancheros found homes in 1975.

By now, of course, buyers of pickups who were serious about downsizing could opt for the four-cylinder Ford Courier. The company had contemplated a subcompact Pinto pickup back in 1970, but in the end went for a rebadged Mazda, the popularity of this mini-pickup being responsible for the eventual end of the Ranchero. The 55-mph (88km/h) speed limit of 1976, part of a national campaign to reduce America's demand for gas, was another nail in the coffin of traditional full-sized V8s. Even the base-model Ranchero 500 now tipped the scales at over 3,900lb (1769kg) and the car was unchanged that year.

A new Ranchero, the final one, as it turned out, appeared for 1977. Throughout its life, Ford's sedan pickup had been based on whatever platform had seemed appropriate at the time. It had started out full-sized in the 1950s, then became a compact in 1960 with the Falcon. As the compact boom waned, so Ranchero switched to the intermediate Fairlane, growing with it through the affluent 1960s before transferring to the sporty Torino for the tail-end of the muscle-car era. Now, as the late 1970s loomed, the Ranchero was downsizing again, adopting the LTD II as its base. Not that this downsizing applied to power units. The base Ranchero, still carrying a 500 badge, came with a 130-bhp 302-ci (4949-cc) V8 and the GT a 148- or 161-bhp 351, though according to *PV4* magazine, which tested a GT in 1977, there was not much to choose between the two. The muscle-car boom may have been over, but buyers could still specify a full-sized 400-ci (6555-cc) power plant. To bolster the performance image, Ford built the Ranchero Viper show truck, with stripes, spoilers and mag wheels, and any Ranchero could be ordered with the GT's Sports Instrument Panel. Options still included items like air conditioning, power seats and power windows, with a Brougham Décor interior to satisfy the most discerning.

The public seemed to like this new, slightly smaller Ranchero, and sales were back up to over 21,000 during 1977, with over 23,000 finding homes in 1978. That year, the big 400-ci V8 was dropped as a standard option, though it appeared in the limited-edition Shelby GT Ranchero, of which only 75 were built to celebrate Ford's 75th birthday. This was the most muscular Ranchero yet, the big-block engine breathing through a large Holley four-barrelled carb and dual exhaust. Finished in black and gold, it came with 7-in chrome Magnum 500 wheels and a white interior.

But the Shelby was something of a swansong. Ford did not advertise the Ranchero that year, a sure sign that it did not see much of a future for its sedan pickup. Significantly, it did not downsize with the LTD for 1979, but kept the 118-in wheelbase,

which was now Ford's biggest. It was now pitched as a luxury pickup, with a long list of standard equipment and a new Limited Production model. This was built in small numbers and came with every conceivable extra, including air conditioning and a red leather interior, but at over $10,000 there were few takers and it was soon withdrawn. Actually, Ranchero sales were holding up

well, at just over 25,000 for 1979. But Ranchero numbers were no longer enough, when the little Courier pickup was selling three times as fast and the Econoline was selling over 184,000. Oversized, undersold and out on a limb, the Ranchero could not survive on its own, and 1979 was its final year.

A restored 1960s Ranchero for sale!

CHAPTER FOUR
GMC: THE REAL THING

General Motors is famous in that, at one time or another, it has offered a car marque to just about every buyer in America. Take an average main-street bank from the days when such things existed. The manager would drive a Cadillac, and the lowly clerk, perhaps a young family man, a Chevrolet. Then for all those in between, depending on income, status and aspirations, there was Pontiac, Buick and Olds, a legacy of William C. Durant's original plan to form his new General Motors empire by acquisition. So successful was this multi-badge strategy that Ford and Chrysler launched sub-marques of their own.

But this empire would have been nothing without a commercial vehicle division, so in 1911 the General Motors Truck Co. (GMC) was formed. Unlike Chevrolet, which Durant began from scratch, or the other General Motors car marques, which had been individually acquired, General Motors consisted of three pre-existing truck-makers which had been swallowed up by it – Rapid, Reliance and Randolph.

The Rapid Motor Vehicle Co. had been

something of a pioneer. Formally incorporated in 1904, it had then been in the business of making trucks for two years, brothers Max and Morris Grabowsky having built their first prototype back in 1900. Assembled in the brothers' Detroit workshop, this was a simple single-cylinder machine, chain-driven and of small size. They formed the Rapid company in 1902

and built around 75 trucks over the next couple of years.

The entire project stepped up a gear in 1904, when new financial backing was offered by the directors of the American Garment Cleaning Co., which had been one of the Grabowskys' earliest customers. Recapitalized and taken over the following year, Rapid concentrated on building a range

of single-cylinder trucks from its new factory in Pontiac. There was also a new two-cylinder machine, its 15-hp engine mounted under the driver's seat. This Model B was a 1-ton truck, with an 80-in (2-m) wheelbase, planetary gearbox and chain final drive. Two hundred trucks and buses were built that first year in Pontiac, and the next few years saw the range expand along with sales. The line-up always featured 1-ton trucks, such as the 1907 E-62, which produced 24hp and cost $1,600 ready to

work. A 1$1/2$-ton version, the E-44, was offered alongside it.

The takeover by General Motors came gradually. Billy Durant began to buy up Rapid stock in 1908, and by the following year his General Motors sales force was promoting the trucks, though it didn't become part of the General Motors family until later in 1909. That year, the company offered 28 different F-models, with an ambulance and fire engine as well as the trucks, with 1- 2- and 3-ton models the

following year, when four-cylinder engines replaced the twins.

Rapid had always made trucks, but the Reliance Motor Truck Co. started out in 1902 as a car manufacturer, only adding a truck to its line in 1906, though it had dropped the cars within 12 months. For 1908 there was a new range of machines, the two-cylinder 1–2-ton Model H, a three-cylinder 3–4-ton version and the 4-ton Model K, powered by a four-cylinder engine. Unusually, all of these were two-stroke units,

RIGHT
The late-1930s GMC pickups were stylish and capable.

OPPOSITE
GMC, General Motors' commercial vehicle arm, built big trucks as well as light pickups.

which in the case of the Model K produced 60hp: advertising stressed that all of them had been designed as trucks from the ground up, 'with a surplus of strength in all parts'.

That same year, Reliance was taken over by General Motors, though the company retained some independence, continuing to produce trucks under the Reliance badge for some time, offering two 2½-ton trucks, a 3- and 4-ton for 1910, priced from $3,150 to $4,400. Not until July of the following year

did the company formally become part of the rapidly growing General Motors conglomerate.

General Motors' third building block was the Randolph Motor Car Co., which enjoyed a shorter period of independence than the first two. It was set up in Flint, Michigan, in 1908, its first product being the splendidly named 'Strenuous Randolph'. This actually encompassed a whole range of trucks, from a light delivery van to a full-

sized 4-ton flatbed. But the Strenuous Randolph had only a short career, as William C. Durant bought the company that same year, absorbing it completely into General Motors by 1910.

By 1911, by which time Billy Durant was out of the picture, having been forced to resign when General Motors hit its first rocky patch, the newly-formed General Motors Truck Co. was able to offer a complete line-up of commercial

ehicles using elements of Rapid, Reliance nd Randolph. The new GMC logo, the big urly 'M' supporting the 'G' and 'C' as if ransporting them elsewhere, first appeared n August 1911, and in January the ollowing year was used on both Rapid and Reliance trucks shown at the New York utomobile Show.

This consolidated range extended from the 3/4-ton ex-Randolph to the 5-ton forward-control Reliance, with electric machines added to the range in 1911 and sold for the next five years, a 1/2-ton being the smallest electric offered. GMC worked hard to promote the electric trucks, but despite price cuts, the trend of the time was towards

gasoline, and most were dropped in 1916.

Of more relevance to the future was the 3/4-ton Model 15 gasoline truck, launched in October 1914 and powered by a Continental four-cylinder engine rated at 19.6hp. The Model 15 was also the first truck to use a bevel-gear drive rear axle instead of a chain, not to mention pneumatic tyres, so it was

OPPOSITE and ABOVE
An early 1950s GMC 150, with 100-bhp
six. It achieved record-breaking sales.

267

OPPOSITE
*GMC's first new post-war pickup was the
FC series, with 'Advance Design' styling.*

quite advanced for its time. The 15 was
followed by larger versions, such as the 1¼-
ton Model 25, which actually reverted to
chain drive, and the 1½-ton Model 31 with
worm-drive transmission. The Model 40 was
a 2-tonner with the choice of chain- or
worm-drive transmission, while 3½- and 5-
ton cousins were added in 1916, along with
GMC's first 1-ton gasoline truck, the Model
21. The 21 used a four-cylinder Continental
engine, like all GMC trucks of the time, this
one of 33bhp. This particular model was
shaft-driven, which within a couple of years
would finally oust the old-fashioned chain.

By now, Billy Durant was back in
charge of the company he had created. The
year 1916 was also marked by a Model 31,
which crossed the continent from
Washington to New York and back again.
After many months and 9,513 miles
(15309km), which included climbing Pikes
Peak, William Warwick and his family were
back home with no major mechanical repairs
needed to the 1½-ton vehicle. The company
made an unsuccessful foray into the tractor
business in 1917, but the First World War
proved to be of particular benefit to the
company, as 90 per cent of its truck
production was given over to war work.

Things were tougher after the war as the
government contracts dried up and army-
surplus trucks began to find their way into
the private market. GMC responded with a
$280 price cut to the ³⁄4-ton Model 16, which
used the same 33-bhp Continental four as the
earlier Model 21. An advertising campaign
emphasized its sterling war record, and the
Model 16 was uprated in 1920, though all

this activity could do nothing to hide a
general recession, with GMC making only
2,623 trucks that year.

The Model 16 went on to form the basis
of GMC's famous K-series trucks in the
1920s, first as the 1-ton K-16, though the
range soon expanded to 5 tons. All of these
abandoned Continental engines in favour of
units built by Northway, another General
Motors division which allowed them to be
described as GMC's own. As for the K-
series, these were generally lighter than their
predecessors and offered a range of special
accessories, such as a power take-off, while
electric lights were standard on all but the
cheapest model. This was the K-15, a ½-ton
truck which was not a success, in spite of the
fact that it shared its 33-bhp Northway-built
four with the K-16, and it was dropped in
1923. The K-16 continued, joined by the
K-16X using a factory-built express body.
Many trucks were still supplied as bare
chassis, or chassis-cabs, but factory-supplied
pickups or flatbeds were becoming
increasingly popular.

Breaking Records
Officially, GMC trucks of the late 1920s and
early '30s were built by the Yellow Truck &
Coach Mfg. Co. General Motors
management planned to diversify into the
coach and taxi market, and arranged that the
the Yellow company, headed by John D.
Hertz, would take over GMC, while General
Motors kept a controlling interest in the
entire enterprise. The upshot of all these
corporate shenanigans was that GMC trucks
were effectively still built by GMC under

the overall ownership of General Motors.

However, Yellow also made 1-ton
trucks, which were sold through GMC
dealers from 1925–26, while GMC's own
light-duty trucks were dropped. Although
relatively powerful, the Yellow 1-tonner wa
too expensive to compete and in 1927 was
replaced by GMC's own T-10 and T-20.
These were part of a new line-up intended t
replace the old K-series which, in 1926,
ranged from the 1-ton K-17 to the 10- and
15-ton 'Big Brutes'. The 1927 T-series
looked altogether more modern, with deepl
crowned fenders and headlights next to the
radiator. Handsome and popular, the T-serie
sold 20,000 from 1927–28, vindicating
GMC's decision to build a brand-new $8
million truck plant at Pontiac, Michigan.

There was a move towards six cylinder
at the time, typified by the GMC T-20 1-ton
'the modern six-cylinder speed truck with
Buick engine'. If there were any doubts as t
the toughness of this new generation, they
were dispelled by the famous racing driver
'Cannonball' Baker in September 1927,
when he drove a T-50 2-ton truck from New
York to San Francisco, covering nearly
3,700 miles (5954km) in less than six days.
Encouraged by the runaway success of the
T-series, GMC launched the ½-ton T-10
soon afterwards, once again six-cylinder-
powered, this time by a Pontiac. And at
under $600 it was less than the price of
many four-cylinder sedans. It was joined fo
1928 by the ½-ton T-11, which was really a
Pontiac De-Luxe Delivery truck with GMC
badges, though it came only as a panel van.

That too was powered by a straight-six.

1931, which may have been why the light truck range was cut back the following year to only four models. General Motors then decided to leave the lightest trucks to Chevrolet, with GMC concentrating on the larger machines. So for 1933 the T-11 was dropped, leaving the 1-ton T-15 as GMC's smallest offering. Still powered by the Pontiac 200-ci six, it came in panel van, chassis form and others, as well as pickup. The T-15 was also dropped early the following year, and for the remainder of 1933 the smallest GMC pickups were the 1$\frac{1}{2}$-ton triumvirate of T-18, T-19 and T-23, all powered by the familiar Pontiac six. The T-16 in 1934, now with a 1$\frac{1}{2}$-ton rating, and an Oldsmobile L head six of 213ci (3490cc) and 84bhp, derated from 90bhp in the Olds sedans. Prices started at $570.

The following year GMC returned to light trucks with a version of the T-16 based on a 131-in (3.3-m) wheelbase. Only bare chassis was offered, at $595, though many of these would have been fitted with pickup bodies. In fact, the whole light/medium range was revamped with sloping grilles and fender-mounted headlights, while hydraulic brakes were standard across the range.

The Depression had still not released it grip, but over 11,000 trucks were sold in 1935 and nearly 28,000 the following year. In fact, 1936 was an important year for GMC light trucks, the company releasing it first-ever $\frac{1}{2}$-ton pickup. The T-14 also cam as a $425 chassis-cab, though the pickup was ready to work for an extra $100. It was

which GMC seems to have decided to concentrate on, though for 1929 the biggest heavy-duty trucks stuck with fours. That year was the company's best before the Depression made itself felt, with over 17,500 trucks sold. This total nearly halved the following year, despite the adoption of a larger 200-ci (3277-cc) 60-bhp Pontiac six by the T-11, T-15 (1-ton), T-17 and T-18

(both 1$\frac{1}{2}$ tons). The heavier-duty T-25 and upwards used a bigger 258-ci (4228-cc) six from Buick. In fact, GMC appeared undeterred as sales continued to slide into 1931, with 16 models and 56 chassis in the T-series, though it did cut prices by up to $600, the T-11 starting at $625 for the basic chassis, the pickup a little more.

Sales bottomed out at just over 6,300 in

breaching 50,000 for the first time. The 1/2-ton T-14 acquired a new short-wheelbased T-14A for 1938, with only 112in between the wheels, while the 126-in model became the T-14B, both of them the only GMC trucks to maintain three- instead of four-speed gearboxes. The T-14 was also re-engined later in the year, with a Pontiac six of 223ci (3654cc) and 81bhp, the same engine appearing in the 3/4-ton T-15.

There were more engine changes in 1939, when GMC began to build its own units of 228ci (3736cc) and 248ci (4064cc) to replace the Pontiac and Oldsmobile sixes. This was to accommodate a new range, prefixed AC for a conventional layout or AF for forward-control, the light pickups keeping their front engines. Typical was the AC-100 pickup at $593, using the same 80-bhp 228-ci six as did all the light-duty GMCs of the time. GMC's increasingly comprehensive range continued into 1940, with 47 models offered and bodies to suit a whole range of uses. The ACs became CCs for 1941, but were otherwise unchanged, with the 1/2-ton CC-100, 3/4-ton CC-150 and 1-ton CC-250. With fender-mounted headlights and split windshields they were up-to-the-minute, though GMC was becoming increasingly preoccupied with fulfilling urgent military orders. This also explains why there were no more changes for 1942, the civilian trucks continuing in 'blackout' trim instead of brightwork because of material shortages. In any case, civilian production had been suspended by June.

When it resumed in 1946, the pre-war CC trucks rolled off the lines, and although

ased on a 126-in (3.2-m) wheelbase and sed the same Olds-designed but GMC-ssembled 213-ci (3490-cc) six as the T-16, ith several other Olds car components eneath the skin. It shared a new streamlined ok with other GMCs, which was also a ature of Chevrolet trucks. With a three-peed gearbox and hydraulic brakes, the new aby GMC was a great success, accounting or 42 per cent of total output in its first ear. There was even a four-wheel-drive ersion developed for the military.

'Dual-Tone Design. Offered only in MC. "Dual-Tone" goes far beyond mere coloring. It is a completely new and entirely different feature – "built-in" – which blends cab, cowl, radiator and radiator grille into one harmonious color design.' The GMC copywriters went wild in 1937, though they were only celebrating all-new streamlined styling, with 12 dual-tone colour options to make the most of the new unified lines. Under the hood, the Olds six was enlarged to 230ci, pushing power and torque to 86bhp and 172lb ft respectively. Whether it was Dual-Tone or not, sales of factory-built pickups were increasing rapidly, and total production was setting a new record,

GMC primarily sold truck chassis for bodies to be fitted by specialists, it still offered a good range of pickups and stakebeds, from the 1/2-ton CC-101 to the 1 1/2-ton CC-302. These pre-war carry-overs continued into the first half of 1947, bearing both CC and slightly updated EC prefixes. It wasn't until June that a genuinely post-war light truck was launched, though the new FC-series still used the 228-ci six. What was new was the styling, which consisted of General Motors' generic 'Advance Design', with built-in headlights, simple three-bar grille and a complete absence of brightwork. Steel-sided pickups were offered in 1/2-, 3/4- and 1-ton forms, as well as 1- and 1 1/2-ton stakesides.

Meanwhile, the post-war appetite for light trucks was increasing, Americans having been starved of them for three years. This allowed GMC to break another new record in 1948, when over 90,000 trucks were sold. This year and the next the new FC-series would be largely unchanged as the company struggled to keep up with post-war demand. The plan appeared to be vindicated when GMC nearly caught its arch-rival, International, overtaking it in 1950 to become America's fourth best-selling truck. With nearly 84,000 units sold in 1949, 'America's finest all-star truck line' was living up to its name. Little wonder that the range had ballooned to 75 model series and 224 different bodies.

The year 1950 saw yet another record, when over 100,000 trucks left GMC's four factories, most of them from the plant in Pontiac. The small pickup, along with GMC's other light trucks, was given a power boost to 96bhp from the same 228-ci six that year. And despite production restrictions in 1951 (the U.S. Government had been seeking to channel raw materials into defence production), the company still reached its target of a 10 per cent share of the truck market. The 228 was uprated again, to 100bhp, while the 1/2-ton received front stabilizer bars and better brakes.

By now, post-war inflation was taking its toll as the price of a 1/2-ton pickup crept to $1,385 in 1952, but there was a significant step forward in 1953 when GMC offered General Motors' Hydra-Matic automatic transmission in its smaller trucks. 'It means freeing the driver of all gear-shifting chores to keep him fresher, more alert to cope with road hazards,' according to the publicity, and 'Small wonder, then, that Hydra-Matic Hauling is redefining trucking.' For 1954, the trucks were restyled with a one-piece windshield and chrome trim returned after a temporary disappearance during the Korean War; even chrome hubcaps were back. The pickup had its own improvements, with higher side panels and a tailgate now over 18in (46cm) above the bed and square tail lights. Meanwhile, a more demanding public was clamouring for more power, so the bigger 248-ci (4064-cc) straight-six engine became standard. With overhead valves and hydraulic lifters, it offered 125bhp from its 7.5:1 compression ratio, making it the most powerful GMC light pickup yet.

Blue-Chip Investment

The whole range of GMC light trucks was transformed in 1955 by the arrival of the Blue Chips. They were late, not unveiled until the spring of that year, for the very good reason that General Motors was renewing its entire car and truck line-up that year, and there was no time to get everything ready at once. But the Blue Chips did make an impact when they finally arrived. According to GMC general manager Phillip J. Monaghan, they were 'the new generation of trucks: designed to haul more payload further, faster, for less money…'. There were 500 major changes in all.

Most obvious was the all-new styling, in which GMC light trucks abandoned their functional, plain appearance in favour of a more flamboyant front end inspired by features from Oldsmobile (the two-bar chrome grille) and Cadillac (the hooded headlights). Panoramic windshield and rear window transformed the pickups, which retained the same model designations as before: 1/2-ton 100, 3/4-ton 150 and 1-ton 250.

There was power to match the new glamour beneath the hood as the base six-cylinder engine was joined by a 287-ci (4703-cc) Pontiac V8 of 155bhp. This was car-type power in a pickup, and proved wildly successful with GMC buyers, 44 per cent of whom opted for a V8 in the first year, while nearly two out of three paid extra for Hydra-Matic transmission; in fact, American trucks were getting more sophisticated by the year.

The most dramatic of all these changes

OPPOSITE
Rounded 1950s pickups make great street rods, as this GMC FC demonstrates.

OPPOSITE and LEFT
There was a new look for 1955, with the
option of a Pontiac V8 and the increasingly
popular Hydra-Matic.

could be seen in the Town & Country Pickup, later renamed the Suburban Pickup after Dodge laid claim to the original name. This had flush-sided panels made of fibreglass to give a smooth profile and deluxe trim. It was GMC's version of a similar Chevrolet pickup, though it was 4.5in (11cm) longer and weighed an extra 130lb (59lb). Opinions differ as to exactly how many of GMC's first flashy pickups were actually made in 1955, but it wasn't much more than 300.

After all that excitement there were fewer changes for 1956 and what there were were mechanical rather than stylistic, the base 248-ci (4064-cc) six having been uprated to 270ci (4424cc) and 130bhp/238lb ft. The Pontiac V8 also gained more cubes, now 317ci (5195cc) for 180bhp at 4,400rpm and 276lb ft peaking at 2,200rpm, while heavier-duty trucks used a detuned version. A significant change was a new four-wheel-drive option on the 100-, 150- and 250-series

pickups, the first time it had been offered as a factory-fitted item.

But just when it seemed that GMC was on an unstoppable upward curve, sales slumped in 1957 to just over 62,000, a drop of 20,000 on the previous year. Market share also fell, the result of a cut-back in defence contracts, which made up 5 per cent of the business that year. Nineteen-fifty-eight was even worse, with less than 56,000 trucks sold, though the front ends of the light-duty

RIGHT and BELOW RIGHT
Oldsmobile inspired the two-bar grille and
Cadillac the hooded headlights.

machines were freshened up with twin headlights. Under the skin was a new 336-ci (5506-cc) V8 of 200bhp, a new automatic transmission and stronger chassis. GMC was working hard to promote diesel power in its big trucks, but this hadn't yet been applied to the small pickups. Meanwhile, the Suburban Pickup was replaced by a similar-looking truck with all-steel sides instead of fibreglass. The following year proved to be the last for the Blue Chip GMCs, and it was a quiet one for the pickups. Not only was GMC concentrating on new tilting-cab trucks for 1959, there were also new light-duty trucks on the way as well.

Into High Gear

GMC certainly made a splash with its new pickups for 1960, which were only part of a completely renewed truck range that year. '34 pickup combinations – with brawn and beauty! … Exclusive, extended-life V6 engines! … 4-wheel-drive with new, lower look!' The 1955 Blue Chips were out – came 'Operation High Gear …The Big GMC Break Through in Truck Engineering!

It was 1955 all over again, with a new look, new engine and new four-wheel-drive system. Lower and wider the before, the new pickups certainly shouted '60s' rather than '50s'. The full-width hood had 'jet-pod' styling, with twin headlights and an upper grille holding two rectangular parking lights.

So it looked different, but the real innovation was beneath the hood, where GMC had abandoned the straight-six layout for the first time in over 30 years. In its place was an all-new V6, a family of engines from

305ci (4998cc), for the light-duty pickups, to 401ci (6571cc). It was designed as a truck engine for high torque, reliability and a long life. In fact, the company paid a great deal of attention to strength and longevity. It is shorter than a V8 made for a stiffer crankshaft and block and the V6 had 33 per cent more cooling area around its valves and cylinders than the old straight-six. At the time, GMC claimed 200,000 miles (321860km) without a major overhaul, and some V6s managed up to 500,000 miles in service before major work, so it looked as though GMC's pioneering work developing a gasoline V6 for trucks had paid off. It also produced a 702-ci (11504-cc) V12 based on the same layout, with 175bhp, though the pickups made do with the basic GMC-305A. This breathed through a one-barrelled Holley carburettor and produced 150bhp and 260lb ft.

The 1960 GMC pickups also had torsion bar independent front suspension, claimed to provide the comfort of a sedan with coil springs to the rear. Double-walled cab construction and a hardwood load bed also featured, as did three- or four-speed manual gearboxes and a four-speed Hydra-Matic transmission, while buyers could choose between Fender-Side or Wide-Side beds, the latter with flush side panels.

Meanwhile, the pickup market was expanding: light trucks were being bought by adventurous families for weekend camping trips, as well as hunters and fishermen. GMC's answer was the new Sports-Cab, a slide-in camper unit that took only minutes to install. Camper units went hand-in-hand with the growing trend towards

four-wheel-drive, which GMC pickups had been offering as a working tool for some years. From 1960, the factory had fitted its own 4x4 system, previously bought in from NAPCO, and made great play of the fact that it had been designed from scratch for all-wheel-drive, not as an afterthought, a mere conversion on stilts. They were so successful that more 4x4 pickups were added for 1961, based on the 1/2-ton 127-in wheelbase truck.

The gasoline V6 clearly had plenty of potential where power was concerned, and some of this was unleashed in 1962, when the light-duty trucks benefited from a 10 per cent increase to 165bhp, with 280lb ft at 1,600rpm. This came courtesy of a two-barrelled Bendix-Stromberg carburettor which replaced the single-barrelled Holley. Meanwhile, that year, GMC announced that 93 per cent of its trucks were now V6-powered (the new-generation power units were a success, and by 1963 over 250,000 had been sold). Some customers thought the V6 a little thirsty, however, so an economy version, the 305-E, was launched for 1963. At the same time, the Hydra-Matic transmission was discarded in favour of the two-speed Pow-R-Flo, actually Chevrolet's Powerglide, and the torsion-bar front suspension was replaced by coils, which were still independent, with leaf springs supporting the load bed.

For 1964, still with an eye on buyers looking for a more economical alternative to the V6, GMC announced the option of a Chevrolet straight-six in the 1000-series pickups. Although far smaller than the 305, this overhead-valve unit still produced

120bhp and 205lb ft, thanks in part to a relatively high 8.5:1 compression ratio. 'GMC breakthrough engineering in action,' went the colourful advertisement. 'Now, a new pickup at a new budget price. GMC quality and durability, with thrifty in-line six engine. Rugged, reliable, all truck … yet you only pay for the power you need … It's new in the GMC line!' In fact, fuel economy was becoming an increasing concern to truck buyers, and GMC, which had been an early champion of diesel in its bigger trucks, now offered a diesel version of the V6 – 'Toro-Flow'. This was only available in the medium-duty trucks, the time for diesel power in light-duty pickups having not yet arrived.

All the pickups – straight-six, V6, Fender-Side, Wide-Side, 1/2-, 3/4- and 1-ton – continued for 1965, a 1/2-ton Wide-Side kicking off the range at $2,025, with a V6-equipped 1-ton with a 9-ft Fender-Side load bed at $2,486 and four-wheel-drive adding around $700 to the price of each. As well as offering a wide range of pickups, GMC sought to distance them from rivals built by Ford or Dodge. The difference, as was emphasized again and again, was that the GMC came from a specialist truck manufacturer rather than a car-maker who happened to build light trucks based on car components. 'That GMC nameplate stands for this – built, sold and serviced by truck people – men who know how to give you a lot of truck for your money.'

The strategy seemed to work, with sales up nearly 18 per cent in 1965 to nearly 124,000 trucks and buses. The following

OPPOSITE and LEFT
Not a pickup, strictly speaking, but heavy-duty trucks like this tipper were part of the GMC line-up, too.

as the 170-bhp base engine. The power-up option was Chevrolet's well-known 283-ci (4637-cc) V8 in 175- or 220-bhp form.

There was new corporate styling to go with the shared engines, simpler and more squared-off than the early-1960s style. There was also some renaming, as the $^{1}/_{2}$-ton became C1500, $^{3}/_{4}$-ton C2500 and 1-ton C3500. Wheelbases of 115, 127 and 133in (2.9, 3.2 and 3.4m) were available, as were Fender-Side, Wide-Side and stakebed rear ends. Add four-wheel-drive (not offered on the 1-ton) and the trucks became K1500 or K2500. These all continued into 1968, though the engine range was expanded to seven, with a 230-ci (3769-cc) six and Chevy's big-block 396-ci (6489-cc) V8 joining the line-up, the 396 offering 310bhp and the promise of near muscle-car performance. Imagine an unladen short-wheelbased truck with a 310-bhp V8 applying its power on wet roads – now that would have been interesting!

This gas-guzzling option was abandoned for 1969 in favour of Chevrolet's 307-ci (5031-cc) or 350-ci (5735-cc) V8, while the bigger six-cylinder option was cut to 250ci (4097cc). The V6 option was dropped halfway through the year, finally severing the connection with the pickups' GMC past. From then on they were rebadged as Chevrolets. To accommodate the ever-growing interest in the great outdoors, or at least to give the impression one was headed that way, a spacious Custom-Camper pickup was announced, which was a C2500 Wide-Side with a 127-in wheelbase and an 8.5-ft bed.

year, GMC built its half-millionth V6-powered truck, the familiar 305 now producing 170bh, and the 351E V6 from GMC's medium trucks an option, producing 220bhp. The Chevrolet 'thrifty' six was dropped.

GMC publicity followed the same theme for 1967, stressing the uniqueness of GMC light trucks because of their truck heritage. The plain fact, however, was that this was becoming less true by the year.

For sound economic reasons, General Motors decreed that GMC would now concentrate on producing medium- and heavy-duty trucks, while Chevrolet would specialize in the lighter-weight vehicles. This avoided duplication, though it meant that from 1967 onwards, GMC pickups were becoming increasingly similar to their Chevrolet cousins. The in-house V6 was still an option that year, but the Chevrolet straight-six returned in 292-ci (4785-cc) form

Uppers & Downers

The 1970s proved to be something of a roller coaster for American-made pickups. Pickup sales in general were on the up, as they continued to gain ground in the leisure and fun markets, and the number of GMC light trucks sold reflected this trend, as did the ones that were loaded with options, such as power steering, automatic transmission and air conditioning. On the other hand, they were also facing increasing competition from imported mini-pickups; the decade had also seen two fuel crises in which soaring gas prices and queues at the pumps would put thirsty V8s at a distinct disadvantage, if only temporarily.

The company launched its first leisure-oriented 4x4, the Jimmy, in 1970. This was really a Chevy Blazer with new badges, though it was always more of a SUV than a pure pickup, so doesn't concern us here. Of more interest was the Sprint, unveiled the following year as a new GMC aimed at combining the comfort and appointments of a car with the practicality of a pickup. Of course, it was again a question of rebadging, this time of Chevrolet's El Camino. It had a

OPPOSITE and BELOW
In 'Operation High Gear' for 1960, there was new styling, torsion-bar front suspension and a new V6 power unit.

eat enough appearance and gave GMC dealers something different to sell, but the Sprint was far less successful than El Camino and only 5,436 of them were sold compared with over 45,000 Caminos. The thinking was, from the marketing point of view, that the GMC badge would give a modicum of tough-truck credibility to the obviously car-based Sprint, but buyers were not deceived and bought an El Camino or Ranchero instead.

Meanwhile, the conventional pickups were having a quiet time, with some new colours added in 1970 and front disc brakes in '71. More interesting in 1972 was the fact that the 307- and 350-ci 'Invader' V8s were offered alongside the 250- and 292-ci sixes. A new option was a Chevrolet 402-ci (6588-cc) V8 of 240bhp, which is rather underwhelming for such a big-block motor; this is because net power was now quoted, with ancillaries attached to the engine, the 402's gross power, measured on the old system, being 300bhp. That year was GMC's best yet, with over 195,000 trucks and buses rolling off the production lines.

The pickups were given a major makeover in 1973, finally losing their 1960s appearance. Though still badged as C1500, 2500 and 3500, they had new styling, with a single-headlight front end, wider bodies and 29 per cent more glass. Reflecting market trends, wood-grain trim for the body was offered, together with the Sierra and Sierra Grande interior packages, the latter also offering the luxury features of a sedan.

GMC also launched its first crew cab – the '3+3' – capable of transporting six in comfort. Engine options still began with the 250-ci (4097-cc) six, now rated at 100 net bhp, the flagship now being the big-block 454-cc (7440-cc) V8 with 240 net bhp. Over 90 per cent of GMC light trucks were sold with a V8 that year, and nearly three out of four came with power steering or automatic transmission, while 40 per cent of buyers opted for one of the fancy trim packages, indicating that not everyone was buying pickups to haul hogs and logs.

Sales dropped in 1974, but even in the aftermath of the first fuel crisis over 194,000 GMC trucks found new homes that year. The company was actually weathering the storm quite well: in 1975, though sales dropped by 10 per cent, many others were faring far worse, and GMC actually emerged with an increased market share. The company was still facing stiff competition from imports in the sub-6,000-lb sector, but bigger pickups were exempt from legislation regarding catalytic convertors, so demand for them actually increased. That year, buyers of full-sized GMC pickups were still able to choose luxury options such as High Sierra, Sierra Grande and Sierra Classic, while one in four ordering a C3500 could opt for the biggest 454-ci V8.

Changes to both the Sprint and the conventional pickups were purely cosmetic for 1976, though sales recovered rapidly; to put the market dominance in traditional pickups in perspective, GMC sold just over 31,000 vans that year, 13,600 Jimmys and over 160,000 pickups. Pickups were benefiting from the post-crisis recovery more than most, making up one in four of all sales

in 1977 when, ten years before, the figure had been 15.4 per cent. Nearly 90 per cent of these were light-duty vehicles, GMC's strength in the sector helping it to gain fourth place in the production pecking order. It celebrated the fact, together with its 75th anniversary, with a series of 'Get Truckin'' advertisements, while the pickups themselves wore a new 'giant ice-cube' grille.

The unsuccessful GMC Sprint was dropped in favour of the new downsized Caballero for 1978. Nearly a foot shorter than its predecessor and nearly 600lb (272kg) lighter, it proved a better seller as well. The base engine was a 231-ci (3785-cc) V6 instead of a V8, but the Caballero offered the same load space as the old Sprint as well as more room in the cab. Coming in Pickup, Diablo Pickup or Laredo guise, it was not a mass-seller, but was an improvement on the the Sprint. Even the full-sized pickups showed a new consciousness of fuel economy and a diesel was offered for the first time. The engine in question was a 350-ci (5735-cc) V8, built by Oldsmobile, and gave 120bhp and 222lb ft. It was not to be a lasting success in General Motors sedans but was the start of a long line of GMC diesel-powered pickups.

GMC production rose by over 13 per cent in 1979 though actual sales dropped. The reason for this discrepancy was that product planners had forecasted another healthy year, failing to predict the second fuel crisis, gas at over a dollar a gallon and a generally stagnant economy. Once again, General Motors' truck division fared less

OPPOSITE and THIS PAGE
A GMC 15 in Sierra Classic trim, lowered,
but otherwise standard.

BELOW RIGHT and OPPOSITE
There was Custom Deluxe trim for this
mildly modified GMC 10.

badly than most of its competitors, but the only pickups actually securing extra sales that year were the small imports. The entire industry was in bad shape and new priorities were being formulated. That's why 1979 saw a couple of trim changes on the GMC pickups, while the company's engineers concentrated on developing electric vans.

The Recovery

The year 1979 proved to be a mere dress rehearsal for the hard times of 1980, as truck sales diminished in a floundering U.S. economy. Sales of GMC pickups fell by 39 per cent and production by more than half. Inflation meant that even the basic $^1/_2$-ton C1500 pickup, with two-wheel-drive and no options, broke the $5,000 barrier, while a C3500 with long wheelbase and Bonus Cab was over $7,400; both the full-sized pickups and the smaller Caballero had only a few trim changes in 1980. A bright spot amid the gloom, however, was that GMC pickups were chosen as the official trucks of the Indy 500 that year.

The C-series was given a new, slightly more aerodynamic front end for 1981, with new bumpers for the Wide-Side, aimed at reducing weight. In fact, the pickups lost up to 308lb (140kg) that year and there were low-drag front disc brakes as a further aid to efficiency. A new engine option was a high-compression (9.2:1) 305-ci (4998-cc) V8 with ESC, which GMC claimed would give the performance of a 350 but with better fuel economy. But some changes were not aimed at increasing mileage per gallon. There were new automatic locking hubs on 4x4s that

allowed the driver to shift into four-wheel-drive on the move at up to 20mph (32km/h), and serious off-roaders could choose a new quad-shock package for the front end.

The effects of the 1979 fuel crisis and America's own economic problems had been savage, but were relatively short-lived. Truck sales recovered slightly in 1982, and by the mid-1980s may even have surpassed those of 1977. GMC's share of this recovery owed much to the new compact S-15 pickup, launched in late 1981 as an '82 model. The company was a latecomer to this market: quite apart from the Japanese-badged imports, Ford (the Courier), Dodge (Ram 50) and Chevrolet (LUV) had all bolted their own badges to Japanese mini-pickups. There had been no GMC-badged LUV – for the reason that it would possibly affect the

credibility of the marque – but the S-15 was designed and built in-house. Well, not quite, as the 117-ci (1917-cc) four-cylinder engine and four-speed transmission were both supplied by Isuzu, though the public didn't seem to mind, and there was one optional power plant, a 135-ci (2212-cc) diesel, also from Isuzu, of 62bhp/96lb ft. Many other components were taken from the General Motors compact cars. The S-15 came in a variety of trims, including Sierra, High Sierra, Sierra Classic and the the sportier Gypsy, with load beds of 6 and 7.5ft (1.8 and 2.3m).

Meanwhile, the full-sized pickups dropped the Oldsmobile 350-ci (5735-cc) diesel in favour of a new 379-ci (6211-cc) V8 from Chevrolet. Offering 148bhp at 3,600rpm and 246lb ft at 2,200rpm, this was

destined to become a regular part of the GMC line-up. Unlike the Olds V8, supply was not restricted, while a four-speed transmission with overdrive was part of the deal.

The S-15, in the meantime, had been a great hit, with nearly 40,000 sold in its first year and slightly more than that in 1983. It effectively killed the Caballero, sales of which slowed to a trickle, though it was still offered for the time being with V6 or V8 gasoline or diesel engines. The S-15's success encouraged GMC to launch variants on the same theme. There was an S-15-based Jimmy for 1983, as well as four-wheel-drive and extended cab versions of the pickups. Buyers could also opt for more power, a 173-ci (2835-cc) V6 offering 125bhp (some sources say 110bhp) and 150lb ft. There were less exciting plans afoot for the full-sized pickups, with changes limited to a new grille, an engine-block heater and galvanization of the front panel of the box.

There was more galvanizing for 1984, this time the interior door panels, and more attention was paid to creature comforts, with power windows, power locks and stereos all joining the options list for Bonus Cab and Crew Cab full-sized pickups. Another new option was Sport Suspension, which included beefier shocks, a special front stabilizer bar and quick-ratio power steering. Once again, GMC was chosen as the official Indianapolis truck, which the company celebrated with an 'Indy Hauler' special edition of the S-15, where previous Indy Hauler specials had been based on the full-sized pickups.

By 1985 it wasn't quite business as usual for GMC, for while sales of light trucks were setting new records, those of medium- and heavy-duty trucks continued to languish: taken together, lump sales of the pickups, the vans, S-15, Jimmy and Caballero made up 88 per cent of GMC sales that year. A new 267-ci (4375-cc) V6, named Vortec, appeared in the Caballero and became the base engine of the C1500 and K1500 pickups as well as some C2500s,

replacing the straight-six. Other C2500s retained the 292-ci (4785-cc) straight-six, while power-up options included the 350-ci (5735-cc) gasoline and 379-ci (6211-cc) diesel, both V8s. The S-15 also received a new base engine in the form of a 151-ci (2474-cc) four-cylinder gasoline, with electronic fuel injection.

Many of these new engines and options were aimed at private buyers, reflecting the fact that nearly 30 per cent of American

OPPOSITE and BELOW
Two faces of the 1980s – an extended-cab
full-sized truck and the rare Caballero.

vehicle sales were classed as trucks by 1986. Just as some experts had predicted, those who had bought pickups in the 1970s as second cars, abandoning them during the fuel crisis, had returned. The American public's growing love affair with light trucks for weekend use may have been interrupted, but it was back to stay, the drawback, from Detroit's point of view, being that increasing numbers of them were now opting for

imported rather than domestic pickups.

There were no changes of note to the full-sized pickups that year, only the S-15 receiving a new instrument panel, and that was about it. This was a sure sign that something big was on the way and GMC unveiled its all-new full-sized pickup as an '88 model mid-way through 1987. This was the Sierra, smoother and more aerodynamic than the old C-series, though with many

parts carried over as well. The range was much the same as before – 1/2-ton C1500, 3/4-ton C2500 and 1-ton C3500, with 4x4 versions carrying the 'K' prefix. There were 117.5- or 131.5-in (3- or 3.3-m) wheelbases, with an extra-long 155.5-in (3.9-m) used when an extended cab was specified.

Anti-lock brakes, improved suspension and better measures for preventing corrosion all featured, while the base engine was still

OPPOSITE
A 1980s C-series full-sized pickup.
However, the compact S-15 alternative was a big hit

BELOW
GMC pickups are capable of pulling tractors, given the right preparation.

the 267-ci (4375-cc) Vortec V6, with 305- and 350-ci gasoline V8s optional, all of them with fuel injection. The meaty 379-ci V8 remained the sole diesel option and a big-cube gasoline returned in the form of the 454-ci (7440-cc) V8. Most Sierras came with flush sides, though there was the option of the Sportside, with steps behind the doors and flared wheel arches.

There were also changes to the smaller S-15, which could now be had with the 160-bhp Vortec V6. It still came in a choice of three wheelbases: 108.3-in short bed, 117.9-in long bed and 122.9-in extended cab – the Club Coupé. As for GMC's heavy-duty trucks, these continued to slide, but with the Sierra having been so well received and the S-15 still selling in healthy numbers, overall sales were up. This did not include the Caballero, only 325 of which were bought in 1988, its final year.

Big trucks may have fallen out of favour, but private buyers liked the tough image that came with them, which may be the reason why the new for 1989 dual-rear-wheel pickups were named 'Big Dooleys'. There were four of them, all with the biggest 454-ci V8s which, along with all the gasoline engines, now had throttle-body fuel injection. For the first time, dual rear wheels could also be ordered on the 1-ton 4x4 pickup, due to a new Borg-Warner transfer case with electronically-controlled synchronizers. The S-15 now had rear-wheel anti-lock brakes as standard, and had also been getting into the record books. A specially modified extended-cab S-15 was taken to the Bonneville Salt Flats in Utah

that year, where it set new class records for the flying mile and flying kilometre, beating a Porsche 928 in the process.

The First Muscle Truck

By 1990 one could have been forgiven for thinking that GMC pickups were no longer being bought for straightforward hauling. Some were, of course, but the increasing importance of the private pickup market was evident in the two new options for the Sierra C1500 that year. The Sports Handling package consisted of Bilstein shock absorbers, beefier front stabilizer bar and high-performance tyres, while if sporty looks to go with those underpinnings were required, the Sport Truck (ST) pack was offered on the 1500 with a short load bed. And as if to underline the pickup's increasingly leisure-orientated applications, GMC built a show truck based on the standard C-series. The GMC Transcend featured a remote-control retractable roof to make it Detroit's first convertible pickup, though it never made it to production.

There was big news the following year when the S-15 pickup was replaced by the new Sonoma. This was about the same size as its predecessor, with 108.3- or 117.9-in wheelbase, plus 122.9in for the extended cab Club Coupé, while styling was brought into line with the Sierra, albeit with single rectangular headlights instead of duals. The engine options were largely unchanged: 105-bhp 151-ci (2474-cc) four, 125-bhp 173-ci (2835-cc) V6, while standard on 4x4 Sonomas and optional on the others was the 160-bhp Vortec V6. By ticking the right

boxes on the order form, however, it was possible to end up with a Sonoma quite unlike any other GMC pickup.

This was the Syclone, one of Detroit's first 'muscle trucks', taking the pickup to its logical conclusion by offering a high-performance, top-spec truck. It was actually a joint venture between GMC and PAS Inc., though the Syclones were all assembled by GMC. At their heart was a turbo-intercooled version of the Vortec V6, with modified exhaust and fuel injection, not to mention 285bhp at 4,400rpm and 350lb ft at 3,600rpm. It came mated to a compulsory four-speed Hydra-Matic, the result being explosive performance: the Syclone could accelerate to 60mph (100km/h) in less than five seconds and deliver a standing-quarter of 13.4 seconds. This was supercar performance and the Syclone had the running gear to match, including anti-lock brakes, four-wheel-drive and modified suspension. It was also loaded with equipment such as air conditioning, sports seats and power everything, which partly accounted for its price tag of $25,000-plus. Only 632 Syclones were built in 1991, each one an instant collector's item. The Syclone was so much of an image-booster that GMC followed it up with a new GT package for the standard Sonoma, complete with a 195-bhp version of the Vortec V6.

Meanwhile, the Sierra had acquired General Motors' latest electronically controlled Hydra-Matic, which was claimed to boost fuel economy by 20 per cent as well as deliver smoother changes and 50 per cent more torque capacity than rival units. For

992, the Sierra had a new four-door long-wheelbased Crew Cab, though it was available only on the top C3500 and K3500 models. Over 250in (6m) long and with a wheelbase of 168.5in (4.3m), it made for a big light truck whose standard power unit was the 350-ci (5735-cc) gasoline V8. The Sierra 1500 was given the GT treatment in 1993, while the electronic Hydra-Matic was made standard, with a five-speed manual

alternative. A significant new option was the arrival of a powered-up diesel, a 395-ci (6473-cc) V8 with turbo and intercooler to produce 190bhp and 380lb ft. It also had electronic injection control, now being applied to diesels engine as well as gasolines for more precise combustion, fewer emissions and greater efficiency.

The extensive Sierra range continued largely unchanged for 1994, though the

Sonoma was revamped with more rounded aerodynamic front end and smoother styling all round. The base engine was now a 134-ci (2196-cc) four of 118bhp, the injected V6 being in 165- or 195-bhp forms. Trim levels included SL (base), SLS (sports) and SLE (luxury), plus a tall High Rider in 4x4 form only for those in need of some off-road image to go with their weekend truck.

GMC achieved yet another sales record

The Sierra, GMC's smoother new face for the 1990s.

293

OPPOSITE
2003 GMC Sonoma with crew cab.

LEFT
The 2003 Sonoma with standard cab,
upholding the GMC badge in the compact
truck market.

in 1995, when it sold not far short of 470,000 trucks. It celebrated the fact by giving the Sierra a new interior that featured a driver's air bag and optional leather upholstery, while trim levels were now similar to those of the Sonoma, covering SL, SLE and SLT forms. Sonomas also received an air bag as well as several other detail improvements. For 1996, the year that GMC

was merged with Pontiac to form a new division of General Motors, both Sierra and Sonoma had the option of a third door on the passenger side in extended cab pickups, while all V6s and V8s were now uprated using Vortec technology, which included sequential central-port injection.

Dual air bags arrived in the 1997 Sierras, while engines ranged from the

200-bhp Vortec 4300 V6 to the 290-bhp Vortec 7400 V8, which included a bi-fuel (gasoline/natural gas) option for the 350-ci unit. The Sierra was approaching the end of its life by now, justifying very few changes for 1998 apart from modified air bags and a refinement of the bi-fuel set-up.

As is often the case, an absence of change one year heralds even more the next

OPPOSITE and BELOW
The GMC Canyon, another new face for the 21st century, features a front end with split lights. The two-door truck is a 2004, the four-door a 2005.

ne around; consequently, for 1999 the
erra was completely renewed. Not only
as the styling new, continuing the rounded-
aerodynamicism that had gathered pace
the 1990s, but the new hydroformed
assis was also designed to be easily
aptable to a whole range of trucks, using
any common parts. Under the hood a new
rtec 255-bhp 4800 joined the range, a
0-bhp Vortec 5300 and a 300-bhp 6000.
e 379-ci (6211-cc) diesel V8 had long
ce been dropped but the 395-ci (6473-cc)
bo-diesel continued unchanged.

There were four-wheel anti-lock brakes
the first time, while the Hydra-Matic
tured a tow/haul mode that increased
ft speeds. The bigger Sierras of over
00-lb (3855-kg) GVW were now built in
exico, keeping the old body for the time
ing. The new cab offered more room than
old, both in regular and extended forms,
there were improvements to the load
d, which came in Wide-side and
ort-Side forms.

GMC entered the new millennium by
creasing power in the Sierra, the Vortec
0 now producing 270bhp and the 5300
5bhp, while some heavy-duty Sierras of
er 8,500-lb GVW now adopted the new
99 body, though the old shape was still
ed in the large Sierra Classic models. The
noma also received some minor changes,
w with 190bhp from its Vortec V6
member how the S-15 had began life as a
odest 82-bhp four?). This demonstrates
w far removed the mini-pickup market
s from its post-fuel-crisis economy
gins. Not all Sonomas packed 190bhp, of

course, though the base four was now a
Vortec 2200 of 120bhp, which from 2000
was compatible with alternative fuels.

There were two new Sierras for 2001 –
the heavy-duty and the C3. The former was
designed for heavy hauling, or at least
suburbanites who liked to look as if they
could, the 2500HD and 3500HD offered
with two- or four-wheel-drive and a wide
range of models including crew cabs and
chassis cabs. There were heavy-duty power
outputs to go with the HD image, including

a new 300-bhp V8 diesel. This was a joint
venture with Isuzu, General Motors' long-
term partner, and was named the Duramax
6600. Gasoline options were the existing
Vortec 6000 V8, giving the same power as
the Duramax, or a new Vortec 8100 with
340bhp. Transmission options were
similarly high-specification, with a ZF
six-speed manual or Allison five-speed
automatic transmission.

The C3 was clearly intended to be more
of a lifestyle vehicle, combining the basic

OPPOSITE
2005 Sierra 1500-series.

BELOW
2005 Sierra 3500HD.

¹/₂-ton pickup with extended cab and four-wheel-drive. With special paintwork and leather interior, it seemed worthy of its $38,305 purchase price, which was confirmed by the 325-bhp Vortec 6000, four-speed automatic transmission and four-wheel disc brakes.

Slightly more affordable was the 2001 Sonoma Crew Cab, with four doors and the Vortec V6 in 180- or 190-bhp guise, the latter if one opted for Insta-Trac four-wheel-drive. The extended cab did encroach into the fairly compact Sonoma's load bed, so a bed extender was optional. By now, a third door was standard on all Sonoma extended-cabs, while the Vortec 2200 four could be had in gasoline or gas/ethanol versions.

As GMC approached its 100th birthday, the division was in a stronger position than ever before. It is true that it had lost out where medium- and heavy-duty trucks were concerned, and had stopped building heavy-duty trucks altogether after an agreement with Volvo. But it had become a leader of the huge U.S. market in light trucks, and in pickups in particular, used either for work or leisure. Moreover, there was no shortage of new product to show in its anniversary year. The Sierra Professional could be equipped as a mobile office for those needing communications equipment on site, and was available in bi-fuel or even pure compressed natural gas forms. Meanwhile, the C3 had become the Denali, with a new feature unique among pickups – four-wheel-steering. GMC's Quadrasteer was intended not as a high-speed aid to performance but to help low-speed

manoeuvring with a trailer, as well as handling at highway speeds while towing. Other innovations such as Displacement on Demand, which allowed the V8 to switch to four-cylinder operation for light loads, or a gasoline/electric hybrid drivetrain for the Sierra, were also in the pipeline. From industrial workhorse to high-tech leisure vehicle, the GMC pickup had come a long way. GMC continued to produce Sierra and canyon models into 2013.

OPPOSITE
2007 Sierra with crew cab.

LEFT and BELOW: Still in demand the 2010 Sierra at Chicago Motor Show.

CHAPTER FIVE
INTERNATIONAL: THE CORNBINDERS

The International Harvester Company
(IHC) has always been better known for
trucks and tractors than lightweight pickups.
But make pickups it did, and from early in
the 20th century. Not only that, but the more
compact Scout of the 1960s and '70s
pioneered the recreational four-wheel-drive
market, succeeding in expanding it where
Jeep failed in the 1950s. The Scout also
inspired Ford to enter the market with the
Bronco, which in turn was the impetus for
Chevrolet to launch the Blazer in 1969. In
short, it has a fair claim to have kickstarted
the whole SUV/pickup leisure revolution.

Such things were far from IHC's mind
when it began building its first commercial
vehicles in the early 20th century. The
company was a straightforward, no-nonsense
sort of concern, making working tools for
working men, its origins lying with Cyrus
McCormick and the reaper he invented in
1845. McCormick the company grew by
acquisition, finally becoming the giant that
was International Harvester in 1902, after
merging with the Deering Harvester
Company plus three smaller concerns.
International Harvester became a one-stop

hop for farmers, offering everything from wagons to ploughs to new-fangled tractors.

Given this wide range of equipment, it wasn't surprising that International was soon building a gasoline vehicle for the road, the International Harvester auto buggies being equipped to carry either goods or people. With their big, artillery-style wheels and mid-mounted two-cylinder engine, the auto buggies looked like the pioneers they were, and from 1907–10 sold well, rivalling even the Ford Model T in their reliability, simple layout and high ground clearance, designed to cope with the uneven roads of the day.

Bodies came in a variety of forms, including the Panel Express van and the Flareboard Express 1/2-ton pickup, named for its angled upper side panels. International Harvester also built a conventional passenger car with smaller wheels from 1910, but this was not a success and was quietly dropped after only three years. This appeared to confirm the company's role as a builder of working vehicles, for apart from the post-war Travelall, it built no other passenger carrier and no private sedans at all.

Instead, it launched a new line of trucks for 1915. Unlike the commercial auto buggies, which were adaptations of an existing design, the new International trucks were designed specifically for heavy-duty haulage, with modern front-mounted water-cooled engines. The transmission was also up to date, with sliding gearbox, shaftdrive and a gear differential. A distinctive feature was the rear-mounted

radiator, sited behind the power unit but in front of the driver, which was said to protect it from irate wagon drivers, who had a habit of backing into these new-fangled gas trucks and piercing the radiator! It also allowed a sloping hood, like the contemporary Mack and European Renault, which gave better visibility. There was a whole range of these trucks from 3/4 to 3 1/2

tons, which were produced up to 1920, the lighter models all using International Harvester's own 20-hp engine.

The range was renewed for 1921, a front-mounted radiator giving it a far more conventional appearance. Trucks, like cars, were developing fast, and customers in the early 1920s demanded conveniences such as electric starting and lighting, not to mention

OPPOSITE and LEFT
The 1930s was an era of streamlined vehicles, and International trucks were no exception.

more speed. International Harvester's ³/₄-ton Model S had all of this, as well as a potential 30mph (48km/h), due to its relatively light weight, higher gearing and a Lycoming four-cylinder engine that produced 35hp at 2100rpm. Pneumatic tyres were standard, as was a battery, electric horn and even a power tyre pump. Many of these ³/₄-tonners were painted bright red by the factory, earning them the nickname 'Red Babies'. They were used by factory representatives as they toured the country, and were also offered at a discount to dealers as a distinctive delivery truck. Over 33,000 Model S Internationals were built in five years. There was also a Model 21 1-ton version, available as the Six-Speed Special from 1928, with a two-speed rear axle in addition to the standard three-

speed transmission. The line-up was renewed as the ³/₄-ton AW-series in 1930, now with 173-ci (2835-cc) L-head four-cylinder engine offering 30bhp. This power unit was bought in from Waukesha, and for 1931 was supplemented by another engine from the same maker of 186ci (3048cc) and 39bhp, which International Harvester fitted to the A1-series, while the 30-bhp AW carried on.

These trucks sold so well that by 1930 International was the third biggest truck-maker in the country behind Ford and Chevrolet. But it still didn't have a ¹/₂-ton model to cover the bottom end of the market, and this arrived in 1933, just as the Depression was at its lowest point. If the truth be told, it wasn't actually an

International at all, at least not in its entirety. Willys-Overland had been badly affected by the Depression, but it also had a new ¹/₂-ton truck which it couldn't afford to produce. International Harvester, meanwhile, desperately needed a ¹/₂-tonner, which it didn't have, nor anywhere to build it. The solution was obvious, and from 1933 Willys-Overland began building little trucks with International badges for sale through International Harvester dealers.

This was the D-1, based on the same 113-in (2.9-m) wheelbase as the Willys original but with a slightly larger L-head six-cylinder engine of 213ci (3490cc). This produced an impressive 70bhp at 3,400rpm, which, to put it in perspective, was nearly twice that offered by International Harvester's existing four-cylinder Series A-1 and ³/₄- and 1-ton M-2, both of 39bhp. The D-1 was well-priced, starting at $360 for the bare chassis, while the pickup was next in line at $475. This meant wafer-thin profit margins, but did it matter? What was important was that it gave International Harvester a full line-up and kept the Willys production lines running, though the company's financial problems meant that D-1s had to be built in batches rather than in a continuous stream. So despite the Depression, International sold 17,000 D-1s in the first year, which was more than its entire in-house truck production.

The D-1 was joined by International Harvester's own in-house ¹/₂-ton truck the following year. This C-1 used the same 213-ci six as the D-1, but was tweaked to produce 78bhp at 3600rpm. It also shared

the D-1's 113-in wheelbase, coming with a long-wheelbased 125-in (3.2-m) option, which added a modest $25 to the price of the basic chassis. Choosing C-1 over D-1 also brought a handsome V-type radiator and more streamlined front end, so it also cost more ($70 for the pickup), but buyers approved and sales expanded. So much so that the Willys-built D-1 was dropped the following year and the C-range expanded to include the four-cylinder ³/4- and 1-ton trucks. In 1936, it was joined by the 133-ci (2179-cc) four-cylinder C-5, producing 33bhp but still rated as a ¹/2-ton, with 113- or 125-in chassis.

The late 1930s saw just about every American consumer durable, from armchairs to coffee cups, assume the Art Deco streamlined look, and light trucks were no exception, featuring split windshields, full fenders and torpedo headlights. But the rakish Internationals that were unveiled in 1937 were not only cosmetically advanced. The bodies of the new D-series were all-steel for the first time and the engines featured full-pressure lubrication. Otherwise, the power units were the 133-ci four and 213-ci six as used by the C-series, which continued in ¹/2-ton form that year, though only with the shorter wheelbase.

International built more than 100,000 trucks in 1937, enough to secure nearly one-third of the American truck market and increase its lead over Dodge, though Ford and Chevrolet, of course, still led the field. Production plummeted the following year, to a little over 50,000, while share of the commercial vehicle cake fell to a little over

OPPOSITE
An International D-series from 1938, with all-steel bodywork.

LEFT
IHC's new K-series pickups came in six-cylinder form only for 1940.

RIGHT and OPPOSITE
Awaiting restoration or left to gradual
decay? This is a 1949 International KB-1.

10 per cent. However, market conditions were such that International Harvester was able to maintain its third place in the industry.

International had concentrated since the mid-1930s on chassis-cabs, leaving specialists, or even the customer, to fit their own bodywork. This changed in 1939, when there was a determination to sell factory-built bodies, marketed as offering 'Beauty Plus Dependability'. These included panel vans and even a station wagon, while pickups were represented by the D-5 and D-2 Stakeside, with vertical wooden stakes around the load bed. The new International Harvester trucks looked good, with all-steel pickups offered alongside the Stakesides, but out in the marketplace, International Harvester was beginning to slip, losing its traditional third place to Dodge in 1940 only to find GMC snapping at its heels.

International responded with an all-new range –the K-series – later in 1940. The K-truck wasn't quite all-new. It still came in the familiar 113- or 125-in wheelbase, and while the little 133-ci four-cylinder engine was dropped, the standard power unit for the 1/2-ton K-1 was the ageing 213-ci six, still in 78-bhp form though now renamed the 'Green Diamond'. There was a 3/4-ton K-2 and 1-ton K-3 as well, all using this motor in place of the big four. However, a feature of the K-series that was new was its full-width styling, with flush headlights blended into the enveloping fenders. There were only minor changes for 1941, though by now International Harvester had slipped to seventh place and by 1942 its market share had fallen to less than 5 per cent. Of course, by now the

company was concentrating on war work, and would contribute thousands of half-tracks and heavy-duty trucks to the Allied effort. This was all very well, but if International Harvester was to regain that coveted third place after the Second World War it would need a new light truck.

A Late Start

If International Harvester's dealers had been expecting a new truck for 1946, they were disappointed, and when production resumed in November 1945, having been suspended the previous year due to the war effort, it was of the 1942-specification trucks with very few changes. Even these were reserved for civilians with essential occupations, farmers and doctors standing a good chance of taking delivery in 1946. The line-up was much the same: the 1/2-ton K-1 was also available in heavy-duty K-1H form (rated at 3/4-ton), and there was the 3/4-ton K-2 and 1-ton K-3. Power still came from the faithful 213-ci six, by now uprated to 82bhp at 3,400rpm plus 160lb ft at 1,200rpm, driving through a three-speed transmission.

There had been a scarcity of vehicles in the early post-war years, which enabled International Harvester to sell over 78,000 trucks, enough to regain fourth position. It maintained this through 1948, the K-series being in mildly updated KB form. International claimed that 97 improvements had been made, but buyers would have been at pains to spot them, though the wider front grille was something of a clue.

Not until January 1950 did International Harvester finally produce the new light truck

that post-war buyers demanded. In fact, it was the last U.S. manufacturer to have come up with such a truck, which may explain why its market share had slipped to less than 10 per cent the previous year. Late though it was, the L-series was undeniably modern. Few could miss the full-width styling, with one-piece windshield and two-piece rear window. Under the hood was an all-new overhead-valve straight-six, which meant that the old side-valve six, its origins in the Willys-built D-1 of 1933, could finally be pensioned off. The new unit was slightly larger at 220ci (3605cc), and considerably more powerful at 101bhp: it was named Silver Diamond. It still drove through a three-speed manual transmission though this now came with the option of floor- or column-shift. Inside the cab, a whole range of new options were specified, including a clock, cigar lighter and seat covers. One could order the basic, affordable L-110 at only $230 for the chassis-cab, plus $93 for the smallest pickup body. It was no surprise, therefore, that for 1950, International Harvester truck production broke the 100,000 barrier once again, and exceeded 150,000 the following year.

The L became R in 1953, with revised styling but the same Silver Diamond six-cylinder power unit. There was a slight power boost to 104bhp for 1954, with 170lb ft, but there were other more significant changes at this time. Four-wheel-drive was a new option, as was an LPG conversion and a three-speed automatic transmission, while tubeless tyres came as standard. Meanwhile, the Travelall station wagon was launched to rival Chevrolet's long-running Suburban.

International Harvester revisited its heritage in 1956, replacing the R-series with the S (remember the S-series Red Babies of the 1920s?), though maybe it was simply that S follows R in the alphabet. Either way, the International Harvester Model S came in the usual choice of 1/2-, 3/4- or the full 1-ton, all immediately recognizable by their squared-off front ends, the headlights having been moved to the top of the fender and with a wider, flatter hood. The bigger windshield was a practical touch, allowing improved visibility, and there were two large parking lights. The pickup could be had with high sides, and other extras included an AM radio, chrome fenders, electric wipers and whitewall tyres.

As a light-duty 1/2-ton truck, the S-series came as a 115-in-wheelbased S-110 or 127-in S-112, but if the longer wheelbase was specified, then a bigger version of the Silver Diamond was part of the package. The bore remained at 3.56in (90.4mm), but the stroke was lengthened to 4.018in (102mm) for a total capacity of 240ci (3933cc), delivering 141bhp at 3800rpm and a meaty 224lb ft at 2000rpm. This four-main-bearing engine was named the Black Diamond, and in basic layout was similar to the Silver original, with a cast-iron block, overhead valves and solid lifters. With sales up by over 5 per cent in 1956 to well over 100,000, International Harvester retained its third place in the industry. But it had learned a valuable lesson: constant improvement was the only way to maintain its position.

This was evident in 1957, when International Harvester's light trucks received several significant upgrades. That year, incidentally, marked the company's 50th anniversary in truck manufacture; in fact, in the half-century since the beginning, 2.6 million trucks of all sizes had rolled off the production lines. According to International, nearly half of these (1.1 million) were still in service in 1957 which, if true, is an astonishing figure for vehicles that had such tough, hard-working lives.

So what changes were made to celebrate this Golden Anniversary? The S-series became the Model A, with all-new styling including a wider cab, wraparound windshield and a flatter hood and roof, indicating that International Harvester trucks were now abandoning the rounded lines that had featured in the 1930s. Underneath, there was a choice of three new variations on the Diamond six, all of which bore the Black Diamond label. The base 220 Black Diamond was really the familiar 220-ci (3605-cc) unit, albeit retuned to produce 113bhp at 3800rpm with 194lb ft at 1600rpm. The 240 Black Diamond was essentially the previous year's 240-ci six, essentially unchanged and with the same 141bhp. But the 264 Black Diamond was new, having been bored and stroked to give 264ci (4326cc), as the name suggests, which provided 154bhp at 3800rpm and 248lb ft at 2400rpm.

All three of these engines were available across the Model A range, from the A-100 short-wheelbased half-ton to the AM-130 long-wheelbased 1-ton. In fact, the range had grown in numbers and complexity, with a choice of ten different wheelbases and many body styles, from a bare chassis-cab to the Metro bus line, ready to transport passengers. All in all there were 58 separate models, which was not counting all the additional options, of which there were plenty. Apart from the bigger Black Diamond power units, most of these were cosmetic or convenience items such as cigar lighters or lockable glove boxes.

All the Model As had 12-volt electrics, but there were two other new features highly significant in the history of the pickup – flush rear panels and a crew cab. Until then, pickup side panels left the rear fenders exposed, but moving the panels out to cover the fenders liberated some of the load bed and looked sleeker into the bargain. But specify the Custom option on the A-100 1/2-ton pickup (114-in wheelbase), and this is what one got. Its appearance was far better, and offered the same load-bed area as the bigger 'Bonus Load' models, with their 7ft long beds. Nor was it expensive to produce, the panels having been taken directly from the two-door Travelall. What was new was the tailgate, which had spring-loaded cables to hold it in the lowered position, and is thought to be the first that could be operated with one hand. So successful was the flush-sided Custom that all International Harvester pickups were soon built this way.

An innovation for 1957 was the crew cab. 'Styled for family travel, built for truck work! The Travelette has an extra curbside door for passenger convenience and full-sized pickup loadspace,' went the publicity. Whether it was named the Travelette, aimed at families, or the Travel Crew, to appeal to men in hard hats, the new International Harvester crew cab could seat six, and as the fulsome copy suggests, had three doors – one on the driver's side, two on the passengers'. It came in 1/2-, 3/4- or 1-ton forms, and was a milestone in the development of pickups.

In spite of all the innovations, International Harvester sales broke no records in 1958, which was the first full calendar year, the truck having been launched in mid 1957, and a little under 90,000 trucks were sold. In fact, it was the slowest for nearly 20 years.

Relief was at hand, however, for sales recovered dramatically to over 108,000 the following year. Here again there were several changes, though not as many innovations. The Model A range became the B, the most obvious change being the addition of a front end with twin headlamps; with large chrome bumper and mesh grille, the International Harvester pickups were altogether more imposing. The Black Diamond engine range was unchanged, while the Custom pickup became an option instead of a model in its own right; the higher-capacity Bonus Load was another new option. More important was the fact that a V8 became available for the first time on an International Harvester light truck. The U.S. pickup industry was going through the same sort of power race as sedans and proto-muscle cars; in the case of the Model B, this brought a 266-ci (4359-cc) power unit, though it offered only marginally more power than the 264 Black Diamond (155bhp) and significantly less

RIGHT and OPPOSITE
This GMC pickup hasn't moved for some
time, but things look more hopeful for the
example opposite.

torque (227lb ft). But the V8, launched as an option in March, was so popular eight months later that it became standard right across the range. The Black Diamond six could be ordered during 1960, but only as a deleted option. Otherwise, the line-up of 1/2-, 3/4-, and 1-ton Model Bs carried on unchanged. But for International Harvester, 1960 was the calm before the storm, for '61 would see the launch of the most significant light truck it ever produced – the Scout.

The Scout Era

Until 1961, International had been a maker of trucks, tractors and farm machinery. Even the Travelall station wagon, the nearest thing to a private car, was aimed more at hotels and taxi companies than families. So the Scout, designed as a genuine dual-purpose vehicle that could be used for hunting trips or desert expeditions as well as everyday work, was a real departure. In fact, the Scout's significance was even greater than

that, for many believe the little 4x4 actually helped to kickstart the four-wheel-drive leisure market, preceding the Ford Bronco by four years and the Chevrolet Blazer by eight: it is true that, later on, Ford and Chevrolet were responsible for the SUV/pickup leisure revolution, but part of their original inspiration must surely be the International Scout.

But what of the Jeep? Surely it was the true pioneer of four-wheel-drive? It was, but

the Jeep was predominantly seen as a working tool throughout the 1950s. Kaiser-Jeep had made some half-hearted attempts at ritzier passenger derivatives, but all were based on the usual hard-riding commercial chassis. A few dedicated off-road enthusiasts – hunters and the like – did buy Jeeps to use at weekends, but they were few and far between. Meanwhile, an increasingly mobile American population had begun to take a renewed interest in the great outdoors. Now they wished to head for the hills at weekends, go camping and hiking in the national parks, and generally escape from city life.

International recognized this need, realizing that a more modern version of the Jeep, with a little more space and power, would sell as a genuine dual-purpose vehicle. It would need to be quieter and easier to drive on-road, and have genuine highway performance while still being tough and chunky enough to be useful off-road.

In September 1959, the team responsible for developing the Scout was given the go-ahead to turn these ideas into reality. At first, it was intended that the Scout should be a limited-production car, with only 50 a day rolling off the lines; for this reason it would be made of fibreglass to save on the cost of tooling steel panels. Ironically, this was found to be more expensive, so a brick-like steel body was substituted, composed mainly of flat panels with a few rounded edges. This was just as well, for it enabled International Harvester to respond more quickly to the ensuing high demand for the Scout.

The next problem was the engine. International Harvester's existing range of sixes and V8s were too big and heavy for the Scout, which needed a torquey, economical four to make it a credible challenger to the Jeep. Not having one of its own, the company considered practically every existing four-cylinder automotive engine available, though none was considered good enough. International Harvester decided to build its own by the simple expedient of chopping the existing V-304 V8 in half and using the right-hand bank as a ready-made 152-ci (2491-cc) four. The advantage in this was that it was using proven components from a well-established power unit, while sharing parts would help to keep costs down. Pontiac followed the same V8-into-four route when it came to its compact Tempest.

International Harvester had no spare capacity to build the Scout at any of its existing factories, so it bought an ex-U.S. Rubber Company plant at Fort Wayne, Indiana, and in November 1960, less than two years after the design process had begun, the first production Scout was built. Given the way it would change the four-wheel-drive market, the car itself wasn't so advanced, having been based on a simple ladder-type chassis with a three-speed manual transmission. It had a 100-in (2.5-m) wheelbase, shorter than any other International Harvester pickup, with a load bed measuring 5ft (1.5m). Four-wheel-drive was extra, as was a dual-range transfer box to double the transmission up to six forward speeds. The Comanche four-cylinder engine offered 93bhp at 4400rpm and 135lb ft at 2400, significantly more than the four-cylinder Jeep's 70bhp/114lb ft.

International Harvester was determined the Scout should be reliable in service, so five prototypes were driven for a total of 200,000 miles (321860km) without problem. When it was finally launched in January 1961, the baby four-wheel-drive was seen as something entirely new. According to the publicity, 'we're selling a vehicle that almost everyone can use', and the press seemed to agree. As standard, the Scout came with a steel cab and pickup bed. However, the cab and doors could be removed by means of 21 capstan screws and four pins; in fact, *Road Test*

magazine did the job in 10 minutes. An optional full-length hardtop was also offered as a quick bolt-on/bolt-off, the inner rear fenders having been extended to offer rudimentary rear seats. Consequently, International Harvester could justifiably claim that a single Scout could be adapted to do the job of four very different vehicles: a Chevrolet Corvair sedan, Ford Ranchero pickup, VW Transporter van and, of course, a Jeep.

This may have been an exaggeration, but if the first press reports are to be believed, the Scout really was adept both on-road and off. *Car Life* tested a two-wheel-drive pickup in June 1961 and was surprised to find the Scout not merely a rehash of the old Second World War Jeep. It could cruise happily on the freeway at a true 65mph (105km/h), while the Comanche four delivered 'great gobs of torque at ridiculously low rpm' and returned 22.5mpg. This two-wheel-drive Scout even acquitted itself well off-road. However, *Car Life* did not like the heavy gearbox and steering ('What Charles Atlas says he'll do for you in just 15 minutes a day is nothing compared to what a little gearbox drill in a Scout will do for your right deltoid.') and the Scout leaked in the rain. It forgave this, recommending the Scout as an economical, adaptable second car for the average family; in so doing, it identified the pickup's appeal, in that the rugged styling had its advantages during the urban commute: 'As sturdy looking as it is, nobody, but nobody, cuts you off in this one. For some reason, it packs more "bluffmanship" in traffic than cars twice its weight.'

A few months later, Tom McCahill of *Car Life* tested a four-wheel-drive Scout with a Powr-Lok rear axle. He was well qualified to do so, being a self-confessed 'four-wheel-drive nut'. It had been a dry few weeks in Florida, too dry for mud to be in evidence, so 'Uncle Tom' headed down to a beach near Daytona to find soft sand. The Scout happily churned through it at 25–30mph, but when he slowed to walking pace, he was stuck. The tide was on the way in, so a Land Rover was brought in to tow the Scout back to terra firma. This also became stuck. Both were winched out by a tow truck minutes before the tide came in. Next day, Tom took the Scout dune-bashing, along with his own Jeep, and found it had the edge when hill-climbing, though it couldn't match the Scout when it came to carrying loads.

In fact, despite its advantage of power and torque, at least on paper, the little International truck didn't quite have the guts of the Jeep. On road, and in four-wheel-drive, it was also significantly slower than the 4x2 version, taking 22 seconds to reach 60mph and topping out at 71mph (114km/h) where the two-wheel-drive could manage a genuine 80.

International recognized this, though it was five years before it offered a turbocharged version of the Comanche, boosting power from 93 to 111bhp. The turbo came in at 2000rpm, so for low-speed off-road work it wouldn't make much difference, but its major advantage was in maintaining power at high altitudes; International claimed that the blown Scout made the same power at 9,000ft (2745m) as the standard car did at sea level.

However, this perceived power deficit did not affect Scout sales, at least not in the early days. It was soon clear that Fort Wayne's 50 cars a day wouldn't be enough to keep up with demand, and production was doubled as a result. Even that wasn't enough, however, and this eventually increased to 133. By the end of the year, over 25,000 had been built and it was clear that International had a hit on its hands. So successful was the Scout that it became International's best-selling line, even though it had originally been envisaged as a limited-production sideline. Most of these early Scouts were ordered with four-wheel-drive and the $128 full-length hardtop, with private buyers in the majority. However, fleets did begin to buy Scouts later – the U.S. postal services ordering 6,745 Scout 800s in 1967.

Given this success, International Harvester made no major changes to the Scout in its first few years, concentrating instead on meeting demand. With production up to 35,000 a year, this seemed sensible, though competition was on the way, the very success of the Scout having encouraged Ford to begin work on its own dual-purpose 4x4, the Bronco. And as ever in Detroit, wherever Ford went, Chevrolet would not be far behind. So not until 1965, when the Bronco was launched, was there any sign of change. That year, the Scout Series 80 became the 800, while the windshield was now fixed rather than fold-down, and measures had been taken to make it

leakproof. There was more soundproofing to go with the full-length Traveltop and some more interior fittings, but that was about all.

It was in 1966 that International Harvester began to do some serious work to keep the Scout up to date, the first priority being more power. The year before, Jeep had launched a 155-bhp V6, and it was known that Ford was working on a Bronco V8. Early road tests had noted that the Scout's engine bay was V8-sized, though it had not yet been filled. Instead, International offered the turbocharged option mentioned earlier, as well as a bored and stroked version of the unblown engine. At 196ci (3212cc), this was significantly larger, though its chief advantage was torque rather than power: according to International Harvester's own figures, power was the same as the 152 turbo but with 180lb ft peaking at a nice, low 2000rpm.

To accommodate an increasingly leisure-oriented market, the 1966 Scout Sportop was given a sporty look, its fibreglass or vinyl top giving it a sedan-like appearance. Inside, there were bucket seats at the front, a proper rear seat, extra trim over the transmission console and rear fenders, while a new instrument panel made the interior seem less sparse. Wind-up windows were also part of the package. *Motor Trend* tested a Sportop and was impressed, especially with its on-highway behaviour. It couldn't match a Jeep V6 on the rough stuff, but on tarmac it was softer, more comfortable and felt more secure.

But it still didn't have straight-line performance, which International tried to

remedy the following year by offering an optional V8. This made the Scout the first ¼-ton pickup available with a V8, which on paper looked good, with 155bhp from the well-proven 266-ci (4359-cc) power unit. In theory, this should have produced Jeep-rivalling performance with a less scary ride. In practice, even this V8 Scout didn't have the off-road guts of its rivals. *Car and Driver* tested one against a Bronco, Land Rover, Toyota Land Cruiser and the inevitable Jeep. None of them had a V8 and according to specification the Scout could pack more power than any of them, apart from the V6 Jeep. In practice, it proved to be sadly lacking, and even the heavier four-cylinder Land Rover could climb hills that defeated the Scout V8.

Over the next few years, International Harvester did its best to keep the Scout abreast of the times. The sad fact, however, was that this pioneer of recreational four-wheel-driving was being left behind by a new generation. In the meantime, two new engine options for 1969 were International's 232-ci (3802-cc) straight-six of 145bhp, while the V8 was upgraded to 304ci (4982-cc) and 180bhp/262lb ft. A limited-edition Scout Aristocrat featured two-tone blue-and-silver paintwork, a chrome roof-rack and all-blue interior. If one failed to catch one of the 2,500 Aristocrats produced, then the standard Scout could be ordered in a choice of metallic colours and, as ever, there was a host of factory- and dealer-fitted options from which to choose. As International's publicity of the time put it, the Scout could be tailored, '…from a

tripped-down workhorse to a jazzy creampuff with color-keyed interiors, buck seats, padding all over and even a stereo tape deck.'

But while International was wowing the public with such largesse, what of its standard line of workaday pickups. Though overshadowed by the excitement generated by the Scout and its rivals, they carried on selling well. After all was said and done, the Scout was only a 1/4-ton mini-truck, and there were plenty of buyers needing rather more capacity than that. The 1/2-, 3/4- and -ton pickups became the Model C for 1961, mechanically similar to the previous Model B but with lower, wider styling emphasized by the four headlights, which were mounted horizontally rather than vertically. The 266-ci (4359-cc) V8 was still standard across the range, which now ran from the 1/2-ton C-100, with a gross vehicle weight of 4,200lb (1905kg) to the 1-ton C-132 of 8,800-lb (3992-kg) GVW. Wheelbases stretched from 115 to 140in (3.6m), putting the 100-in (2.5-m) Scout into perspective.

More changes came in 1963, when the C-100 became C-1000 and so on, right through the range, distinguished by its single headlights and new grille. In a reversal of what had gone before, the 220- and 240-ci straight-sixes were now standard, with the 266-ci 155-bhp V8 offered at extra cost. Having made a gesture to the more economical thinking of the times (Detroit was in the midst of a compact-car boom), International Harvester had its best year yet. In fact, what with that and the runaway success of the Scout, compacts seemed to have taken a hold at International. For 1964 it launched the smaller C-900 pickup, combining a 107-in (2.7-m) wheelbase with the Scout's Comanche four-cylinder power unit. In effect, this was the first downsized pickup, still with a 1/2-ton payload but costing nearly $200 less than the full-sized 1/2-ton C-1000.

At the time, International pickups came in Fenderside or Bonus Load flush-sided form, though the D-900 was offered with Bonus Load only from 1965. Meanwhile, the big C-series trucks also adopted the D suffix for 1965, along with a new grille, while International's 304-ci (4982-cc) V8 became an option on certain models. For 1967, the compact pickup spawned the new 908B, with longer 115-in wheelbase and the 266-ci V8 as standard. Both Fenderside and Bonus Load models were available with the same 6ft 8-in (2-m) load bed. Its bigger brothers became the B-series that year, with yet another new grille, and there were few changes the following year.

The conventional pickups finally had a complete facelift for 1969, having been given the slab-sided styling similar to the Scout. It looked well on the workaday pickups, perhaps better than on the Scout, which was in need of more cosmetic changes to accomodate the leisure market. Once again, there were three basic models: ¹/2-ton 1000D (115–134-in wheelbase), ³/4-ton 1200D (115–164-in wheelbase) and 1-ton 1300D (131–156-in wheelbase). By now there were more engine options, the 1000D adopting International's own 232-ci straight-six and the familiar 240-ci (3933-cc) six, now in the heavier-duty 1100D. The bigger-payload 1200 and 1300 now had the 266-ci V8, standard once again, with International's 304-ci V8 an option on the the big six BG-265. An LPG version of the 304 was listed for 1971, along with International's own 345-ci (5653-cc) V8, mustering not far short of 200bhp, not to mention 304lb ft.

A new dashboard and grille characterized the pickups updated as the 10-series the next year (1010, 1110 and so on). However, there were very few changes for 1973, though all engines were now tuned to run on low-lead fuel. These full-sized International pickups were by now actually nearing the end of their lives while, behind the scenes, the company was slipping badly, trailing Chevrolet, Ford, Dodge and GMC in truck sales. Nineteen-seventy-five proved to be the final year, with the renamed ¹/2-ton 150 and ³/4-ton 200 flying the flag though the 1-ton had already gone.

This left the Scout as International's only light truck. It had been facelifted and relaunched in 1971, as the Scout II, partly as a result of the new sales campaign masterminded by ex-Chrysler executive Keith Mazurek, convinced the Scout could do better in the leisure market. Over $1 million was spent on prime-time TV and

other publicity, in an attempt to persuade buyers that a Scout II was as trendy as a Bronco, Jeep or Blazer.

At first glance, the Scout II, launched in 1971, seemed not much different from the original. Certainly, the hardtop had a rakish new rear-window line, but otherwise, little seemed to have changed apart from slightly more rounded lines. In fact, the Scout II had been completely re-engineered. Three inches lower and nearly a foot longer, it was an attempt to offer more space on the same 100-in wheelbase. The doors were wider and the floor was lowered to ease entry/exit – always a problem in high-riding off-roaders, especially for women in short skirts.

To satisfy drivers and to give it a fighting chance of keeping up with the Blazers, a 345-ci (5653-cc) V8 was listed, which had little more power than the more familiar 304 but a lot more torque (209lb ft at 2200rpm). At least one magazine writer remarked that this was a power unit from a truck-maker, and bode well for off-road performance. Otherwise, the 196-ci (3212-cc) four, 232-ci (3802-cc) six and 304-ci (4982-cc) V8 were still available. Inside, the Scout II had a whole range of luxury equipment, some of it optional, otherwise standard, including air conditioning, pile carpet and automatic transmission. It had come a long way from its beginnings as the spartan, dual-purpose little truck of ten years earlier, but that was the way things were going in 1971. The Scout now seemed more luxurious than a Bronco, as *PV4* magazine remarked when it tested them back to back in 1975. When one

compared the base four-cylinder Scout with the V8 Bronco, it found the International to be slower, but also quieter and more comfortable while using less low-lead gas. However, the Bronco was thought to be better off-road.

International scored a first for 1976, when it offered the first diesel engine to appear in a U.S.-built 4x4. The range was rejigged that year, as with the full-sized pickups gone, something was needed to replace them. So International extended the Scout's wheelbase to 118in (3m) to create the Traveler SUV and Terra pickup. The old short-wheelbased Scout continued only as a Traveler, the stubby little pickup having been dropped. As for the Terra, it offered something that was almost unique in the U.S. market, not only bigger than the smallest pickups but also more compact than the full-sized trucks. Despite which, it had a 6-ft load bed and could even carry 11cu ft in the cab behind the seats, which for taller drivers tended to restrict seat travel and legroom.

There was a Nissan six-cylinder diesel option to go with the new longer pickup body. International Harvester did not have a suitable small diesel of its own, and considered the Japanese-made six to be the pick of the bunch. Measuring 198ci (3245cc), it delivered 92bhp at 4000rpm and 138lb ft at half that speed, International claiming that economy was 50–60 per cent better than the gasoline equivalent. As well as the diesel, the Terra could also be had with the same engine/transmission combinations as any other Scout. *PV4*

magazine tested the diesel in May 1976 and found it could cruise at 70–75mph (113–121km/h) along with big rigs – this was the 'Convoy' era, of course – and averaged nearly 17mpg around 11 for a Terra V8. Off-road, PV4 considered the diesel Scout a rock crawler second to none. It was less impressed, however, when sub-zero temperatures turned the fuel to a waxy consistency during a transcontinental trip.

An interesting variation on the Scout Terra was the Suntanner, which PV4 tested in the summer of 1977. It was simply the standard Terra with the cab removed and a soft top in its place, with a tonneau cover over the load bed. With a 304 V8 under the hood, this was at the leisure end of the 4x4 pickup market for sure, as opposed to the workaday diesel. However, five days in the California desert with the Suntanner turned into a love/hate relationship for the journalists from PV4. They loved top-down off-roading but hated the awkward, ill-fitting soft top, the noise, and the fact that the Terra's longer wheelbase compromised off-road manoeuvrability. But the Suntanner could sprint to 60mph (100km/h) in 13.7 seconds, when the 304 V8 was fitted, which partly compensated for its on-road thirst of 12.7mpg and around 8.2mpg off-road.

The Scout SSII, launched the same year as this test, was based on the old short-wheelbased Scout pickup, though aimed primarily at leisure off-roading. On the outside, there were stripes, wide wheels and a soft top, while inside was a spartan interior with a metal floor, that could be hosed down, and a single driver's bucket seat. The

economical diesel was not an option, and SSII buyers were obliged to choose between the ageing 196 four or the two V8s. With the biggest 345 V8 bolted in, the SSII could run to 60mph in 11.7 seconds on its 3.73:1 rear axle.

By 1979, the Scout was still getting good reviews but was looking undeniably old, viewed as slab-sided and boxy and a little plain next to younger, leisure-oriented 4x4s. Over 25,000 of them sold the previous year, which may have been a good average for the early 1960s, but in America's now vast 4x4 market made the Scout one of the smaller players. Incidentally, less than 10 per cent of 1978 Scouts were ordered with the 196-ci four-cylinder engine, demonstrating how much market priorities had changed. People who bought 4x4 pickups for work were increasingly choosing diesel, but nearly everyone else went for gas-guzzling V8s, which were more fun and to hell with the cost. For 1980, there were a few changes, notably the dropping of the two-wheel-drive Scout and the addition of a turbocharger to the Nissan diesel, which now offered 101bhp at 3800rpm and 175lb ft at 2200rpm. Power steering became standard, and there were taller rear axle ratios.

The 1980 Scouts and Terras looked good in their own no-nonsense way but, behind the scenes, International Harvester was in trouble. Consequently, it decided to revert to its core business of heavy trucks, attempting to sell off the entire Scout line-up as a going concern. When that came to nothing, Scout production ceased in October 1980, bringing an end to International's long career in pickups.

Or so it seemed, until 2003, when International launched what it claimed to be the biggest pickup truck in the world. 'The International CXT brings new meaning to "everything is big in Texas",' said Bob Day, Mayor of Garland, Texas, where the giant pickup was built. The CXT was quite simply a 20-ton heavy-duty hauler disguised as a civilian pickup. Perhaps the only surprise, given the success of the ex-military Hummer, was that no one had done it before.

It could haul three times as much as conventional 'full-sized', or perhaps one should say 'under-sized', pickups, had air brakes and four-wheel-drive, and was built on the same platform as snowploughs and dump trucks. But instead of the normal one- or two-man cab, there was a full crew cab to seat five in spacious comfort. Options included a leather interior, flat-screen TV and reclining captain's chair.

International's official line was that the CXT was something that would allow businesses to promote themselves, but it was clearly also a giant Tonka toy for rich adults, who had trouble escaping their inner child. 'If you brought this truck to the playground,' remarked Rob Swim, director of the company's marketing strategy, 'you'd be king of the dirt pile.' Power came from an authentic, heavy-duty DT 466 turbo-diesel delivering 220bhp and 540lb ft, coupled to an Allison 2000-series automatic transmission. And if anyone argued that a Dodge Ram 3500 had a lot more power and torque, there was one thing they could not dispute – the International CXT was the biggest pickup truck on the block.

OPPOSITE
The Scout (including this rare right-hand-drive version) looks bare and spartan by today's standards, but appealed to leisure users in the early 1960s.

CHAPTER SIX
JEEP: SON OF A HERO

RIGHT and OPPOSITE
How it all began: later Jeep pickups owed much to the original CJ-series. This is a 1947 CJ2A.

Compared with the long-lived, highly-successful and frankly iconic CJ-series – the famous 'Jeep' that everyone knows – the later pickup range has tended to be overshadowed by its more illustrious namesake. Yet Jeep pickups were produced from 1947 to 1992 and were an important part of the company's line-up for 45 years.

Immediately after the Second World War, Willys-Overland found itself in a unique position. It had produced its final wartime Jeep on 20 August 1945, which didn't mean the end of all military contracts. Quite apart from the usual replacement orders, the export market, and American military involvement in Korea, Vietnam and elsewhere, post-war demand for the fighting Jeep was maintained, with military sales commanding the lion's share, if not all of Jeep profits for many years. Not only that, but although the Jeep had been designed from the ground up as a military reconnaissance vehicle, it also had potential for civilian use as well. It remained a tough, lightweight little four-wheel-drive that had no obvious rivals, and farmers, forest rangers and weekend hunters were its main

customers. Moreover, the Jeep had another ace up its sleeve: it had emerged from the war covered in glory, fondly remembered by thousands of GIs and a symbol of the Allied effort. As such, it began its civilian career on a huge tide of good will, ready to tap a market that in America in the late 1940s had been starved of new civilian transport.

What the Jeep didn't have was load space, having been designed to accommodate no more than a 1/4-ton payload, and the standard Go-Devil four-cylinder engine of 134ci (2196cc) and 60bhp did not have sufficient muscle for serious towing. Neither did weather protection come as standard on the basic Jeep, GIs having no choice in the matter though the buying public did. So, at first, sales of the civilianized CJ2A were largely restricted to farmers and others needing four-wheel-drive above all else.

Willys' determination to broaden the Jeep's appeal was underlined in 1946 when the station wagon and Panel Delivery van were launched, both based on a longer 104-in (2.6-m) wheelbase. Jeep's first pickup appeared the following year, based on an

OPPOSITE and ABOVE
The early Jeep pickups of the 1950s were tough working tools.

OPPOSITE and LEFT
Jeep's pickup was offered in two- or four-wheel-drive forms, and was the first post-war 4x4 pickup to reach the market.

even longer 118-in (3-m) wheelbase, which gave a respectable amount of load space. Like the van and station wagon, the pickup had been styled by Brooks Stevens, whose artistic sense was limited by the capabilities of Willys' sheet-metal plant. The company also wanted its new generation of long Jeeps to bear a strong family resemblance to the original, which the pickup did, looking surprisingly attractive into the bargain.

A whole range was offered right from the start, with the choice of stepside box or stake beds and a bare chassis or chassis-cab on which customers could build their own rear body. Uniquely, the Jeep truck came in both two- and four-wheel-drive forms, making it the first American four-wheel-drive pickup of the post-war era. It also came with slightly wider 7-in tyres. Some sources list only the four-wheel-drive version, but it seems unlikely that Willys, anxious to expand Jeep sales and appeal,

would have failed to offer a two-wheel-drive as well. All the new pickups were rated at one ton, so they were significantly heavier-duty than the 1/2-ton Panel Delivery. Cheapest of the line-up, at only $1,175, was the bare chassis, which weighed less than 2,000lb (910kg), and the steel pickup came in at $1,620.

The Go-Devil four-cylinder L-head was rated at 63bhp, slightly more than in the CJ2A, though torque was unchanged at

OPPOSITE and LEFT
With 63bhp from its Go-Devil four-cylinder
engine, the Jeep pickup was no muscle
truck, which was not important in 1952.

105lb ft at 2000rpm, while compression ratio and carburettor were also to the same specification as the CJ, so the story behind the extra three horsepower remains a mystery. With an all-up weight of over 3,400lb (1540kg), plus payload, for the stakebed version, performance was never going to impress hot-rod enthusiasts, which didn't matter in 1947 when the simple availability of a tough, four-wheel-drive

pickup, ready to work, was reason enough to buy one.

Whatever their exact power, all Jeep pickups utilized the same three-speed synchromesh transmission with a floor-mounted shift, while Bendix hydraulic brakes were fitted as they were to all the Jeeps. The pickup proved to be a minority seller for Willys in its first year, the company selling over 33,000 station wagons

and not far short of 80,000 Jeep CJs. As for pickups, the actual figure is open to dispute, varying from a little under 5,000 to 8,787. What is not in doubt was that Willys had successfully introduced America's first four-wheel-drive pickup. From here on, sales could only increase.

This proved to be the case, with over 40,000 pickups sold in 1948, contributing greatly to Jeep's total of over 135,000,

BELOW
The interiors of the pickups were neat though spartan, and the Go-Devil engine was well-proven and reliable.

OPPOSITE
This truck is derelict though intact and ready to restore.

helped by two-wheel-drive versions of the chassis-cab, pickup and platform, the bare chassis without cab being no longer listed. The two-wheel-drive pickups were a little over $300 cheaper than the 4x4s, though in the meantime prices had taken a significant hike, with the 4x4 stepside up to $1,743, the 4x2 version costing $1,427. Mechanically, they were unchanged, but with over 40,000 sold and customers clamouring for anything with an engine and four wheels, was there any need to change them?

However, the company was acutely aware of its need to expand civilian sales to reduce its dependence on military orders,

and for this reason introduced the Jeepster in 1948. This was another Brooks Stevens design, an open four-seater with the familiar Jeep front end but two-wheel-drive and with all the normal comforts of a car apart from a steel roof. But the Jeep style was proving less than tempting to private buyers, especially coupled with the pickup's 63-bhp Go-Devil engine. Moreover, it was possible to buy a Ford Super Deluxe Club convertible, which was quite luxurious and had a V8 engine, for the same price. Only 10,326 Jeepsters were sold and 3,350 the following year, despite a six-cylinder option, making it clear that Willys would be

continuing to depend on its military and commercial Jeeps for the time being.

In 1949 it needed these more than ever, as initial interest in the Jeepster dwindled and U.S. vehicle production finally caught up with demand. As a result, Jeep production slumped to around 83,000, while profits halved. There were no changes to the pickups, and no sign of the L-head six-cylinder engine becoming available. At 72bhp, this 149-ci (2442-cc) unit offered usefully more power than the Go-Devil, but was only offered on Willys' passenger vehicles – the station wagon and Jeepster.

THIS PAGE and OPPOSITE
The Jeep pickup changed little in ten
years, though the ID on this 1957 model
shows that it used the later 72-bhp
Hurricane four.

Military Backing

When Willys-Overland launched its 1950 range on 3 March that year, it must have been clear to the assembled dealers that it was making a concerted effort to deal with criticisms of poor performance. The six-cylinder engine, now named 'Lightning', was boosted to 161ci (2638cc) for an output of 75bhp at 4,000rpm, though it still wasn't offered in the pickups. Neither did they benefit from 'Hurricane', a development of the Go-Devil with overhead inlet side exhaust valves, which allowed larger inlet valves and better breathing, with 72bhp at 4,000rpm: pickups wouldn't be able to utilize that power until 1951.

There was a new ¹/₂-ton variant, in the meantime, mechanically identical to the 1-ton and offered in the same chassis-cab, pickup and platform series, with two- or four-wheel-drive. All pickups, along with the station wagons and vans, had revised front styling with a V-shaped grille surmounted by five chrome bars, plus a redesigned instrument panel. Sales recovered a little, with over 22,000 pickups finding customers, though Willys still sold more station wagons and standard Jeeps, the latter now the updated CJ3A.

Military sales began to revive as orders for Jeeps began to flow in as a result of the Korean War. Overall sales soared to over 119,000 in 1951, seeing a 168 per cent increase in the first half of the year. The pickups played little part in this, with sales slipping by around 10 per cent to just over 20,000. The ¹/₂-ton pickup had been a short-lived experiment and was dropped, though a

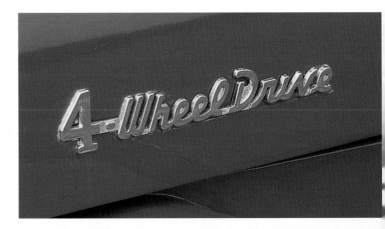

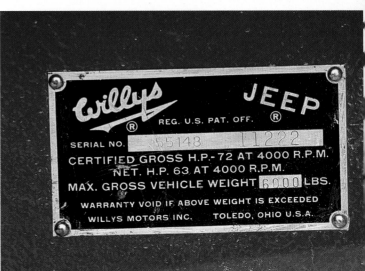

½-ton van was still available. A significant improvement, however, was the fitting of the Hurricane four to all the pickups, offering 114lb ft at 2,000rpm due to its deeper breathing and a higher 7.4:1 compression ratio. Four-by-four versions now bore a '4-Wheel-Drive' badge on the hood, and the bare chassis was introduced at $865 for the two-wheel-drive model.

The production lines at Toledo, Ohio, were running at top speed to cope with the continuous backlog of military orders, with Willys selling vehicles worth over $300 million and numbering 148,000, over 30,000 of which were pickups. The two-wheel-drive pickup was dropped and though still available to special order, Jeep would not list another 4x2 pickup until 1963. The plain fact was that with capacious, good-value two-wheel-drive pickups offered by Detroit, there was no reason to choose the Jeep truck unless one needed four-wheel-drive. Fortunately for Willys, no big-league competitor was building a 4x4 light truck at the moment.

Once again, buyers of pickups saw other Jeep customers benefiting from a power boost they could not have. This time, for 1952, the 149-ci (2442-cc) six was given the Hurricane overhead inlet valve treatment, which boosted power dramatically to 90bhp at 4,200rpm, though this most powerful Jeep engine yet came only in station wagon form. Willys management also made a fresh bid for the private car market in 1952, launching the compact-plus Aero Willys, which proved no more successful than the Jeepster and was dropped that year.

There were no changes to the pickups for 1953. In any case, Willys was busy launching the CJ3B, which finally brought the more powerful Hurricane four to the basic civilian Jeep. There were new military projects, too, such as a 1,400-lb (635-kg) Aero Jeep designed to be dropped by parachute into war zones, and a front-line ambulance based on a stretched wheelbase. As well as the new products, Willys-Overland had been taken over by Kaiser Automobiles, which caused disruption as all Kaiser and Willys production was concentrated at the Toledo factory. Less than 18,000 pickups were sold that year.

For 1954, however, customers for Jeep pickups finally got the substantial power boost for which many had surely been waiting. The four-cylinder trucks continued as before, with chassis-cab, pickup or platform all powered by the Hurricane F-head four-cylinder engine. But for an extra $90, one could now opt for a pickup powered by the new 'Super Hurricane' six. Unlike the previous F-head six, this engine used side valves, but with a capacity of 226ci (3703cc) produced a substantial 115bhp at 3,650rpm, backed by 190lb ft at 1,800rpm. Torquey and low-revving, it was ideally suited to the heavy off-road work to which Jeep trucks were often subjected. The engine was actually a result of the Kaiser takeover, an existing power unit already produced by the new parent company. All pickups had another new grille that year, now with three bright horizontal bars and nine vertical bars in the body colour. However, despite the new engine

option, sales of pickups dropped below 10,000 in 1954.

So popular was the Super Hurricane that Willys dropped the four-cylinder pickup the following year. With the range now trimmed to three – chassis-cab, pickup and platform, all four-wheel-drive and all using the big Kaiser six – over 17,700 were sold. More than half of Willys' output now used a six-cylinder engine of one sort or another. The company was now realigning itself as a maker of trucks rather than cars, as the Aero Willys was dropped and the station wagon was referred to as the utility wagon, the pickups, of course, being unaffected by any of this. But although only three standard models of truck were offered, there were plenty of special models based on the same chassis and running gear. The Commando, for example, was a four-wheel-drive fire truck, while an open-top personnel carrier was another special on the familiar 118-in wheelbase. Even the basic CJ5 Jeep could be turned into a small pickup using an option to extend the load bed to give an extra 6sq ft of space.

For 1956, in one of the rejigs to the range to which Jeep trucks were often submitted, it was possible to buy a four-cylinder Jeep pickup once again, but only with a shorter 104.5-in wheelbase and a payload of ½ ton. Power came from the familiar 72-bhp Hurricane four, while the 1-ton pickup kept the big 226-ci six and 118-in wheelbase. All of these were four-wheel-drive, of course, and though Jeep did extend its two-wheel-drive range that year with the CJ-based DJ Dispatcher, the company's focus was increasingly on 4x4s. All the pickups, whatever their wheelbase, payload or engine, had a new grille that year, though one needed to be a Jeep expert to spot the difference, the middle bar of the three having been moved from the centre of the grille to nearer the top.

Nineteen-fifty-seven was a significant year for Jeep pickups, when the first genuinely new model for a decade made an appearance. This was the FC (Forward Control) which placed the engine under the cab, like many modern light commercials, allowing a longer load bed within more compact overall dimensions. The 1/2-ton FC-150 and 1-ton FC-170 both offered reasonably large load beds, despite relatively short wheelbases of 81 and 103.5in (2 and 2.6m). The 150 was a full 3ft shorter than the standard Jeep pickup, with a narrower 9-in (23-cm) tread.

With their novel 'upfront' styling – unremarkable compared with later light trucks but an innovation in 1957 – the FCs embodied Jeep's new idea, though they retained the four-wheel-drive; in fact, all the running gear was familiar, the FC-150 being powered by the 72-bhp Hurricane four and its bigger brother by the 115-bhp Super Hurricane. A three-speed transmission was standard, with four speeds optional. There were chassis-cab, pickup and stakeside models, with an optional deluxe cab offering extra trim, foam rubber seats, cigarette lighter and small rear three-quarter windows among other things.

As for the more conventional pickups, the range was rejigged to avoid conflict with the radical new FC. The four-cylinder short-wheelbased pickup was upgraded to 1 ton, while the long-wheelbased six continued as before, though now with extra chassis options for those wishing to fit their own bodywork: bare chassis, chassis and cowl, and chassis and windshield were offered as well as the usual chassis-cab.

Given the excitement of the FC launch, it was hardly surprising that Jeep opted for a quieter life in 1958 with no important new features at all. Twelve-volt electrics became standard on all models, as did a one-piece windshield. Jeep could still claim to be the largest producer of four-wheel-drives in the world, and Kaiser announced that 1958 sales, although a pale shadow of the glory days of the late 1940s, were sufficient to make it the third biggest maker of commercial vehicles in America.

Which was all very well, except that the standard Jeep pickups were now distinctly long in the tooth: the FC-series had been a fine addition to the range, but it could not be denied that its conventional cousin had been in production for over ten years and looked it: when driven, it also felt it too. The 1950s was the era of the V8, and by 1958 Ford and Chevrolet pickups were available with overhead-valve V8s of 160–170bhp. The Jeep's 226-ci six was tough and torquey but it simply didn't have the same get up and go. Of course, it didn't have four-wheel-drive, but the Dodge Power Wagon did, and Dodge also offered the option of a 200-bhp V8 on its 4x2 pickups. Whichever way one looked at it, Jeep pickups were under increasing pressure to shape up.

However, no one seemed to have told Jeep management, as changes for 1959 were limited to the new Jeep Gala, a two-wheel-drive Dispatcher with a fringed top and striped seats, while the hard-pressed pickups had to continue as they were. There were more cosmetic changes for 1960, with the two-tone paintwork and special trim used on the Maverick two-wheel-drive station wagon now offered on all Jeeps, apart from the FCs. In the absence of anything new, it was an attempt to spruce up the outdated pickups and station wagon; pickup buyers could also choose a deluxe cab in place of the standard one, an option pioneered by the FCs. This was sold alongside more practical options that had long been available on the pickups – namely, a power take-off and pulley drive.

The stakeside truck was discontinued in four-cylinder form for 1961, which still left a choice of four pickups – one four-cylinder and three sixes. Price-wise, the conventional 1-ton pickups were a little cheaper than the FC-150. There was a new FC variant, however, with a twin rear-wheel option offered on the FC-170 for the first time. Available in the usual chassis-cab, pickup and stakeside forms, it was intended for heavy work, though the rated payload remained at one ton.

Tornado Power
Two-tone colour schemes, twin rear wheels – they weren't exactly the sort of thing to set the market alight, especially when the basic pickup had been around for 15 years and parts of the running gear for longer still. However, Jeep (Kaiser was about to officially drop the

Willys part of the name) was working on a solution, though it wouldn't appear until October 1962. In the meantime, the first sign that something important was on the horizon was unveiled in May of that year – the all-new Tornado 140 power unit.

Now this was big news. Not only was the new 230-ci (3769-cc) straight-six impressively powerful, at 140bhp and 210lb ft, but it also had an overhead camshaft, the only ohc engine built in America at the time. It had a relatively high compression ratio of 8.5:1 and made extensive use of aluminium to save weight, though the cylinder block was still cast iron. Moreover, it came not from the experimental department of Pontiac or Chrysler, but from little Willys, which hadn't produced a new engine in years! The Tornado was intended for an all-new Jeep, due for launch later in the year, but in the

OPPOSITE and THIS PAGE
FC (Forward Control) pickups were new for 1957, though the standard models carried over little changed.

RIGHT
*Part of a new era for Jeep pickups, the
Gladiator was derived from the new
Wagoneer, complete with overhead-cam
Tornado six.*

OPPOSITE
*Unstoppable? It may well have been true,
with four-wheel-drive and an unheard-of
140bhp from the Tornado engine.*

meantime the company decided to offer the
Tornado on its older trucks, providing some
valuable customer mileage in the process. It
also gave Jeep a much-needed publicity
boost, the journalists being duly impressed
by the new high-output six; one writer
referred to it as the '140-hp bomb'.

But the new engine wasn't compulsory,
and for 1962 one could still order the 1-ton
pickup in short-wheelbased form with the
ageing Hurricane four, which produced
almost precisely half the power of the
Tornado, or as a long wheelbase powered by
the Super Hurricane six.

Jeep finally launched the car for which

"UNSTOPPABLE" 'JEEP' GLADIATOR 4-WHEEL DRIVE

the Tornado had been designed in October, as planned, which turned out to be a milestone in the company's history and the most significant new model for many years. In fact, there were two of them, both based on the same chassis. We are only concerned here with the Gladiator pickup, but the Wagoneer also deserves a mention. As a roomy six-seater station wagon with optional four-wheel-drive, the Wagoneer can be regarded as the ancestor of the SUVs of today. Automatic transmission was an option, as was independent front suspension, while the Tornado six provided punchy performance. It was plain that Jeep had realized there was a market out there for a

family four-wheel-drive luxury station wagon, but in 1963 the Wagoneer was undoubtedly ahead of its time.

Alongside the Wagoneer was a new range of Gladiator pickups, known collectively as the J-series. Unusually, there was no attempt to detune the Tornado for a more workaday role, and the pickups had exactly the same high-compression six. Also shared with the Wagoneer was the new chassis, which had been carefully designed to offer a lower step-up height while retaining good ground clearance. This made dignified entries and exits from a Wagoneer easier; more to the point for the Gladiator, the load bed was lower and thus easier to

load. In fact, Jeep claimed it was over 7in (18cm) lower than that of some of its rivals.

There was a whole range of Gladiators right from the start – clearly intended to supplant the traditional pickups – there being 46 model options in all. These came in two wheelbase sizes, the 120-in (3-m) J-200 and 126-in (3.2-m) J-300. These two basic models came in a variety of payloads – 1/2-, 3/4- and 1-ton – and with the choice of two- or four-wheel-drive.

The return of a two-wheel-drive pickup was significant in that Jeep had effectively abandoned this market several years earlier, recognizing that the old pickup, its roots stretching back to 1947 and beyond, simply couldn't compete with younger rivals from Detroit. Four-wheel-drive was still a feature almost unique to the marque, but now Jeep finally had a modern, competitive two-wheel-drive pickup as well. The Gladiator pickups came in the usual chassis-cab and stakeside forms, but the steel pickup was offered in two versions. The Thriftside, its narrower bed and exposed rear fenders presenting a traditional stepside look, was a nod to the past, while the Townside had a wider load bed, and flush sides and fenders hidden behind the rear panels. The Gladiator was the up-to-the-minute pickup that it promised to be, particularly with the Townside body, its boxy, chunky styling suggesting toughness and a capacity for hard work.

Meanwhile, what of the traditional Jeep pickups? They were not discarded altogether, and one could still opt for the Hurricane four engine, now with the full 118-in wheelbase,

It was not a pickup, but the late-1960s Commando was Jeep's attempt to buy into the recreational SUV market.

or the Super Hurricane six, the latter on a chassis-cab, pickup or stakeside base. For an extra $100 or so, Jeep would also fit the Tornado 140, which still made the 1-ton pickup hundreds of dollars cheaper than the equivalent Gladiator. However, the FC-150 and 170 were not allowed access to the new engine.

It was during that first year that complaints about the Tornado began to filter in concerning its tendency to pink on its high compression ratio. Jeep responded with what it called the Economy Option, which provided a lower 7.5:1 compression, allowing the Tornado to run happily on regular fuel, even in mountainous regions. There was a slight drop in power and torque, to 133bhp and 199lb ft, but it was a small price to pay for the added dependability. There were no other changes to the Gladiators, though it is worth recording that the luxury status of the Wagoneer was underlined when air conditioning was added to the options list, which already included power steering and power brakes. Meanwhile, the traditional Jeep pickups also carried over unchanged.

Both Wagoneer and Gladiator were good-sellers, obvious from the production totals. A little over 85,600 Jeeps of all types were built in 1962 and over 110,000 the following year, when the Gladiator was launched, with over 120,000 in '64. Interestingly, these higher totals were divided about 50/50 between four- and six-cylinder production, indicating that the basic four-cylinder CJ Jeep was still an important part of the range.

Nineteen-sixty-five was a year of change for Jeep. It finally bade farewell to the old pickup, whose lineage stretched back to 1947 and beyond. That also meant farewell to the Hurricane four and Super Hurricane six power units, though the four would soldier on in the CJ Jeep. But that wasn't the end of the pickup's production life. By now, Jeep had subsidiary factories building Jeeps under licence in many parts of the world. When U.S. production of the 1947 pickup ended, it had simply transferred overseas. The same fate befell the FC-series, which was dropped by Jeep in America the following year, but continued to be produced

in India for far longer. Neither did Jeep overseas plants concentrate on outmoded models: that same year, Mexican subsidiary VAM began producing the Gladiator and Wagoneer under licence.

Meanwhile, the J-series received a new flagship power option in the form of the American Motors 327-ci (5358-cc) V8. At last there was a V8-powered Jeep pickup, in this case offering 250bhp at 4700rpm, a near-80 per cent increase, and a strong 340lb ft at 2600rpm. The new power unit was named 'Vigilante' and transformed the Gladiator's performance from sprightly to something far more exciting. Naturally, Jeep's main motivation in fitting the V8 was to keep the Wagoneer competitive with conventional station wagons, but it did the Gladiator a power of good nevertheless. To go with the new V8 came a new automatic transmission (at least, new to Jeep): General Motors Turbo Hydra-Matic was regarded as one of the best available and could only add to the J-series' appeal.

The following year, the Tornado six found itself sidelined by another American Motors unit, this time an overhead-valve straight-six of 145bhp and 215lb ft. Named the 'Hi-Torque', it was impressively smooth and durable, and its arrival only two years after the Tornado's introduction suggested that Jeep's own foray into high-output sixes had not been a success.

It wasn't all about engines, however, and the Gladiator was also renumbered later in 1965, the only changes appearing to have been slightly higher gross vehicle weights. The J-200 and 300 were replaced by the J-

2000 and 3000, the entire range comprising J-2500, J-2600, J-2800, J-3500, J-3600, J-3700 and J-3800. Wheelbase lengths was unchanged, as was the split between Thriftside and Townside pickups.

Nineteen-sixty-six was a quieter year, though the Gladiators did receive a whole list of standard safety items, including a padded instrument panel and sun visors, dual-circuit self-adjusting brakes and reversing lights. There was also an impact-resistant windshield, seat belts, external mirrors, dual wipers and washers, reversing lights and four-way flashers. What it didn't get was an ultra-luxurious option to mirror the new Super Wagoneer, with its 270-bhp four-barrelled Vigilante V8, auto transmission, air conditioning and power everything. But the Gladiator, after all, was still a working vehicle, the age of the pickup as a leisure toy having not yet arrived.

Not that Kaiser-Jeep, now its official name, was suffering too much. Continued strong military production (over 86,000 military trucks) contributed to a profit of over $14.5 million in 1967, a new military product that year having been the M715 truck, derived from the Gladiator. But this fat surplus was concealing the fact that most of it came from military contracts and that the civilian range was falling behind despite the improvements. Soon, Kaiser-Jeep actually found itself in debt, and to raise cash sold off two of its highly successful subsidiaries in Brazil and Argentina. This helped to ease cash flow, though it also ended the flow of annual profit-sharing from south to north, but was only a short-term

solution: Jeep really needed to dramatically expand its sales on the home market.

It attempted to do this with the 1967 Jeepster, which incidentally, and contrary to popular belief, was not based on the tooling of the original 1940s Jeepster; the new one may have looked similar, but was in reality completely different. Although the Jeepster was primarily intended as a fun car, meant to exploit the booming interest in off-road leisure, there was a useful pickup as well. Like the four-seater roadster and station wagon, this came as standard with the venerable Hurricane four of 75bhp, plus three-speed transmission and four-wheel-

344

drive. However, the 'Dauntless' V6, which Jeep had taken over from General Motors, was an option, offering 155bhp in this relatively compact car. By contrast, the Gladiator range was cut back, all the two-wheel-drive versions having been dropped apart from the J-3500, which combined the $1/2$-ton payload with the longer 126-in (3.2-m) wheelbase. It was as though Jeep's brief reacquaintance with two-wheel-drive pickups was already on the way out.

The Gladiator range was reduced again in 1968, and the long-wheelbased Thriftsides were dropped altogether: the stepside style was in any case looking increasingly outmoded as most pickups were adopting the sleeker flush sides which Jeep already offered on the Townside. However, this still

OPPOSITE
A well-used Gladiator at work.

ABOVE
New and old, a 1974 Jeep pickup next to one from 1957.

left a choice of 24 Gladiators, ranging in price from the $3,119 J-2500 chassis-cab to the J-3800 platform stake at $4,429. The remaining two-wheel-drive Gladiators had also been dropped and, interestingly, Jeep also dropped the two-wheel-drive Wagoneers in 1968 to concentrate on its core unique feature of offering four-wheel-drive across the range.

Of course, four-wheel-drive was rapidly becoming a must-have item in certain leisure markets, and Jeep made renewed efforts to appeal to this sector in the face of stiff competition. This meant a new 132-in (3.3-m) wheelbased model for the Gladiator, all the better to accommodate a large camper unit which could be easily mounted and demounted. In theory, one could now use the Gladiator all week as a working pickup, then fit the camper on a Friday night and head for the hills. There was also a smaller, lighter camper unit for the existing 126-in Gladiator. These units were also offered fully-equipped: that for the CJ5 came with a double bed, two singles, a sink, stove, toilet, icebox and heater, offering the prospect of a cheap vacation for families which didn't mind roughing it. The camper package was priced at $148.

AMC Expansion
The 1970s proved to be the start of a new era for Jeep. In February 1970, the company was taken over by American Motors, which under Roy D. Chapin Jr. realized, even more than Jeep, the huge potential of four-wheel-drive. Chapin expanded Jeep's dealer network into urban areas, much of the old

network having been one-horse workshops out in the sticks, and updated the range, giving a new fun/sport emphasis to the CJ-series with special editions like the Renegade. It also took the Wagoneer further upmarket and launched the two-door Cherokee to plug the gap between. As a result, Jeep sales soared as never before, though AMC's own car range ironically continued to flounder.

There were only modest changes to the Gladiator pickup. It acquired the Wagoneer's multi-toothed grille, making it look lower and wider, and there was a new option of two-tone paint. A side-mounted spare tyre was another choice, bolted in between the passenger door and rear fender. Mechanically the Gladiator was unchanged, the AMC 232-ci (3802-cc) straight-six being the standard power unit. The optional V8 was now a Buick 350-ci (5735cc) of 230bhp and 314lb ft, though the engine range for both Gladiator and Wagoneer would soon mushroom and a range of V8s would be offered. Jeep's other pickup, the Jeepster, continued with the familiar 72-bhp Hurricane four, while the optional engine remained the rough but punchy ex-Buick 225-ci (3687-cc) V6, now with 160bhp and 235lb ft.

There was more news of powertrains the following year, when the Gladiator received AMC's 258-ci (4228-cc) six as its base engine, giving 150bhp and 195lb ft, slightly more than the smaller 232-ci six used previously. Not surprisingly, the Buick V8 was dropped, as AMC had suitable V8s of its own, which could be supplied in-house

without contributing to General Motors' profits. In fact, two V8s were now optional on the big Jeep pickups: a 304-ci (4982-cc) unit of 210bhp/300lb ft and a top-line 360-ci (5899-cc), the biggest ever fitted to a civilian Jeep, offering 245bhp/365lb ft on a two-barrelled carburettor.

The line-up was rejigged and simplified and loading ratings were cut from ten categories to five. The range now started with the Gladiator J-2000, offered as a chassis-cab as well as the Thriftside or Townside pickups, both having a 7-ft (2.1-m) load bed and 5,000-lb (2268-kg) GVW. The heavy-duty J-4000 came in four GVWs of 5–8,000lb, all of them with the choice of chassis-cab or Townside pickup with 8-ft bed. The 8,000-lb (3629-kg) model was new, named the Camper Truck, and was designed specifically for carrying a portable camper unit. It had the 360-ci V8 as standard, plus four-speed transmission and heavy-duty cooling system, battery, springs and shocks. The fact that Jeep offered a special Gladiator specifically for campers demonstrates how important this market had now become.

In 1971 *Road & Track* tested the J-2500, which was loaded with several options, including the 360-ci V8, four-speed transmission, Townside body, power steering and the Custom trim package, which meant a fancier cab. It noticed the advantage possessed by the Gladiator since 1963: because it was designed for four-wheel-drive from the start, all the running gear was tucked neatly away, allowing a reasonably low ride height and decent ground clearance.

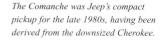

The Comanche was Jeep's compact pickup for the late 1980s, having been derived from the downsized Cherokee.

By contrast, according to *Road & Track*, a Ford 4x4 pickup looked as though it was 'on stilts'. The Gladiator was clearly a working vehicle, the heavy-duty springs giving a bouncy ride, which settled down nicely when a 1,000-lb load of sand was on the bed. Testers also thought the 'heavy-duty' transmission well named, i.e. heavy but seemingly durable enough to outlast the rest of the truck, while automatic transmission was an option for those unwilling to wrestle

with a macho stick-shift. All in all, *Road & Track* considered it 'A tough, no-nonsense 4wd pickup ...not only satisfactory on the highway but thoroughly capable off the pavement as well.'

The Gladiator name disappeared in 1972 and the full-sized pickups were simply called Jeep trucks, the range of 13 models starting with the J-2500 and J-3500 on a 120-in (3-m) wheelbase, while the heavier-duty J-4500, J-4600, J-4700 and J-4800 all shared a

longer 132-in (3.3-m) wheelbase. The top two trucks had the 345-bhp 360-ci (5899-cc) V8 as standard, while the others continued with the 258-ci (4228-cc) six, with optional 304-ci (4982-cc) or 360-ci (5899-cc) V8s. A new model was a 6,000-lb (2722-kg) GVW version of the J-2000, the J-2600. The Jeepster Commando also got a name check, now referred to as the Jeep Commando to coincide with new, more conventional slab-sided styling. The Hurricane four had been

OPPOSITE and LEFT
The CJ pickup returned in the 1980s: this is
a U.K.-registered CJ10.

finally pensioned off and AMC engines were now used, with 232-ci (3802-cc) and 258-ci (4228-cc) sixes, plus the 304-ci (4982-cc) V8 now offered. A pickup remained part of the range.

Nineteen-seventy-three saw a significant step forward in four-wheel-drive technology. Until then, four-wheel-drive had only been used on the rough, as keeping it connected on tarmac caused wear, tear and even damage, not to mention inefficiency. Freewheeling front hubs were a partial solution, but in the early 1970s had to be switched manually on and off. Jeep's revolutionary solution to this problem was Quadra-Trac, which allowed full-time, fully-automatic four-wheel-drive. This was simply a third limited-slip differential, allowing power to be fed to each of the four wheels as it was needed, regardless of whether the truck was running on mud, snow, wet or dry tarmac. Nowadays we take full-time four-wheel-drive for granted, but in 1973 it was a huge step forward, and made the big Jeeps no more complicated to operate than a two-wheel-drive sedan, especially if also equipped with automatic transmission, power steering and power brakes.

Quadra-Trac was only available on the trucks with lighter payloads, the 5,000- and 6,000-lb GVW models, but all Jeep trucks had the new option of an aluminium hardtop to cover the load bed. Complete with side and rear windows, it was an extra $200, though as a first-year promotion Jeep offered it as a no-cost option on the J-4500 and J-4600. All pickups had new double-walled boxes and tailgates to match, with a new

dashboard in the cab. Many in-cab items were now also colour-co-ordinated, including the floor mats, steering wheel and the new dash. And if even the 360-ci V8 wasn't powerful enough, a four-barrelled version now topped the options list. Power was now measured in net terms, with all ancillaries attached, instead of gross, so the 360 four-barrel's power was more impressive than it seemed: the 360 two-barrel was now listed at 175bhp and the base 258-ci (4228-cc) six at 110bhp.

Meanwhile, AMC's hard work seemed to be paying off, with Jeep retail sales up 44 per cent in 1973 to nearly 67,000. Moreover, the press liked the latest pickups. *PV4* magazine noted that the J-4500 was 'not a stylish truck by today's standards' though it was now ten years old, after all. On the other hand, journalists were most impressed by Quadra-Trac, praising it as 'the best full-time 4wd system on American vehicles, and has the ability to make for confident motoring under any conditions'. As the only full-time 4x4 pickup on the market, the Jeep truck, they concluded, had a distinct advantage over the competition.

For 1974 there were new designations for the short-wheelbased J-10 pickup and long-wheelbased J-20. Oddly, both lost an inch of wheelbase compared with the previous trucks, now at 119 and 131in (3 and 3.3m) respectively. The base engines were unchanged (258-ci six, plus the 360-ci V8 in two- or four-barrelled forms) but were joined by a 401-ci (6571-cc) V8 with single four-barrelled carburettor and a net output of 235bhp at 4,600rpm. All Jeep trucks now

had front disc brakes, which was a particularly worthwhile improvement, given the performance of the top 235-bhp V8. Even the two-barrelled 360 was respectably fast. *PV4* magazine tested a J-10 with this motor under the hood and found it could sprint to 60mph (100km/h) in 13.4 seconds and run the standing quarter-mile in less than 20 seconds. Not exactly muscle-car performance, but neither was it slow for a brick-like Jeep.

Of course, there was a price to be paid for performance, and a 360 V8-equipped J-10 returned only 9–11mpg on the road and as little as 8mpg on the rough, which was all very well when gas was cheap, the oil crisis having not yet occurred, and when no one, apart from a few scientists, had heard of global warming. However, even when the first oil crisis was over, and during the recession that started to bite during 1975, Jeep sales didn't suffer all that much and actually improved a little. Not only that, but they carried on increasing right through the 1970s, peaking at over 140,000 in the U.S. and Canada alone in the 1979 calendar year.

Jeep would be obliged to pay more attention to fuel economy in the 1980s, but during the '70s, with Detroit sedans desperately downsizing all around, the big Jeeps were left to continue their gas-guzzling habits, and buyers didn't seem to mind one way or the other. Of course, Jeeps were classified as light trucks, even the Wagoneer, which was nothing of the sort, which exempted them from the EPA's new CAFE fuel regulations as a result of intensive lobbying by the motor industry. So maybe

OPPOSITE
Standard CJs hardly qualified as true pickups, having very small load beds. It is hard to believe, but this is a 1990s model.

concluded *Four Wheeler* magazine, after testing a Honcho, 'now it's pretty too.' So popular was the Honcho package ('Jeep Honcho – Mucho Macho', according to the publicity) that it remained part of the range for several years.

After a quiet year in 1977, the pickups received yet another option package the following year. This was the era of CB radio, Smokey and the Bandit and Convoy, so this latest pickup package was inevitably labelled '10-4'. Echoing the Honcho, this added chunky fat tyres, in this case 10 x 15-in Tracker A-Ts, to white spoked wheels, plus two-tone orange decals and a roll bar. The exterior was given extra brightwork and there was deluxe trim and extra sound insulation inside. The Golden Eagle package had been popular on the Jeep CJ, so it was extended to the pickups as well, though once again, only to the short-wheelbased J-10, in anticipation of it being more popular with weekend drivers than the larger, less wieldy J-20. Many Golden Eagle features were shared with other packages, notably the big tyres and wide wheels, the extra brightwork and roll bar. Off-road driving lights were unique to the Golden Eagle, however, and the colour scheme was highlighted gold and black, while beige Levis were the interior theme.

Meanwhile, Jeep production continued to climb, reaching its highest civilian level in 1978, with over 150,000 built during the fiscal year. So high was demand, that AMC decided to turn its Brampton, Ontario, plant over to Jeep production, increasing capacity to 200,000 vehicles a year. AMC itself was still losing millions of dollars a year,

OPPOSITE and LEFT
Sounds (and looks) familiar? Jeep revived the Gladiator name for this 2005 concept pickup, heralding a return to retro style.

he continued rise in Jeep sales throughout his period is not so hard to understand, specially with the fashion for family and eisure 4x4s growing every year.

Jeep responded to this growing leisure market by beautifying the big pickups: just as he basic CJ Jeeps had been transformed into un cars with bright colours and alloy wheels, now it was the turn of the J-series. The first ign of this was the Pioneer option, offered on both J-10 and J-20. This was primarily an ppearance package, including wood-grain xterior trim, with instrument panel to match, hick carpeting, and brightwork for the front ender, hubcaps and other details.

The Pioneer was followed in mid-1976 by the Honcho package, offered only on the short-wheelbased J-10. While the Pioneer reflected something of a country club image, the Honcho was very much a macho type and sported white slotted wheels mated with fat A-T Goodyears with the fashionable raised white lettering. It had stripes and decals, a rear step fender and even a Levi's denim interior to match one's jeans. A sports steering wheel, engine-turned instrument panel, dual horns and other detailing completed the package, which cost $699. Even air conditioning was on the options list, so Jeep was clearly making an effort to steer the big pickup towards the leisure market. 'The Jeep pickup was always tough,' consequently Jeep could be regarded as something of a godsend.

It wasn't until the final quarter of 1979 that the cracks began to show. Record sales continued through the first three quarters, falling sharply in the last three months of the year – a portent of things to come. Meanwhile, most of Jeep's attention was focused on emissions compliance, the engine range having been trimmed to make it quicker and cheaper: the 360-ci four-barrel and 401-ci V8s were dropped from the trucks, leaving only the 258-ci six and 360-ci two-barrel. That meant fewer changes to the cars, though the trucks, along with the Wagoneer and Cherokee, gained new grilles with rectangular headlights. But the second fuel crisis, which hit an already weakened U.S. economy in 1979, proved disastrous for the American motor industry, kicking off a recession and a new wave of downsizing. For AMC, it meant that Jeep, which for a decade had been the goose that laid the golden egg and kept the whole enterprise afloat, was finally on a downward curve. The 1980s, to paraphrase the Chinese proverb, would be interesting times.

The 25-mpg Jeep

By 1980, the race was on to improve fuel economy, and every model in the Jeep range was modified with that aim in mind. The CJ even came with a new 2.5-litre four-cylinder option, which in homage to the past was named 'Hurricane'. The pickups saw nothing quite so drastic, though free-wheeling hubs were made standard to cut drivetrain losses and improve efficiency on the highway.

Quadra-Trac still cost extra, and the standard manual transmission was now four-speed rather than three in a further bid to boost economy. This would not be a late-model Jeep pickup with some sort of special trim package, so while the 10-4 and Custom packages were dropped, the new Laredo took their place. Offered only on the J-10, this brought extra sound insulation, a front sway bar and fender guards, plus cosmetic items such as a chrome grille and wheels, special interior trim, and a leather-wrapped steering wheel.

Despite efforts to improve economy (the four-cylinder CJ now made 25mpg on the highway), Jeep sales slumped by more than 50 per cent in 1980, forcing AMC's partner, Renault, to increase its holding in the business merely to keep things going. The following year it was even worse as sales fell to a little over 63,000, while AMC posted a $138 million loss. The trucks, along with the other big Jeeps, were given small front spoilers, to improve aerodynamics, and a new 258-ci (4228-cc) six-cylinder engine which was 90lb (40kg) lighter than the old. The J-20 still had the 360-ci V8 as standard but could be ordered with the lightweight six.

In 1982 there were yet more attempts to economize. A five-speed overdrive manual gearbox and a new wide-ratio automatic helped the six-cylinder J-10 to achieve 18mpg in town and 25 on the highway; in other words, it was now using about half as much fuel as a V8-powered J-10 from a few years before. The Pioneer trim package returned, a new option being the Sportside pickup, with roll bar, flared wheel arches

and chunky T/A tyres. It also had stepside side panels, which clearly distinguished it as a sport rather than a working pickup. Available only with the Honcho package, *Four Wheeler* magazine decided it transformed the humble truck's image. 'Ten years ago, Jeep pickups used to be laughed at ... only doddering old men, old hunters and fishermen and farmers bought Jeep pickups ...In 1982, instead of laughs, the Jeep Honcho gets admiring glances from all sides.'

There were few changes to the Jeep trucks for 1983, the J-10 continuing in base, Custom, Pioneer or Laredo trim, plus the Sportside Honcho. The J-20 (a J-10 with the optional long bed) came as basic, Custom or Pioneer. AMC was still losing money by the hour, but Jeep sales recovered to over 82,000 that year – back to over 150,000 the year after. The early 1980s had been a trying time, but it looked as though Jeep had survived. Nineteen-eighty-four was another quiet year for the pickup, unless one regarded the colour-keyed instrument panel as exciting, and the Honcho and Sportside were dropped. But there was good reason, as Jeep was busy launching the radically downsized Cherokee and Wagoneer, which used four-cylinder or V6 power with a turbo diesel added the following year. It was the same story for 1985, the pickups having now been reduced to only two models, the $1/2$-ton J-10 and $3/4$-ton J-20, both on the same wheelbase.

But in 1986, for the first time in years, Jeep finally offered a genuinely new pickup. It was the Comanche, and logically enough was a pickup version of the newly downsized Cherokee and Wagoneer, which were proving wildly successful. Like them, the Comanche was based on a unitary body (without a separate chassis) and Quadra-Link front suspension (a solid axle on coil springs). Power choices were the same as the two-door Cherokee on which it was based, with a 150-ci (2458-cc) four of 117bhp and 135lb ft and options including a 173-ci (2835-cc) V6 and the efficient 126-ci (2065-cc) turbo-diesel. Five-speed manual and three-speed automatic transmissions were also on the options list.

Though classed as a compact pickup, the Comanche was one of the larger ones, with a 119-in wheelbase and 7ft 4-in load bed. Trim levels included the Custom, aimed at business users, and the X and XLS with better trim for private buyers. Meanwhile, the big 131-in wheelbased J-series pickups carried on as before.

The Comanche was well received, one magazine proclaiming it truck of the year. *Four-Wheel & Off-Road* magazine did not but was impressed by its long-term Comanche V6 after it had covered 10,000 miles (16090km). It praised Quadra-Link for providing the best ride/handling combination of any pickup and averaging 17mpg, which included plenty of hard off-road use. The chief weakness, however, was a lack of power from the V6 – but then, like all motoring writers who did not need to pay for gas or insurance, that wasn't so unexpected.

A short-wheelbased Comanche joined the line-up in 1987. It was priced to sell at $6,495, which made it $1,000 cheaper than a Dodge Dakota. Of course, the new baby Comanche came only in two-wheel-drive, but with the 150-ci four now fuel-injected with 121bhp, offered more power than any other compact pickup. It also had a usefully large 6-ft load bed, so the 113-in wheelbase didn't intrude too much on the little truck's usability. The existing Comanches all reverted to Jeep's traditional trim levels that year, the new-fangled X and XLS having been dropped in favour of base, Pioneer, Chief and Laredo. The Laredo was given bucket seats and a special trim, clearly not intended for a working life or anything remotely dirty. But this was evidently what the public wanted and Jeep set a new sales record that year, with over 208,000 sold in the U.S. alone.

So when Chrysler bought AMC in August 1987 for $1.1 billion, it was a pretty good deal. The AMC car line-up was swiftly dropped, for what Chrysler really wanted was Jeep. By now, the marque really was riding the crest of a wave, to the extent of introducing a new 242-ci (3966-) six of 177bhp, as gas prices fell again and memories of the fuel crisis began to fade. This was offered in the Comanche for 1988, notably in the new Comanche Eliminator, a short-wheelbased two-wheel-drive truck aimed at the youth market. As well as Power-Tech and a five-speed transmission, the Eliminator also sported stripes, flared fenders and silver detailing. The Comanche Chief, by contrast, was aimed squarely at the off-roaders, offered only as a 4x4 with chunky Goodyears, spotlights and a roll bar. Meanwhile, the ancient J-10 and J-20 full-

sized trucks kept on selling in small numbers, still listed for 1988 with the 360-ci (5899-cc) V8 and auto transmission standard from later in the year. The following year, however, the J-series finally took a bow, an astonishing 26 years after the Gladiator had been launched. They had transformed Jeep's standing in the pickup market.

Chrysler executives must have given themselves a pat on the back in the light of Jeep's continuing success: over 250,000 Jeeps were sold in 1988 and only slightly less than that in 1989, while Chrysler announced that it was increasing capacity to 400,000 to meet an ambitious expansion plan. The Comanche saw few changes that year, the short-wheelbased version offered as base, the good-value SporTruck, Pioneer (now with power steering) and youthful Eliminator. The long-wheelbased pickups came in base or Pioneer trim only, while all Jeeps now came with a seven-year/70,000-mile warranty.

It was becoming clear, however, that pickups were not a feature of Chrysler's plans for Jeep, and 1990, '91 and '92 saw no changes of note to the Comanche, which in base four-cylinder form remained Jeep's cheapest vehicle. Chrysler saw more profits in the development of Jeep passenger SUVs as the market for them continued to expand through the 1990s. In any case, Comanche sales slowed down, so it was no surprise when Jeep's final commercial was dropped in 1993. The marque's 45-year history of building four-wheel-drive pickups beloved by Americans was finally at an end.

OTHER MANUFACTURERS

RIGHT
2003 Cadillac Escalade EXT, unlikely to be
used for hauling straw or rubble.

OPPOSITE
The Caddy pickup was derived from this,
the Escalade SUV.

AMERICAN AUSTIN/BANTAM

Based on the English Austin Seven, the American Austin was produced through much of the 1930s, offering a miniature truck for urban deliveries. A panel van was offered from 1930, with the first pickup arriving in 1934, powered by the same 14-hp four-cylinder engine and with a diminutive 75-in (1.9-m) wheelbase. The price of the American Austins started at $330, which wasn't much cheaper than a full-sized Ford. Bankruptcy loomed in 1934, though production did resume three years later, the little trucks now attractively restyled and renamed the American Bantam. Still based on the Austin engine and wheelbase, they survived through to 1941. It was Bantam which designed the Second World War Jeep, though its limited facilities could never fulfil the military's massive orders, and production was handed over to Ford and Willys. The little Bantam never reappeared.

CADILLAC

Twenty years ago, it would have been hard to believe that Cadillac would eventually

launch a pickup truck. Cadillac has always been a producer of upscaled sedans, but it declined through the 1980s as BMW, Mercedes and Jaguar poached increasing numbers of American customers. Meanwhile, the popularity of luxury SUVs was rocketing and Cadillac's reply was the Escalade. It may have been a rebadged,

retrimmed Chevrolet, but it finally allowed Cadillac to partake in the SUV revolution. It would also seem that where there is a luxury SUV, a luxury pickup can't be far behind. Announced for 2003, the Escalade EXT was really no more than the standard SUV with a shorter passenger compartment and a load bed mounted on the back. But like the Lincoln Blackwood, it proved attractive to people for whom the usual station wagon-shaped SUV was no longer exclusive enough.

There was no lack of power, equipment or fittings in the EXT. Beneath the hood was General Motors' Vortec 6000 V8, here in 345-bhp form, its 380lb ft giving it an unquenchable thirst for gas so that it delivered only around 12mpg. With the Vortec driving through General Motors' Hydra-Matic four-speed autotomatic transmission, the EXT could tow up to 8,000lb (3630kg), and had been given every latest electronic gadget to aid handling. Road Sensing Suspension allowed electronic control of the shock absorbers, with body roll, pitch and wheel motion all monitored, the damping being adjusted to suit, while StabiliTrack traction control adjusted brake pressure, engine torque or throttle setting in the event of wheelspin being detected. The EXT also utilized a viscous-coupled four-wheel-drive system that required no input from the driver whatsoever.

Based on the Chevrolet Avalanche, the EXT shared its Midgate feature, a flap between load bed and cab that extended the bed from a stubby five to a far more useful 8ft (2.4m) in length. In fact, the EXT's load bed, unlike the carpeted Lincoln Blackwood, proved surprisingly practical, in that it came in standard hose-down form. Therefore, all that was missing from the American luxury market in the early-21st century was a pickup from the likes of BMW, Mercedes and Jaguar.

CROSLEY

The American-made Crosley was small even by European standards, so it must have seemed exceedingly so to an ordinary customer looking for an American pickup in the late 1940s. In fact, millionaire Powel Crosley wasn't trying to sell his mini-trucks to them at all. He began building two-cylinder mini-cars in 1939, adding a pickup to match – the Parkway Delivery – the following year.

At 10ft (3m) long, the Crosley Parkway was powered by an air-cooled Waukesha engine measuring 39ci (639cc) and delivering 12bhp at 4,000rpm. Payload was a scant 350lb (160kg), and the Parkway was barely capable of 50mph (80km/h). On the other hand, fuel consumption was around 50mpg and it cost only $324, ready to work, making it suitable for light deliveries, particularly in cities. Engine size was

OPPOSITE
The Escalade EXT's load bed is neatly concealed on this 2005 example.

LEFT: In 2013 little has changed in the general appearance of the Escalade EXT.

361

2002 Isuzu 4 Sport, a typically robust
Japanese pickup.

actually reduced for 1941, when it was given a shorter stroke to cure a weak crankshaft. Nevertheless, over 2,000 were sold and another 1,000 in the few months before the Second World War intervened.

The war gave Crosley the opportunity to give his mini-trucks a boost once peace was restored. The company had developed a small overhead-cam four-cylinder engine for the Navy, designed to power refrigeration units and the like. It was unusual in that its cylinder block was made of sheet-metal stampings, copper-brazed together. Named the COBRA, this high-revving 44-ci (721-cc) unit seemed just the thing to power the new generation of Crosley cars and trucks after the war had ended. Crosley had completely redesigned the mini-cars for 1946, with the pickup following in January 1947, so with an engine delivering nearly 50 per cent more power than the old Waukesha twin, the payload was increased to a full 1/4-ton. Once again, the mini-truck's most important feature was its modest fuel consumption, together with great manoeuvrability and ease of parking, though it still lacked capacity, being 15in shorter than a VW Beetle.

Alas COBRA proved unsuitable for peacetime use: the steel/copper cylinder block began to develop problems when electrolysis caused holes to form in the cylinders. A more conventional cast-iron block replaced it for 1949, fitted to a restyled range of cars and trucks. This made them more reliable, but the price had crept to $900, when the price of a full-sized Chevrolet 1/2-ton pickup was only $1,253.

Despite all the improvements, Crosley sales were now steadily declining from their peak in 1948 until, by 1952, only 243 trucks had been sold. Production ended that year.

DIAMOND T

Diamond T is usually associated with the heavy-duty trucks it built with Reo as part of the White empire; but it did build a variety of smaller pickups up to 1951, some of which were stylish indeed. C.A. Tilt built his first sub-1-ton truck in 1916, the 3/4-ton Model JA, which by 1919 had become the 1-ton J-5, both with four-cylinder engines. Other 3/4- and 1-ton trucks followed through to 1936, when much of the range was given new streamlined styling, including the 3/4-ton Model 80 pickup. This was powered by a Hercules six, and by 1939 was offered in 80S (standard) and 80D (deluxe) models.

Diamond T introduced a 1/2-ton for the first time in 1941, the Model 91 and Model 117 offering two wheelbase lengths but sharing the same six-cylinder engine. Also new was a 1/2-ton version of the existing 1-ton, which itself was offered in pickup form. All of these developments were cut short by the Second World War, however, and when it ended, Diamond T decided to drop its light-duty trucks altogether, allowing it to concentrate on larger vehicles.

FARGO

Dodge hasn't always had the monopoly of Chrysler's truck line-up. De Soto was a badge used in some export markets, and Fargo actually predated both of these, having been offered from the corporation's earliest

days. The original Fargo 1-ton didn't last long, however, as the acquisition of Dodge, not to mention Graham, resulted in some rationalization, and in the early 1930s the badge was simply a means of selling Chrysler trucks into big fleets.

A new era dawned in 1936, however, when Fargo was reinvented as a line of trucks for the Canadian market. The Fargo 1/2-ton pickup of that year was based on Plymouth sedan running gear with a Dodge cab, and the new trucks were built in Detroit, alongside the Dodges. Within a few years, a complete line-up of up to 3 tons was offered, though Fargos remained for export from the U.S.A. After the Second World War they became closer in resemblance to the Dodges with which they were built, until only the badges were different. Thus typical Fargo post-war pickups included the 1/2-ton Utiline and FW100 Power Wagon that were Dodges in all but name.

ISUZU

Isuzu pickups are more common that one might think. As a long-term partner of General Motors, Isuzu pickups have been sold in Europe with Bedford or Opel badges, and in the U.S.A. as the Chevrolet LUV. Either way, it means that Isuzu-badged pickups appear to be rarer than they really are.

The basic vehicles have long been straightforward and conventional, with two- or four-wheel-drive and four-cylinder petrol or diesel engines. In 2004/5 the latest Isuzu Rodeo certainly impressed the media, picking up a

OPPOSITE
A 2002 Isuzu 4 Sport in four-door crew-cab
form. At times, Isuzu pickups have also
worn Chevrolet and Bedford badges.

LEFT: The ISUZU D-MAX 2nd Generation
brings Isuzu pickups into 2013.

string of awards in Britain, and promising car-like comfort from its optional air conditioning.

Isuzu the company has a long and respected history as a maker of diesel engines. It produced Japan's first-ever V8 in 1950, and the country's first diesel engine for passenger cars in '61. Isuzu also pioneered direct-injection diesels for light trucks and electronic control for all diesel engines.

An early Land Rover Series I, its pickup body fitted with vehicle recovery equipment.

LAND ROVER

Land Rover is Britain's equivalent of the Jeep, and was even inspired by the American original. Immediately after the Second World War, Rover needed a new car

that it could export and put into production quickly. Company boss Maurice Wilks had been using an ex-army Jeep on his farm, which was food for thought, and the rest all came together.

Within months of Wilks' idea, the first prototypes were running, and the new Land Rover went into production in July 1948. It was of similar size and concept to the Jeep, but with four-speed dual-range transmission

Short-wheelbased Land Rovers, like CJ Jeeps, have long had limited load-bed space.

and smaller 1.6-litre engine. Like the Jeep, its compact dimensions made it of limited use as a pickup, but it soon gained respect as a tough, capable, go-anywhere workhorse and a legend was born.

It was eight years before a long-wheelbased Land Rover was added, with a 107-in (2.7-m) wheelbase adding a useful 41in (104cm) to the load-bed length. A new diesel option arrived the following year, but like Jeep, Land Rover seemed reluctant to change its workhorse too often. It was another ten years before a six-cylinder petrol option arrived, and an ex-General Motors 3.5-litre V8 joined the range in 1979, giving the leaf-sprung, drum-braked Land Rover surprising performance. In the meantime, Rover launched its own Forward Control pickup, with the same running gear but a far bigger load bed than the standard model.

The 1980s saw a more determined effort to keep the ageing Land Rover up to date, a High Capacity pickup answering criticisms of the 109's long but narrow load bed early in the decade. Nineteen-eighty-three saw the substantially new One-Ten, with coil-sprung suspension, disc brakes and permanent four-wheel-drive, plus a turbo-diesel option soon after. In 1991, the One-Ten became the Defender, shortly before exports to the U.S.A. commenced, now with an efficient Tdi diesel engine and the petrol V8; the Tdi was replaced by a five-cylinder diesel, the Td5, in 1998. By the late 1990s, the Land Rover was selling in the proportion of one in six alongside the popular Range Rover and Discovery, the company having now decided to concentrate on the profitable SUV market. But as a workhorse pickup, the Land Rover was as capable as ever.

Like Jeep, Land Rover produced its own Forward Control, with four-wheel-drive and a long load bed.

LEFT
Short-wheelbased Land Rover pickups are still favoured in off-road competition.

RIGHT
Defender was the much updated Land
Rover offered from 1991, with the same
rugged build and fine off-road ability as
before.

OPPOSITE
2004 Land Rover Defender Td5, with crew
cab and five-cylinder turbo-diesel engine.

This 2009/10 model is a Defender 90 SVX pickup. This is to be the last of the Defenders before a major overhaul from 2012.

Therefore it was widely understood that the 2012MY upgrades would be the last made to the traditional Defender design before it was replaced. Whilst emissions and safety regulations had threatened the Defender since the early 2000s these had either been avoided through 'grandfather rights' or Land Rover had found ways to modify the vehicle to economically meet the new requirements. However safety regulations due for introduction in 2015 requiring minimum pedestrian safety standards and the fitment of airbags to commercial vehicles cannot be met without a wholesale redesign of the Defender.

The main change for the 2012 models was the installation of a different engine from the Ford Duratorq engine range. The 2.4-litre engine introduced in 2007 was not capable of meeting the upcoming Euro V Emissions Standards and so was replaced with the ZSD-422 engine, essentially a 2.2-litre variant of the same engine. Although smaller than the existing unit the power and torque outputs remained unchanged and the same 6-speed gearbox was used as well. The engine included a Diesel particulate filter for the first time on a Defender. The only other change was the reintroduction of the Soft Top bodystyle to the general market. This had been a popular option for the Land Rover Series but by the introduction of the Defender had been relegated to special order and military buyers only. Land Rover stated that the option was being brought back due to 'customer feedback'.

In August 2011 Land Rover announced an update of the Defender for the 2012 model year. By this time Land Rover had publically acknowledged that it was working on a project to produce an all-new replacement for the Defender. This would lead to the unveiling of the first DC100 concept vehicle in September that year.

LINCOLN

If Edsel Ford had seen the Lincoln Blackwood he would have been very surprised indeed. His vision for Lincoln was that it should be Ford's upper-class marque, and for over 70 years this had been the case. But Lincoln yielded to the pressure of the times in 1998 and launched its own super-luxury SUV, the Navigator, powered by Ford's 5.4-litre V8 Triton and loaded with every option imaginable.

It was a great success, and once Lincoln had broken with tradition and applied its badge to a light truck, there was no reason not to go one step further and build a super-

RIGHT
This 2002 Lincoln Blackwood needs its
waterproof cover as the load bed is
carpeted!

OPPOSITE
The 2006 Lincoln Mark LT continues the
luxury pickup theme.

From this angle there's no way of knowing the Mark LT is a pickup.

luxury pickup. Announced in April 2001, the Lincoln Blackwood was based on Ford's F-150 Super Crew, despite the price tag of $50,000 and the long list of standard equipment. The pickup bed was certainly different. When it was first shown as a concept car, the Blackwood featured a cargo box made of African wengewood, which was found to be too difficult to work with in production, and plastic laminate was substituted instead, which, in any case, was claimed to be twice as stiff as a box of steel. Also, even though no one was likely to use their Blackwood for hauling hogs to market, the bed had a removable carpet and stainless-steel walls, while a remote-control tonneau cover hid valuables from the public gaze.

The F-150's bench seating for six was banished, and four Connolly leather bucket seats were put in their place, each of them heated and air-conditioned, while the dashboard was recognizably F-series but with oak trim. The Blackwood was so loaded with equipment that there was only one option – GPS.

But the luxury was not merely cosmetic – the Lincoln Blackwood had also been re-engineered beneath the skin. The four-wheel discs had ABS, and to keep the usually unladen rear end under control, the shock mountings were moved and there were additional air springs and an anti-windup bar. There was traction control as well as the ABS, controlled by reducing power from the 331-ci (5424-cc) dohc V8. Assuming that the traction control wasn't interfering, the V8 could offer 300bhp and 355lb ft, driving through a four-speed automatic at an average fuel consumption of around 13mpg.

Ford ceased sales of the Lincoln Mark LT in the United States and Canada after the 2008 model year. In its place, Ford created an upper-end trim of the 2009 F-150 called Platinum. Sales continue in Mexico, because the Ford F-150 is sold as the Ford Lobo. The Lincoln Mark LT will be a rebadged Ford F-150 Platinum for Mexico beginning in the 2010 model year.

If there was any doubt that luxury pickups were intended for hard work, the Mark LT confirmed it.

1999 Mazda B-Series.

MAZDA

The story of Mazda's pickups, at least in the U.S.A., is inextricably linked with that of Ford, though there is an interesting twist. Ford's Courier of the early 1970s was a rebadged Mazda, of course, designed, engineered and built in Japan before it was shipped across the Pacific. And very successful it was for Ford too, providing it with a competent compact truck at a time when sales in this market were soaring. Toyota made a similar deal with General Motors, building its own U.S. sales on the back of the liaison, while Mitsubishi also profited from selling its Forte pickup via Plymouth and Dodge dealers. Nissan, meanwhile, ploughed a furrow of its own, later building its own factory in the U.S.A.

But somehow Mazda seemed to have lost out. The Courier was eventually dropped and Ford and Mazda went on to design their own compact pickups. But while the Ford Ranger sold by the thousand, Mazda's own B-Series was something of a flop in

America. Mazda had a problem in that, unlike Toyota or Nissan, it had no significant presence in North America before the Ford Courier deal in 1970, and apart from enthusiasts, few people knew or cared that the Courier was a Mazda in disguise. Consequently, the new B-Series had to establish itself as a little-known brand, which is no easy task.

So when Mazda came to renew the B in 1994, it turned to Ford. In a reversal of history, the latest Mazda pickup was no

LEFT and BELOW
2003 Mazda B-Series, looking up to date but based heavily on the Ford Ranger.

A selection of 2003 and '04 B-Series pickups, all of them based on the Ford Ranger. This was ironic as Mazda originally sold pickups to Ford!

more than a modified Ranger, with minor styling the only feature to set them apart. Only from 1998 did the B-Series become a little more distinctive, with flared fenders and a new name – the Truck – for 2002.

By the early-21st century, there were criticisms that the Truck was now outdated: after all, the Ranger, on which it had been based, was now an old design. But it did offer a wide range, including two-door regular or four-door extended cabs, two- or four-wheel-drive and three levels of trim – base, SE and Dual Sport, the latter with raised suspension to give a 4x4 look but with 4x2 under the skin to give more economy. Engine options were a 141-ci (2310-cc) four (143bhp/154lb ft), 184-ci (3015-cc) V6 (150bhp/180lb ft), and 245-ci (4015-cc) V6 (207bhp/238lb ft). Even so, this was an increasingly outdated design.

In 2006 the BT-50 was launched bringing it much more up-to-date. The model has continued to be modified into 2010 to produce a stylish mid-sized pickup.

OPPOSITE: Mazda either needed a new pickup of its own, or a more modern base vehicle.

The Mazda pickup got a facelift in the late 2000s with the BT-50, this model is from 2009.

Mitsubishi's L200 was a useful compact pickup of the 1980s, offered with either two- or four-wheel-drive.

MERCURY

Like Lincoln, Mercury was conceived as one of Ford's more upmarket marques, yet it too was used on pickups and even on heavy-duty trucks. The badge was fitted to Ford F-series pickups built in Windsor, Canada, after the Second World War, the first Mercury pickup having been announced on 20 March 1946. The F-based Mercury M-series was launched in January 1948, only a week after the Ford original went on sale. But there were some differences, apart from trim, all of the Mercuries being V8-powered until the final year, when a 223-ci (3654-cc) six was offered as well. Until then, Ford's familiar 239-ci flathead V8 came in light- and heavy-duty forms, one emphasizing power, the other torque. Two-tone paint was another feature unique to Mercury pickups at the time: 'Mercury Trucks. Smartest Truck Line Ever Built,' went the publicity. Smart maybe, but by 1957 it was deemed unecessary by Ford, and the line was dropped that year.

MITSUBISHI

As far as the American pickup market is concerned, Mitsubishi's most significant contribution were two compact trucks that were actually sold with American names – the Dodge 50 and Plymouth Arrow. Both were well-regarded, highly successful, and made in Japan. However, Mitsubishi already had over ten years of pickup history under its belt, its first pickup having been launched in 1967 as the Colt, a conventional compact rated at 1/2 a ton, followed by the 1-ton L200, which also enjoyed success.

By now, Mitsubishi was heavily involved with General Motors, and the two began to design a compact pickup that would appeal to American taste, the front end looking more like a sedan than a small truck, and with plenty of equipment. When it was finally launched in 1978, the new Forte justified the effort, having been under development for an astonishing eight years. In the first year alone, 45,000 were sold, and sales more than doubled the following year, the U.S. market taking around 60 per cent of production. Reflecting the general mood, *PV4* magazine voted the Forte, in its American guise, Pickup of the Year.

Small by American standards, the Forte

Mitsubishi L200 4x4 pickup.

had all the ingredients of success. As well as a comfortable cab, it boasted a 6-ft (1.8-m) load bed with double-walled tailgate: as Chrysler would later discover in its own front-drive Rampage/new Arrow, intended to replace the Forte, compact pickups needed some credibility where load-carrying was concerned, even if they were only leisure vehicles. The Forte came with 123-ci (2016-cc) or 160-ci (2622-cc) four-cylinder engines in the U.S., though other markets had 141-ci (2310-cc) diesel or 98-ci (1606-cc) gasoline alternatives. U.S.-market pickups also demanded four-wheel-drive, or at least the option, and the Forte offered this from 1980.

RIGHT and OPPOSITE
By 1999, the L200 had grown. But with or without the fibreglass hardtop, it makes a reliable workhorse.

PAGES 390 and 391
The later L200 also came in leisure crew-cab guise, with or without hardtop.

Later on, however, American sales were hit by an increase in import tax, which is why Chrysler launched a home-grown replacement. But Mitsubishi carried on developing the Forte long after Chrysler had stopped selling it. Larger tyres and a bigger 153-ci (2507-cc) diesel were only a few of

OPPOSITE and THIS PAGE
A 2003 Mitsubishi L200, with covered
load bed, GPS and intercooled turbo-diesel
engine.

BELOW & RIGHT
Mitsubishi offers the new retro-styled
Raider for 2006, a natural for the U.S.
market.

OPPOSITE
The late 2000s saw an updrade to
Mitsubishi's pickup truck with the launch of
the L200 which has curvier cleaner lines
than previous models, but still with the
toughness and durability which is expected
of Mitsubishi pickups.

the improvements, and sales remained
buoyant to the very end, at around 130,000
units a year.

It was replaced by the Strada in 1991,
which paid more attention to the SUV
lifestyle than the Forte, though it also
boasted the largest load bed in its class and a
153-ci turbo-diesel of 85bhp. This achieved
its second generation five years later, now
built in Thailand and sold as the L200,
available as Standard, Club or Double Cab
on two- or four-wheel-drive platforms. In
fact, the L200 became something of a
standard where pickups were concerned, still
sold in Britain in 2005 in two-wheel-drive
Single Cab form or Club Cab and Double
Cab as 4x4s, all powered by a 153-ci
intercooled turbo-diesel four, offering up to
113bhp and 177lb ft.

A European-market Nissan Navara with King Cab.

NISSAN

Of all the compact pickup trucks imported into America, Nissan can probably claim to have the biggest clutch of 'firsts': first to be imported in 1959; the first ¹/₂-ton compact pickup ten years later; the first long-load bed compact in 1975; the first compact with an extended cab two years later.

It is an impressive track record, but few could have forseen this back in 1959, when the U.S. pickup market was dominated by heavyweight ¹/₂-tonners from Chevrolet, Ford and Dodge. America's home-grown mini-pickups, like the Crosley and American Bantam, had long since faded away, and the idea of a mini-pickup equalling the success of the VW Beetle in North America would have seemed absurd.

It must have seemed that way to Nissan itself, at first. At the time, there was nothing to equal the Datsun 1000 pickup – able to carry a ¹/₄-ton load and powered by a 61-ci (1000-cc) 37-bhp four-cylinder engine. It was sufficiently promising for Nissan to rapidly upgrade it to 74ci (1200cc) and 60bhp, then to the revised 320 of 1961.

However, sales were still relatively small until the bigger 520 pickup arrived in the U.S. in 1965. Over 15,000 of these were sold each year, transforming Nissan from an insignificant specialist to a major importer. In fact, in its first year, the 520 became the best-selling imported pickup, which Nissan maintained until the mid 1970s.

This success, and the shock effect of the first fuel crisis, caused Ford and General Motors to seek Japanese imports of their own, Ford rebadging a Mazda its compact Courier pickup and Chevrolet doing the same to the Toyota-sourced LUV. Faced with such a response from these household names, with their big dealer networks, Nissan was in danger of losing the initiative. But it kept up with the top-sellers' list by launching a string of innovations which are now standard practice in pickups: the ¹/₂-ton compact, the long-bed compact and the King Cab extended-cab compact.

The first of these was based on the highly successful 520, but the latter two were developments of Nissan's fourth-generation pickup, the 620, which was launched in 1972. At this time, Nissan pickups were still badged as Datsuns in the U.S., as well as in Europe, the final pickup to bear the name being the all-new 720 announced in 1979.

The effect of a second fuel crisis, and a firmly-rooted reputation for quality and reliability, saw sales of the 720 surpass even those of its predecessors: the company was exporting so many pickups across the Pacific that it decided on another first – it would build an assembly plant in the U.S. Based at

A 2003 Navara with double cab. The four-door, five-seater cab is quite different from the extended two-door King Cab.

At that time, Nissan, along with the other Japanese manufacturers, seemed disinclined to build full-sized pickups to challenge the Ford F-series and Dodge Ram, but that changed when the Nissan Titan was announced. With a 344-ci (5637-cc) 305-bhp V8 standard across the range, it clearly had ambitions beyond the Frontier. King and Crew Cabs were available, and a five-speed automatic transmission was standard, as was permanent four-wheel-drive. Meanwhile, the

OPPOSITE and THIS PAGE
For the U.K., the Navara had four-wheel-drive and a powerful intercooled turbo-diesel engine.

Smyrna, Tennessee, the Nissan Motor Manufacturing Corporation (NMMC) produced its first pickup in 1983, and by the early 21st century over 1.7 million had rolled off the line.

The 720 proved to be long-lived as well as a good-seller, and its replacement didn't appear until 1987. The Hardbody turned out to be another record-breaker, averaging 100,000-plus sales a year. Ten years later, the Hardbody gave way to the Frontier, which boasted the largest standard load bed of any compact pickup. Given Nissan's history, it naturally came with a King Cab option, not

to mention a six-cylinder power unit and four-wheel-drive. As ever, it proved to be well-built, topping the JD Power quality survey in 1998, with fewer problems than any of its rivals. That same year, for the fifth year running, NMMC emerged as the U.S.A.'s most productive automotive factory. New Frontiers were soon expanded with the cheaper two-wheel-drive Desert Runner and the Crew Cab, both launched in mid 1999. When it was announced, the latter was a four-door compact pickup with no direct competition, which was yet another first.

BELOW, OPPOSITE, PAGES 402 and 403 Nissan has long campaigned modified pickups in the gruelling Dakar Rally in Africa.

Frontier had developed into a large range-encompassing two-door King Cab and four-door Crew Cab, with four levels of trim (XE, SE, NISMO and LE). Power choices were between a 153-ci (2507-cc) four of 154bhp/173lb ft and a 245-ci (4015-cc) V6 (the only option on the Crew Cab) mustering 265bhp and 284lb ft, while transmissions consisted of a five-speed automatic or a five- or six-speed manual. The little Datsun 1000 had certainly come a long way.

PLYMOUTH

The existence of Plymouth trucks appears to have been unnecessary, with Dodge, after all, already being Chrysler's commercial division. However, the complexities of Chrysler's dealer network, ensuring that every area had easy access to Plymouth, De Soto, Dodge and Chrysler, and that every dealer had two lines to sell, made it all worthwhile.

The first Plymouth light trucks were actually two-door sedans with blanked out windows and a third door in the back for loading. The first true pickup arrived in 1937, based on the 116-in (2.9-m) Commercial Car chassis which was shared with Dodge. This came in chassis-cab form as a station wagon or sedan delivery as well as a pickup. All were powered by the same L-head six-cylinder engine used by Dodge, measuring 201ci (3294cc) and producing 70bhp.

Nearly 15,000 Commercial Cars were sold in 1937, but sales halved the following year due to higher prices and a severe recession. The Plymouth trucks had been restyled, retaining their resemblance to Plymouth sedans, which changed for 1939, when the latest PT81 Commercial Cars moved closer in appearance to the Dodge truck, which suited the pickup in particular. The cab had been moved forward, but the wheelbase was unchanged at 116in, while the L-head and three-speed transmission were the same as that of the previous year. Power was boosted to 79bhp for 1940, but sales of the Plymouth pickups were slow and only 800 found homes in 1941. This was

their last year, and it would be over 30 years before another Plymouth pickup made an appearance.

The Trail Duster was launched in 1974, again based on Dodge components, though it was an SUV rather than a pickup. For the first post-war Plymouth pickup we have to proceed to 1979, though once again it was hardly an in-house design. In fact, the Arrow compact pickup was a Mitsubishi, imported from Japan by Chrysler and fitted with either Dodge 50 or Plymouth Arrow badges, depending on which dealer was appropriate.

In fact, this conventional, clean-looking little truck was considered to have been one of the best compacts of its time. Powered by a 122-ci (1999-cc) four-cylinder engine of 90bhp, it offered a four-speed transmission and 81.5-in (2-m) load bed. The cab was of decent size and the payload was the best in class. There was also an upscaled Sport version, with five-speed box, white spoked wheels, flashy stripes and extra instrumentation. It also offered a larger engine of 156ci (2556cc) and 105bhp. The good-looking Arrows continued almost unchanged through 1980 and '81, though a mid-range Custom was added for 1981, filling the gap between the base model and the Sport. It had the Sport's bigger engine and five-speed transmission, plus carpeting and a chrome front fender to justify a near-$500 premium over the basic pickup, the Sport now costing over $1,000 extra. Custom became the entry model for 1982, supplanted by a slightly flashier Royal and the evergreen Sport.

It was the final year for the Arrows,

replaced for 1983 by the Scamp. This was yet another example of Chrysler badge engineering, the Plymouth Scamp being the same as the Dodge Rampage. Both were based on the front-wheel-drive Chrysler Omni and powered by the company's own 135-ci (2212-cc) four-cylinder engine. The result was that it was quite sporty, or as the Scamp brochure put it: 'The dashing good looks of a sporty car … the carry-all utility of a small truck.'

But the public was not convinced, and so few Scamps were sold that it was listed for only a year, though the Rampage lasted for two. While the Arrow had been a genuine pickup in miniature, the Scamp had obviously derived from a modern front-wheel-drive hatchback, which was too radical for the average pickup buyer to accept, and in America probably still is.

POWELL

Not much is known about the Powell Sport Wagon, the slab-sided pickup having been built mainly out of flat panels. It was based on old Plymouth components and was produced in Compton, California, between 1954 and 1956.

REO

Ask most Americans to define the Reo Speedwagon, and they'll think it is a rock group. But the Reo Motor Car Co. of Lansing, Michigan, was building trucks from 1908, and the aptly-named Speedwagon was its most famous model. In the late 1920s, Reo was the fifth biggest truck-maker in the U.S. Naturally, pickups featured highly on its list, with a 1/2-ton junior Speedwagon offered from around that time, prior to which, the lightest-duty Reos were 3/4- and 1-ton models. The company also built cars, and some of the lighter Reo pickups were built on sedan running gear. Reo was taken over by White in 1957, when it concentrated on heavy-duty trucks.

STUDEBAKER

Studebaker was in the vehicle business long before anyone else. Henry and Clem Studebaker set up a blacksmith's shop in South Bend, Indiana, in 1852, building two farm wagons that year. The business thrived, and by 1876 they were the largest producer of horse-drawn vehicles in the world. Studebaker the company was also a pioneer of the motor car, experimenting with various designs in the 1890s and producing electric- and gasoline-powered cars in the 1900s.

It wasn't until late 1911, however, that light trucks began to emerge from the South Bend factory. The Flanders 20, powered by an L-head four-cylinder engine of 155ci (2540cc), was originally offered as a panel van, but some were built as pickups and used at the firm's Detroit factory. The first pickup on general sale arrived in 1914 as the 3/4-ton Delivery Car, which also came in Express Body form. Again, an L-head four provided the power. These early pickups continued to sell until 1917, but production was low and when they ended, Studebaker would not offer another pickup for 20 years.

The Coupé-Express of 1937 was a different beast from those early pickups, converted from the stylish Studebaker

Dictator instead of a light truck. It was well-equipped, with an adjustable seat, twin sun visors and two windshield wipers, among other things, with a 6-ft (1.8-m) double-walled all-steel cargo box mounted behind the cab. The Dictator – an odd name, given

events in Germany, Spain and Italy at the time – was powered by a six-cylinder L-head engine measuring 218ci (3572cc), also used by the pickup. With 86bhp and 160lb ft, it was usefully powerful, Studebaker selling over 3,000 in the first year.

The 1947 Studebaker pickup had a certain bulbous charm.

It carried through into 1938, restyled to match the equivalent Studebaker sedan, the same happening in 1939, with power increased to 90bhp from an enlarged 226-ci (3703-cc). Sales, however, fell to 1,200, and Studebaker dropped the pickup for 1940. It was back for 1941, but as part of the new M-series line-up of light trucks. Although it shared many components with the Champion sedan, the pickup, together with the rest of the M-series, had its own front-end styling. Reflecting its more truck-like demeanour, the latest Coupé-Express was far more spartan than the original, and came with a smaller 170-ci (2786-cc) L-head six of 80bhp. Its advantage was a price of $664, despite a longer 6.5-ft load bed, and Studebaker was able to sell over 4,600 as a result.

Studebaker concentrated on heavier military trucks during the Second World War, but the little M5 pickup was back for 1946, little changed from the 1941 original, though a useful addition was the use of larger 6.00 x 15-in six-ply tyres, allowing a 300-lb (136-kg) hike in GVW. With the home market desperate for trucks of any description, Studebaker sold over 14,000 M5s that year and it was the same through 1947 and '48 as the company concentrated on production rather than new features.

But there was something new for 1949. Mechanically, the 2R-series was much the same as its predecessor, but it also had advanced new styling by Robert Bourke, none other than Raymond Loewy's chief of styling. With its low stance, no running boards and a smooth double-walled cargo

OPPOSITE and LEFT
This mildly customized pickup is a 1947 Studebaker M5, a continuation of the company's pre-war truck. The Bourke-designed 2R replaced it in 1949.

OPPOSITE and LEFT
In the 1930s, Studebaker's pickup was the
sedan-based Coupé-Express, but this
purpose-built pickup was launched in 1941
as part of the new M-series. It failed to
equal the sales of Chevrolet or Ford but
was quite a success nevertheless.

RIGHT and OPPOSITE
Studebaker's heavier-duty trucks benefited
from the new styling, seen on this 1950
stakeside, for example.

box, the 2R pickup was well ahead of the competition. It came in ¹/₂-ton 2R5 and 1-ton 2R10, as well as with a chassis-cab or stakeside rear end. With the advanced styling and a large-capacity ex-aircraft engine

factory at South Bend, many were sold, with over 110,000 ¹/₂-ton pickups and nearly 38,000 1-tonners leaving the production line. Given this success, the trucks were hardly changed from 1950 to '53, by which time

the price for the basic ¹/₂-ton pickup had risen to $1,404.

They were facelifted for 1954 as the 3R-series, with a new grille, curved one-piece windshield and some trim changes. Now a

OPPOSITE and ABOVE
A 1950 Studebaker with original interior.

RIGHT and OPPOSITE
Before and after? Both these 1950 2R
pickups show the Robert Bourke styling
influence. The 2R transformed Studebaker
into a major producer of light trucks.

OPPOSITE
A 1951 2R, when the pickups were hardly
changed, thanks to Studebaker's post-war
success. But the end was approaching by
the early 1960s.

LEFT
A 1955 Studebaker 3R, now with one-piece
windshield and split grille.

OPPOSITE

1955 was a year of change, with the 224-ci (3761-cc) V8 offered on the light-duty pickups for the first time.

LEFT

1958 Studebaker Transtar Deluxe: the new name had arrived in 1956 to replace the E-series badge.

V8 was offered, but only on Studebaker's heavy-duty trucks, the smaller pickups coming with the familiar 170-ci (2786-cc) six or a 245-ci (4015-cc) version offering 102bhp and 205lb ft. This was rectified the following year, when the 245 six was dropped, the 170 enlarged to 186ci (3048cc), due to a longer stroke. A V8 was fitted to light-duty pickups for the first time, the 224-ci (3671-cc) unit producing 140bhp and 202lb ft. Several other changes, including a larger rear window, made these the E-series trucks, though they changed again for 1956, rebadged as Transtars.

Newly merged with Packard, Studebaker

OPPOSITE and LEFT
1958 Studebaker Transtar Deluxe, showing
the larger rear window (opposite) from
which all Studebaker pickups had benefited
since 1955.

was in poor shape by now, so the pickups were promoted with the new name and duo-tone colours rather than any major engineering changes. However, it was able to stretch to a new fibreglass grille for 1957 and a bigger 259-ci (4244-cc) version of the V8. A four-wheel-drive conversion was launched the following year, available in both the V8 and reintroduced 245-ci (4015-cc) six, and a new stripped-down low-priced pickup was introduced, eschewing

even the buck-toothed fibreglass grille to save money. It was named the Scotsman.

Meanwhile, Studebaker had been enjoying some welcome success with the Lark compact sedan, which provided a few dollars to invest in the trucks, plus new front-end styling for the pickups in 1960. Now named the Champ, this latest pickup used the Lark's modern squared-off front end, though it retained the old cargo box and was based on a truck chassis: as before, the

Champ wasn't simply a Lark with a load bed. Now there were four engine options, ranging from the standard 90-bhp six to a 210-bhp 289-ci (4736-cc) V8 on the heavier-duty Champs. The L-head six even gained overhead valves for 1961, with a higher compression ratio helping it to 110bhp. The load bed was also updated as a new flush-sided box called the Spaceside, the tooling for which had actually been obtained from Dodge. The Champ made an arrractive,

modern pickup, and at $1,870 with a 6.5-ft bed, was the cheapest U.S.-built pickup of 5,000-lb (2268-kg) GVW. Unfortunately, many Studebaker dealers weren't geared to sell trucks, so sales weren't as high as they could have been.

The end came in December 1963 as Studebaker was facing some terminal restructuring in order to survive. Those final 1963 and '64 model-year Champs had shown some improvements, notably to the suspension and steering, while a Conestoga camper was a new option. The rights to the Champ were sold to Nathan Altman in 1964, along with the Avanti sports car, though only the Avanti survived.

OPPOSITE and THIS PAGE
The 1958 Transtar, one of the last traditional Studebaker pickups. For the last few years of its life it became the Champ, complete with Lark front end.

SUBARU

Subaru of Japan hasn't as high a profile in the world of pickups as Nissan, Toyota or Isuzu, let alone Ford, Chevrolet or GMC. Yet this vehicle arm of the Fuji Corporation pioneered the concept of lightweight four-wheel-drive pickups with car-like characteristics.

Beginning with Japanese microcars in the 1950s, it progressed to larger cars with wider appeal, though it wasn't until the 1970s that Subaru began to offer selectable four-wheel-drive on its 1.6- and 1.8-litre pickups, as well as on the equivalent sedans and estates.

OPPOSITE
The Champ, one of the very last of Studebaker's pickups, still a purpose-built truck but now with styling borrowed from the Lark sedan.

LEFT and BELOW
Subaru's lightweight four-wheel-drive pickup of the 1980s was popular with farmers.

OPPOSITE and LEFT
Subaru revived the concept of a lightweight
four-wheel-drive pickup, and prospered as
a result.

These proved most successful, light in weight, easy to drive and much cheaper to buy than a full-sized off-road pickup from Land Rover or Jeep. Subaru pickups didn't have the ultimate off-road ability of these more specialized vehicles, but a dual-range transmission gave them a useful edge on the competition.

Subaru later concentrated on more upmarket four-wheel-drive performance cars, but its go-anywhere pickups were almost unique in their day.

THIS PAGE and OPPOSITE
Toyota's Hi-Lux proved to be one of the longest-lived and best-known names in pickup history, whether they were in base or extended-cab form, two- or four-wheel-drive.

TOYOTA

Unlike its arch-rival, Nissan, Toyota was not a pioneer of compact pickups in North America, though the market was still in its infancy when the little Toyota Stout was launched in the U.S.A. in 1964. It lasted five years, when it was replaced by the Hi-Lux, perhaps one of the best-known and long-lived names in the history of pickups.

The Hi-Lux's original four-cylinder engine was replaced by a smaller 110-ci (1802-cc) four in 1970, which nevertheless offered more power, and was later replaced by a 123-ci (2016-cc). A long-bed version was added in 1973, which is interesting, as Nissan also claims to have offered the first such compact two years later. At the same time, the Hi-Lux acquired a still bigger engine, now of 135ci (2212cc), and a five-

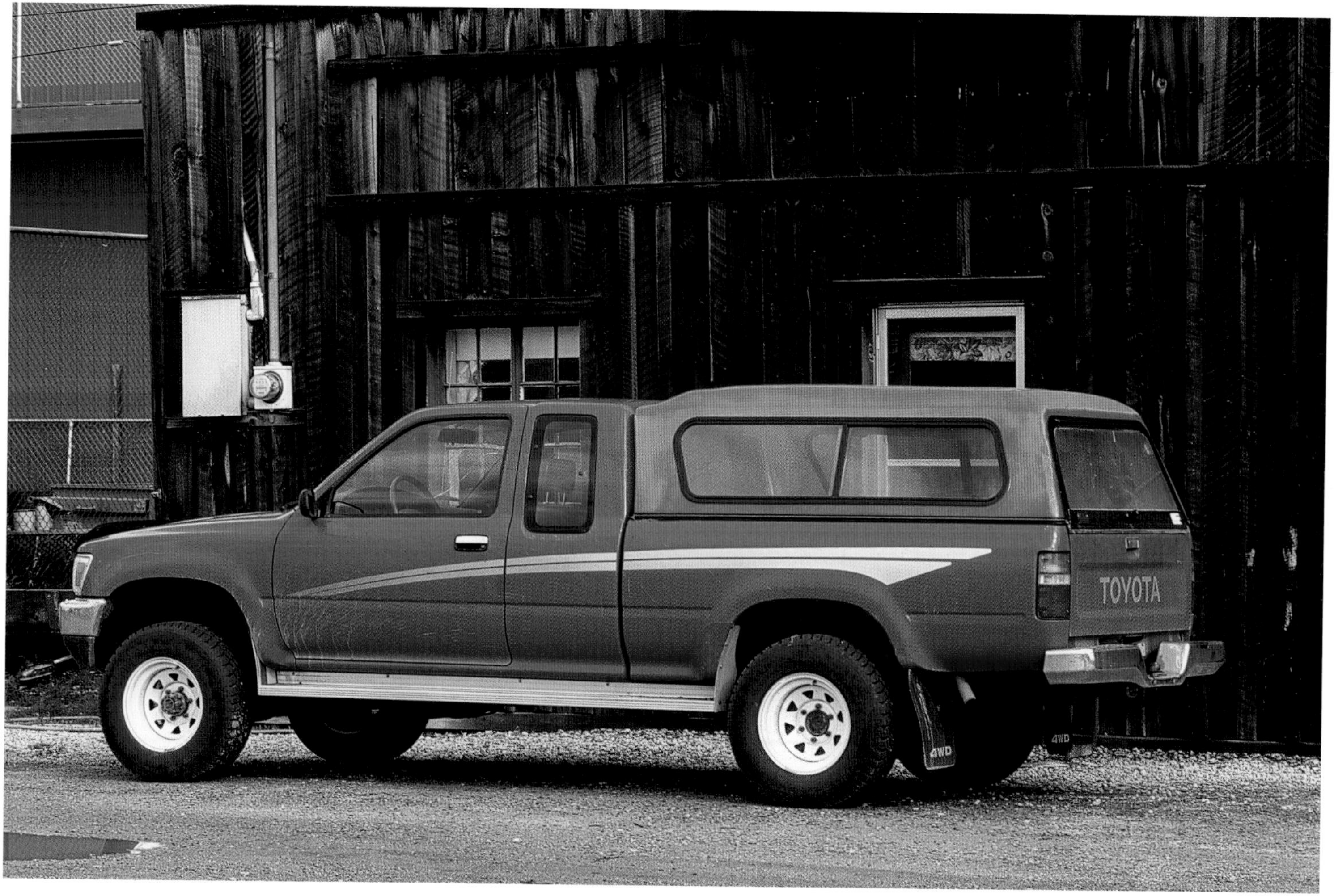
TOYOTA
4WD

OPPOSITE
1995 Toyota Hi-Lux with crew cab. Most Hi-Luxes were sold with four-wheel-drive, and this has obviously used it!

LEFT
The new-generation Toyota Tacoma was designed especially for the U.S. market, shown here in 1996 Xtra cab form.

speed transmission. The Hi-Lux name was actually dropped in 1976, though it was retained in other markets, and it was simply named Toyota's 'compact truck' for many years thereafter.

Until the late 1970s, the little Toyota had no ambitions to become a leisure or luxury toy. It was a working tool, with live axles and leaf springs at both ends. But it did get a new SR-5 option in 1979, with various sporty additions, plus another power boost two years later, with the 147-ci (2409-cc) 22R four-cylinder engine. And just to show that Toyota hadn't forgotten its truck's working origins, there was a new diesel option as well – a 135-ci four-cylinder unit.

By now, the Hi-Lux also had a four-wheel-drive option, though this was of a fairly workaday kind, with a compulsory four- rather than five-speed transmission, though it was necessary to stop before switching between two- and four-wheel-drive. That changed in 1984 with a more modern shift-on-the-fly version, with the

OPPOSITE and THIS PAGE
Meanwhile, the Hi-Lux carried on. This is a
2001 crew cab with VX trim, four-wheel-
drive and diesel power.

front hubs lockable from inside the cab. In
fact, there were several convenience touches
added that year, including an Xtra cab with
storage space behind the seats, this being
Toyota's response to the extended cabs that
most compact pickups now offered as an
option. A four-speed electronically-
controlled automatic transmission was
another new option, rare in a compact
pickup at that time.

Nineteen-eighty-five saw some minor
changes to the cargo box, but the big news
came the following year, when independent
front suspension, using double-wishbone
torsion bars, was fitted for the first time.
This greatly improved the pickup's ride and

now, Toyota had continued to ship pickups into the U.S., but in the early 1990s it decided to design a new compact pickup specifically for the U.S.A., and to build it there as well. Thus the Tacoma was born.

It still came with a four-cylinder engine as standard, though this was a 166-ci (2720-cc) unit with a meaty 142bhp and 160lb ft and 150bhp/177lbft optional. Also on the extras list was a 209-ci (3425-cc) V6 offering 190bhp and 220lb ft, while other more familiar Toyota options – Xtra cab and SR-5 – were available too. Front suspension was now independent with coil springs, with

OPPOSITE and THIS PAGE
Seen here in U.K. specification, the Hi-Lux remained a working vehicle, with hose-down rubber mats on the floor instead of carpets.

handling. By way of a celebration, the brakes were upgraded to match, while alloy wheels and fat tyres became part of the SR-5 package, which was still going strong.

One of the most far-reaching effects of the independent front end was that it gave Toyota the space to fit a V6. This was something it had to do, as Ford (Ranger) and Chevrolet (S-10) were already offering a V6 option in their compact pickups. Toyota's

184-ci (3015-cc) V6 dramatically improved performance, and increased the towing limit to 3,500lb (1588kg), complementing the interior upgrades from the previous year.

But despite the V6 and independent front suspension, not to mention Toyota's reputation for toughness and reliability, the Japanese-made compact never approached the sales of either the S-10 or Ranger, which brought about a change of strategy. Until

leaf springs retained at the rear on both two- and four-wheel-drive versions. After two years on the market, the California-built Tacomas were given some upgrades, notably a locking rear differential on the 4x4s, and bucket seats on the extended cabs.

A cheaper two-wheel-drive Tacoma, the PreRunner, was launched in 1999, named after 4x2 trucks used in off-road racing.

OPPOSITE and THIS PAGE
2004 Toyota H2J Land Cruiser pickup.

PAGE 438
Jeff Kincaid racing a Tacoma.

PAGE 439
Racing a Toyota Tundra.

LEFT and BELOW
The Toyota FTX concept: something else to
tempt the American buyer?

PAGE 440
Less svelte than some of its rivals, the
XRunner was certainly imposing.

PAGE 441
The 2009 Hilux is ever popular and just as
tough.

The Stepside was a sporty new package offered for 2000, aimed at younger buyers, while in 2001 a four-door Double Cab joined the line-up. By 2005, the Tacoma had more power as well, and with the latest 245-ci (4015-cc) V6 beneath the hood, drove 245bhp through the standard six-speed transmission, enough for 0–60mph in 7.5 seconds and with a towing limit of 6,500lb (2950kg). Now it seemed that the Toyota pickup was a compact no longer, and had left its working origins far behind.

TRIVAN

To prove that not all American-built pickups were thoroughly conventional four-wheelers, the Trivan offered something quite different. It had three wheels, two at the front, one at the rear, and was rated at $1/2$ a ton. It was built by the Roustabout Company of Frackville, Pennsylvania and featured a three-speed transmission and air suspension, with a steel tube frame. Only around 150 were made between 1962 and 1964.

WILLYS-OVERLAND

Best-known for the Jeep, Willys also built conventional pickups, with an Open Express body offered as early as 1913, having a 30-bhp motor driving through a three-speed transmission. Similar basic light trucks were produced for several years, often using components from the Willys car range, and by 1917 there was a range of three payloads: 750lb, 800lb (on a longer 106-in/2.7-m wheelbase) and 1,200lb.

For 1920, the Light Four used a much smaller 140-ci (2294-cc) four-cylinder engine, though it was still able to haul 800lb (360kg), and would be used by Willys for the next 40 years. All of these trucks were replaced by the small, advanced Whippet in 1927, itself based on the successful Whippet car. Light in weight, but with ample power from the 30-bhp four or 40-bhp six-cylinder engines, the Whippet proved a useful pickup, and had the advanced feature of four-wheel brakes.

That was followed by the Series 77 of 1933, sharing streamlined styling with the equivalent Willys car, though it was only

OPPOSITE
New for 2009/10 the Toyota Hilux Power limited edition.

LEFT and PAGES 444 and 445
Willys-Overland made the Jeep, but had a history of producing pickups stretching back to 1913.

offered as a panel van for the first two years. In the meantime, Willys-Overland had been in and out of receivership but still managed to offer a pickup version for 1935, based on the same 100-in wheelbase and 1/2-ton rating. The Series 77 was completely restyled for 1937, now with an integral grille and headlights faired into the rounded fenders. Power was supplied by a 134-ci (2196-cc) L-head four of 48bhp, this modern-looking pickup carrying through to 1938, with a more conventional grille and built-in headlights for '39. A powered-up 61-bhp version of the L-head four was also offered, to which hydraulic brakes were fitted. But that proved to be the final Willys pickup, the arrival of the Jeep changing the face of the company forever in 1940.

INDEX